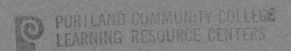

SONG WITHOUT MUSIC:
Chinese *Tz'u* Poetry

RENDITIONS **BOOKS**

are issued by the Comparative Literature and Translation Centre
The Chinese University of Hong Kong
publisher of *Renditions*, a Chinese-English Translation Magazine

General Editors

Stephen C. Soong
George Kao

This book is published
with the aid of the
WING LUNG BANK FUND
for Promotion of Chinese Culture

SONG WITHOUT MUSIC:
Chinese *Tz'u* Poetry

Edited by Stephen C. Soong

A *RENDITIONS* Book

The Chinese University Press
Hong Kong

Distributed by
The University of Washington Press
Seattle and London

Printed by South China Printing Co. Hong Kong

CONTENTS

1 PREFACE

5 Twenty Selected Lyrics *(Translated by D.C. Lau)*

25 MIAO YÜEH: The Chinese Lyric *(Translated by John Minford)*

45 Eleven *Tz'u* by Wei Chuang *(Translated by C.Y. Hsu)*

57 CHANG TSUNG-SU: Behind the Lines: *Tz'u* Poets and Their Private Selves *(Translated by Frederick C. Tsai)*

62 Thirteen *Tz'u* by Liu Yung *(Translated by Winnie Lai-fong Leung)*

83 CHIA-YING YEH CHAO: An Appreciation of the *Tz'u* of Yen Shu *(Translated by James R. Hightower)*

100 Twenty-one *Tz'u* by Ou-yang Hsiu *(Translated by Teresa Yee-wha Yü)*

121 RUTH W. ADLER: Confucian Gentleman and Lyric Poet: Romanticism and Eroticism in the *Tz'u* of Ou-yang Hsiu

143 CHENG CH'IEN: Liu Yung and Su Shih in the Evolution of *Tz'u* Poetry *(Translated by Ying-hsiung Chou)*

157 KU SUI: Interpretation of Su Tung-p'o's *Tz'u* *(Translated by Huang Kuo-pin and Teresa Yee-wha Yü)*

177 Nine *Tz'u* by Chou Pang-yen *(Translated by Julie Landau)*

190 YÜ P'ING-PO: Appreciations of *Tz'u* *(Translated by Ying-hsiung Chou and Winnie Lai-fong Leung)*

199 Ten *Tz'u* by Lu Yu *(Translated by James P. Rice)*

211 LIANG MING-YÜEH: The *Tz'u* Music of Chiang K'uei: Its Style and Compositional Strategy

247 Three *Tz'u* Songs with Prefaces by Chiang K'uei *(Translated by Huang Kuo-pin)*

252 Eleven *Tz'u* by Nalan Hsinteh *(Translated by John C.H. Wu)*

265 WAI-LEUNG WONG: "The River at Dusk Is Saddening Me": Cheng Ch'ou Yü and *Tz'u* Poetry

280 Notes on Contributors

Preface

When Walter Pater produced his famous dictum: "All art constantly aspires towards the condition of music", he might well have had the Chinese *tz'u* 詞 poetry in mind. More probably than not, he had never heard of this form of versification. But *tz'u*, in fact, was written to music, and to be sung; the word itself means "*song words*" in Chinese. Scholars disagree as to the exact date when *tz'u* originated and the manner in which it came into being. It would not be wide of the mark, however, to say that these "songs", or "lyrics" (as they are sometimes referred to in English), began to take shape and develop their characteristic style in the T'ang dynasty, although the very first piece in this genre could be traced further back. At that particular juncture, three streams of music coexisted: the songs collected by the Music Bureau beginning in the Han; the folk songs preserved since the time of the Wei, the Chin and the Six Dynasties; and the popular songs introduced into China mostly from Central Asia through Turkestan. Some of the songs came from as far as India and Burma. *Pu-sa man* 菩薩蠻, one of the most popular tunes, was actually a song in praise of the hairdresses of the Burmese empresses of the time.[1] From the literature and source materials available to us today, we can assume that the literary aspect of *tz'u* was derived from the five-syllable and seven-syllable lines of the regulated verse, or *shih* 詩, which reached the peak of its splendor in the T'ang dynasty, while the musical aspect of *tz'u* was the triumph of popular foreign songs over traditional native songs, which had grown too stereotyped to excite continued interest. Because of its musicality, the appeal of *tz'u* was not confined to the intellect and the imagination, nor for that matter did it find favor among only the educated and initiated. Instead, this form of poetry-making spread far and wide, reaching everyone who had an ear for a pleasant tune.

The neglect of the musical aspect of *tz'u* often leads to questionable conclusions. Professor Kojiro Yoshikawa, the eminent Japanese scholar, for example, denies *tz'u* its rightful place in the development of Chinese literature. He wrote:

> The rise and spread of the *tz'u* form, because it represented a new development in the history of Chinese poetry, has been regarded as of great importance by recent literary historians. It is probable that they have in fact attached too much importance to the form. As its other name, *shih-yü* or remnants of *shih*, suggests, it is no more than an off-shoot of the *shih* form.[2]

For one thing, *shih-yü* 詩餘 is not the other name, but rather one of 18 other names for *tz'u* in its early stages.[3] Then, again, the word *yü* should not be translated in the sense of off-shoot, remnant, left-over, branch off, annex or extension, all smacking of the derogatory. Several Ch'ing critics pointed out that *yü* should not be inter-

---

[1] Hsieh Sung 謝葑, *Shih tz'u chih-yao* 詩詞指要 (The Essence of Shih and Tz'u), Hong Kong, Chung Hua, 1979, p. 91.

[2] Yoshikawa, Kojiro (Tr. B. Watson), *An Introduction to Sung Poetry*, Cambridge, Mass. 1967, p. 9.

[3] Liang Jung-chi 梁榮基, *Tz'u-hsueh li-lun tsung-k'ao* 詞學理論綜考（上篇）(A General Survey of Tz'u Theories, Part I), *Kuo-li pien-i-kuan kuan-k'an* 國立編譯館館刊, (Journal of the National Institute for Compilation and Translation), Taipei, 1979, Vol. 8, No. 1, p. 31.

preted as 賸餘, *left-over*, but 贏餘, *surplus*. The crux of the matter is that the one interpretation is confined to the stylistical treatment of *tz'u*, while the other deals with the musical dimension in addition to the literary. Thus, the proper rendition of the word *yü* here is *overflow*, which embraces both the literary aspect and the musical aspect. When the grandeur of T'ang poetry could no longer express adequately the more refined and delicate feelings and the simple quatrains could no longer contain the spirit of song, it was natural for a new genre to emerge.

Perhaps the following description of *tz'u* would throw light on its *raison d'être*:

> In composing *tz'u*, it would be unbecoming to pile color upon
> color; nor should it be just a plain sketch. There will be no sub-
> stance if there is too much color and there will be no attraction
> if it is a plain sketch. *Tz'u* should be like a beautiful lady engaged
> in making herself up. Without the aid of pearls and jades, she
> looks bright and luxuriant by herself; without the aid of rouge
> and powder, she is yet fresh and elegant and has natural grace.
> That is how a good *tz'u* poem should look.[4]

This is a fitting description especially of the shorter *tz'u* songs, known as *hsiao-ling* 小令. When the cup of *shih* overflowed, *tz'u* came into existence, and in time matured and evolved into longer and more elaborate tunes of equal beauty.

T'ang Kuei-chang 唐圭璋's monumental work, *Ch'üan Sung tz'u* 全宋詞 (Complete Sung *Tz'u*), first published in 1940 and revised in 1964, collects more than 1,330 *tz'u* writers and 19,900 *tz'u* poems.[5] They are a far cry from the 3,812 poets mentioned in Li O 厲鶚's *Sung-shih chi shih* 宋詩紀事 (Notes on Sung Poetry). According to Yü P'ing-po 俞平伯, if *shih* were to be compared to squares and circles, then *tz'u* would be polygons; if *shih* were to be thought of as straight lines, then *tz'u* would be curves, more diversified and multifarious than the regulated 5-syllable and 7-syllable *shih*. He further cites the *Ch'in-ting tz'u-p'u* 欽定詞譜 (Imperial Register of *Tz'u* Poetry), completed in 1715 during Emperor K'ang Hsi's reign, which lists 826 tunes, with 2,306 variations, and comments that it would not, therefore, be factually wrong to say that there are about 2,000 tune patterns.[6] Thus, it can be seen that *tz'u* poetry has widened the scope and enriched the content of *shih* poetry—it has created another "world" in the poetic universe. Since its genesis, *tz'u* has become a major genre in its own right and has coexisted with *shih* down to the present day.

It is a pity that the popular *tz'u* compositions sung and enjoyed by the common people were not recorded in musical notations; they were so well known that there seemed no need to do so. As *tz'u* grew with time, it became more stylized and sophisticated and could only be mastered by the literati and the elite. It could no longer be composed and written by the uninitiated. In writing to the various

---

[4]Shen Hsiang-lung 沈祥龍, *Lun tz'u sui-pi* 論詞隨筆 (Notes on *Tz'u*) published in the Ch'ing dynasty.

[5]New edition published by Hong Kong, Chung Hua, 1977, 5 vols.

[6]Yü P'ing-po 俞平伯, *T'ang Sung tz'u Hsuan-shih* 唐宋詞選釋 (Annotated Anthology of T'ang and Sung *Tz'u*), Peking, 1979, p. 5.

tune patterns, the poet must observe strict rules regarding rhyme, the number of lines, the number of characters in each line and whether each should have an even or uneven tone. Gradually, the *tz'u* form itself became decadent and oblique so that the longer tunes with their esoteric idiom and pattern were more and more the products of a chosen few. Musically, they had grown to be even harder to record and, with only a few exceptions, what notations that might have existed are irretrievably lost. This state of affairs was made more difficult by the traditional Chinese musical notation which did not record the rhythm, but only the melody.

Even with its music all but lost to our ears, the musical aspect of *tz'u* can still be detected and felt today in its purely literary form. The *hsiao-ling* at their best are delightful, melodious and harmonious. The best long tunes, on the other hand, very much resemble chamber music, set in a minor key. In the three or four stanzas of a long tune, one hears a motif first introduced and then imperceptibly replaced by another motif. These motifs reappear in different guises or variations, by slight hints and the echoing of key words which appeared previously. The feelings are tightly interwoven and developed in themes just as a piece of music observes the rigid rules of counterpoint. The total effect of the best *tz'u* poem is endearing and haunting. It often lingers on and achieves in varying degrees what Pater describes as the effort "to obliterate the distinction between the matter and the form".

Scholarly interest in Chinese literature has been increasing steadily over the past years, and it seems timely to make available a volume of essays and translations devoted to *tz'u* as a separate literary genre. Besides dealing with *tz'u* in a comprehensive fashion, and with some of its individual exponents, such a treatise should lead to a better and deeper appreciation of the uniqueness of this poetic form, as distinct from the traditional *shih*, of which there are biographical and critical studies and anthologies without number. It was decided from the beginning that the approach to this collective study should be an intimate rather than a pedantic one. As John Minford, one of our contributors, puts it, "The purpose is to take the poetry-loving reader by the hand and welcome him into this new world."

Accordingly, the historical and explicative treatment is deliberately played down to allow space for as many translations of *tz'u* poetry as possible. Chinese texts are printed alongside the translations to enable students of Chinese language and literature to savor the original at the same time. It is natural that such a presentation does not permit the inclusion of all major *tz'u* writers. However, most of the essays in this volume deal with individual poets, while the remaining few discourse on *tz'u* in general; in each case there are copious citations from famous *tz'u* poems by way of illustration. Whenever a piece of *tz'u* is quoted in translation, the Chinese original is also given. We hope the essays would thus compensate for any unintentional omission. The reader is expected to find further delight in cross-referencing as much as possible while perusing the essays, since they are complementary to the independent groups of translations. He would also likely encounter a *tz'u* poem in the translations and the same poem, in quite different wording, in the essays. Translated by different hands, they might appear to be different works in the original. It is not our policy to adopt one unified version, as a poem is open to different interpretations by different readers, and sometimes even by the same reader at different times. This is especially true of *tz'u*, because it is highly condensed and does not follow the usual grammatic structure. However, as the names of tunes, which used to be *tz'u* titles, are no longer associated with the content of individual pieces, they have, together with the names of authors, been romanized in the Wade-Giles system for the benefit of the readers.

The Editor takes great pleasure in introducing to the Western world for the first time four important contemporary *tz'u* critics, who are either scholars in this verse form or *tz'u* writers themselves. Of the four, Professor Ku Sui is the only one who has died. Professors Yü P'ing-po, Miao Yueh and Cheng Chien, though advanced in age, are very much alive and still engaged in writing and research. In their writings, we find a fusion of the traditional "*tz'u* talk" form of literary criticism and a modern sensibility tinged with Western influence. The pleasure is doubled when we see that the younger generation of *tz'u* scholars, whether from China or from the West, treat their topics with a reverence that bespeaks precious tradition and continuity.

In putting together such a volume, no one person could presume to be able to handle the work all by himself. It has to be a collective effort. First and foremost, I would like to pay tribute to Professor D.C. Lau of the Department of Chinese Language and Literature of our University, whose expertise and wise counsel contributed much to the gradual shaping of this book. His experience in translation and his sensitivity to both Chinese and English languages and to the niceties of *tz'u* endow him with that rare combination of sureness and lightness of touch which, so essential to the study of *tz'u*, has been invaluable to the present venture.

Professor Chia-ying Yeh Chao of the University of British Columbia has given me support and has involved herself in this project from the very beginning. Besides supplying the essay by her former teacher, Professor Ku Sui and one of her own, she has solicited articles and translations from her colleague and students. Their contributions in this volume are an eloquent testimony to her generous help.

Invaluable and continuous assistance, editorial and otherwise, has been received from my colleagues, Mr. Frederick Tsai, Dr. Ying-hsiung Chou and Mr. K.B. Wong. To them the Editor owes profound gratitude. Mr. C.H. Sheung, Head of the Chinese Department, has graced the pages of this volume with his calligraphy. Advice has been kindly given without reserve by Mr. M.J. So of the Chinese Department, Miss Louise Ho of the English Department, Dr. Bell Yung of the Music Department and Mr. T.H. Fok of the Philosophy Department. Mrs. Y.Y. Lo, my associate for many years, went over the final drafts of each article with meticulous care and planned the layout and the production with ingenuity. Without the support, encouragement and help from my colleague, Mr. George Kao, this volume could hardly have become a reality. It is also difficult to imagine embarking on such a project without assistance from many other quarters, especially the able staff at The Chinese University Press.

Finally, I would like to thank all my contributors, be they veterans or newcomers to the field, for their cooperation and patience in spite of my constant prodding. They have made the present volume as profitable an editing experience as, I hope, it will be an enjoyable and memorable one for the reader.

—Stephen C. Soong

Twenty Selected Lyrics

Translated by D. C. Lau

女冠子　韋莊

四月十七
正是去年今日
別君時
忍淚佯低面
含羞半斂眉

不知魂已斷
空有夢相隨
除却天邊月
沒人知

To the Tune of _Nü kuan tzu_

The Seventeenth Day of the Fourth Month
Was the very day a year ago
When we said goodbye.
Holding back my tears, I feigned looking down
And in bashfulness I puckered my brows.

Little did I know that my soul was crippled
And dreams would be left to follow you in vain.
Apart from the moon on the edge of the sky
No one knows of this.

Wei Chuang (826-910)

5

生查子　牛希濟

春山煙欲收
天淡稀星少
殘月臉邊明
別淚臨清曉

語已多
情未了
回首猶重道
記得綠羅裙
處處憐芳草

To the Tune of *Sheng-cha-tzu*

From the spring hills the mist was about to lift.
The sky was pale, the scattered stars were scanty.
The fading moon by her cheeks shone,
Parting tears at the break of dawn.

Much had been said
But love lingered on.
Turning round, she said yet once again,
'Remember my green silk skirt
And be kind to the sweet grass where you go.'

Niu Hsi-chi (died after 925)

生查子　牛希濟

春山烟欲收
天淡稀星少
殘月臉邊明
別淚臨清曉

語已多
情未了
回首猶重道
記得綠羅裙
處處憐芳草

清平樂　李煜

別来春半
觸目愁腸斷
砌下落梅如雪亂
拂了一身還滿

鴈来音信無憑
路遙歸夢難成
離恨恰如春草
更行更遠還生

To the Tune of *Ch'ing-p'ing yüeh*

Spring is half gone since we parted.
Wherever I turn the sight breaks my heart.
Below the steps plum blossoms fall confusedly
　　like snow.
Brushing them off, I am covered all over again.

The migrant birds come but where is the sign of
　　a message.
The road is too long for homeward dreams to be
　　dreamed.
The grief of parting is just like grass in spring:
The farther you go, the more it seems to grow.

Li Yü (937-978)

清平樂　李煜

別來春半
觸目愁腸斷
砌下落梅如雪亂
拂了一身還滿

雁來音信無憑
路遙歸夢難成
離恨恰如春草
更行更遠還生

踏莎行　晏殊

小徑紅稀
芳郊綠遍
高臺樹色陰陰見
春風不解禁楊花
濛濛亂撲行人面

翠葉藏鶯
朱簾隔燕
鑪香靜逐游絲轉
一場愁夢酒醒時
斜陽却照深深院

To the Tune of *T'a so hsing*

On the narrow path a touch of red,
In the fields an expanse of green,
By the tall tower the trees show a darkish hue.
The spring wind has not the sense to restrain the
　　willow catkins
Which rush wildly in a drizzle at the faces of
　　passers by.

The green leaves enfold the oriole,
The red blinds shut out the swallow.
The incense from the burner chases the gossamer
　　quietly around.
As I awake from a troubled dream, the wine
　　wearing off,
There goes the slanting sun shining on the inner
　　courtyard.

Yen Shu (991-1055)

浪淘沙　歐陽修

把酒祝東風
且共從容
垂楊紫陌洛城東
總是當時攜手處
游遍芳叢

聚散苦匆匆
此恨無窮
今年花勝去年紅
可惜明年花更好
知與誰同

To the Tune of *Lang t'ao sha*

Raising my cup, I plead with the east wind
To stay with us for yet a while longer.
East of Loyang, the willows drooping, the fields
    purple,
There is no spot but we visited, hand in hand,
Where flowers bloom in abundance.

Having met, we parted, only too soon.
What would have been will never be.
Flowers this year are redder than last.
What a pity, flowers next year will be finer still
But goodness knows who will share them with me.

Ou-yang Hsiu (1007-1072)

浪淘沙　歐陽修

把酒祝東風
且共從容
垂楊紫陌洛城東
總是當時携手處
游遍芳叢

聚散苦匆匆
此恨無窮
今年花勝去年紅
可惜明年花更好
知與誰同

蝶戀花　歐陽修

誰道閒情拋卻久
每到春來惆悵還依舊
日日花前常病酒
不辭鏡裏朱顏瘦

河畔青蕪堤上柳
為問新愁何事年年有
獨立小橋風滿袖
平林新月人歸後

To the Tune of *Tieh lien hua*

Who says idle love has long been cast aside?
Whenever spring comes round I am melancholy
    as ever.
Day after day, overcome by wine among the
    flowers,
I accept a youthful face haggard in the mirror.

Green grass by the river, willows on the bank,
But why, I ask, is there new grief year after year?
Alone I stand on the little bridge, the wind swelling
    my sleeves,
After she is gone in the moonlight across the wood
    in the plain.

                                        Ou-yang Hsiu

蝶戀花

誰道閒情拋棄久
每到春來惆悵還依舊
日日花前常病酒
不辭鏡裡朱顏瘦

河畔青蕪堤上柳
為問新愁何事年年有
獨立小橋風滿袖
平林新月人歸後

Flowers and Birds
by Jên Po-nien 任伯年 (1840-1896)

生查子

太牟元夜昔
花市燈如畫
月上柳梢頭
人約黃昏後

今年元夜時
月與花依舊
不見去年人
淚濕春衫袖

To the Tune of *Sheng-cha-tzu*

Last year on the Night of the Lanterns
The flower market was bright as day.
The moon climbed to the tip of the willow tree;
I awaited my love at the hour of dusk.

This year on the Night of the Lanterns
The moon and the flowers are as they were.
My love from last year is nowhere to be seen;
Tears drench the sleeves of my spring dress.

Ou-yang Hsiu

生查子

去年元夜時
花市燈如畫
月上柳梢頭
人約黃昏後

今年元夜時
月與花依舊
不見去年人
淚濕春衫袖

采桑子

羣芳過後西湖好
狼籍殘紅
飛絮濛濛
垂柳闌干盡日風

笙歌散盡游人去
始覺春空
垂下簾櫳
雙燕過來細雨中

To the Tune of *Ts'ai-sang tzu*

采桑子

羣芳過後西湖好
狼籍殘紅
飛絮濛濛
垂柳闌干盡日風

笙歌散盡遊人去
始覺春空
垂下簾櫳
雙燕歸來細雨中

The West Lake is lovely when the blossoms are
    gone,
The ground littered with fallen red,
Catkins flying in a drizzle,
All day the wind blows on the railings by the
    drooping willows.

Only after the merry-making when the revellers
    are gone
Does one feel the emptiness of spring.
I lower the blinds on the window:
A pair of swallows come back in the fine rain.

Ou-yang Hsiu

鷓鴣天　晏幾道

彩袖殷勤捧玉鍾
當年拚却醉顏紅
舞低楊柳樓心月
歌盡桃花扇影風

從別後
憶相逢
幾回魂夢與君同
今宵賸把銀釭照
猶恐相逢是夢中

鷓鴣天　晏幾道

彩袖殷勤捧玉鍾
當年拚却醉顏紅
舞低楊柳樓心月
歌盡桃花扇影風

從別後
憶相逢
幾回魂夢與君同
今宵賸把銀釭照
猶恐相逢是夢中

To the Tune of *Che-ku t'ien*

Embroidered sleeves never let my jade cup go dry.
Then was I willing to risk a face flushed with wine.
She danced till the moon sank below the Willow
    Tower
And stilled the breeze coming off the Peach Fan by
    her song.

Ever since we parted,
Thinking of our meeting,
How often has my soul shared with yours the same
    dream!
Tonight I keep holding the silver lamp to you
For fear even now our meeting is but a dream.

Yen Chi-tao (?1030-?)

采桑子　晏幾道

西樓月下當時見
淚粉偷勻
歌罷還顰
恨隔鑪煙看未真

別來樓外垂楊縷
幾換青春
倦客紅塵
長記樓中粉淚人

To the Tune of *Ts'ai-sang tzu*

The time we met under the moon in the West
    Lodge
In stealth you powdered over your tears
And you sang only to frown after your song.
A pity I could not see you clearly across the
    incense!

After we parted, the threads of the willow outside
Have time and again renewed their fresh green,
While the weary traveller in the mundane dust
Can never forget the girl in the Lodge with the
    powdered tears.

Yen Chi-tao

采桑子

西樓月下當時見
淚粉偷勻
歌罷還顰
恨隔鑪烟看未眞

別來樓外垂楊縷
幾換青春
倦客紅塵
長記樓中粉淚人

臨江仙　蘇軾

夜飲東坡醒復醉
歸來髣髴三更
家童鼻息已雷鳴
敲門都不應
倚杖聽江聲

長恨此身非我有
何時忘却營營
夜闌風靜縠紋平
小舟從此逝
江海寄餘生

To the Tune of *Lin-chiang hsien*

On the East Hill I sobered up only to get drunk
    again.
When I returned it must have been the third watch.
The servant boy was by then snoring like thunder.
He never answered however hard I knocked.
Leaning on my staff I listened to the sound of the
    river.

I constantly regret not being my own master.
When can I leave behind this life of care?
The night spent, the wind drops and the ripples
    subside.
I will go away on a small boat never to return,
Spending the rest of my days upon the seas.

Su Shih (1036-1101)

浣溪沙　蘇軾

山下蘭芽短浸溪
松間沙路淨無泥
蕭蕭暮雨子規啼

誰道人生無再少
門前溪水尚能西
休將白髮唱黃雞

To the Tune of *Huan hsi sha*

Below the hill the short orchid shoots soak in the
    stream,
Amongst the pines the clean sandy path is un-
    sullied,
To the sound of rain drizzling at dusk, the cuckoo
    cries.

Who says for man youth never comes a second
    time?
Even the stream by the door is able to make for
    the west[1].
Sing not with your white hair of the cock im-
    patient for dawn.

Su Shih

浣溪沙

山下蘭芽短浸溪
松間沙路淨無泥
蕭蕭暮雨子規啼

誰道人生無再少
門前溪水尚能西
休將白髮唱黃雞

[1]It used to be the belief in China that in its nature water always
flows east.

少年遊　　蘇軾

去年相送
餘杭門外
飛雪似楊花
今年春盡
楊花似雪
猶不見還家

對酒捲簾邀明月
風露透窗紗
恰似姮娥憐雙燕
分明照
畫樑斜

To the Tune of *Shao-nien yu*

Last year when I saw you off
Outside the city gates,
The fluttering snow was like willow catkins.
This year spring has drawn to a close
And willow catkins are like snow.
Still there is no sign of your return.

I roll up the blinds and ask the moon to share my
　　wine
And the wind and dew come through the window
　　gauze.
It's as if the Moon Maiden, out of pity for the
　　nesting birds,
Lights up clearly
The painted beam aslant.

Su Shih

少年遊

去年相送
餘杭門外
飛雪似楊花
今年春盡
楊花似雪
猶不見還家

對酒捲簾邀明月
風露透窗紗
恰似姮娥憐雙燕
分明照
畫樑斜

蝶戀花　蘇軾

花褪殘紅青杏小
燕子飛時
綠水人家遶
枝上柳綿吹又少
天涯何處無芳草

牆裏秋千牆外道
牆外行人
牆裏佳人笑
笑漸不聞聲漸悄
多情却被無情惱

To the Tune of *Tieh lien hua*

Flowers slip off their faded red and green apricots
　　are small.
When the swallow takes to its wings
The green water round the homestead winds.
The catkins on the willow branches dwindle with
　　each gust of wind.
Where to the ends of the earth is there no sweet
　　grass?

Within the walls a swing, without a path;
Without the walls a wayfarer,
Within the laughter of a fair maid.
The laughter grows faint; the sound dies away.
One who cares is vexed by one who cares not.

Su Shih

蝶戀花

花褪殘紅青杏小

燕子飛時

綠水人家遶

枝上柳綿吹又少

天涯何處無芳草

牆裏秋千牆外道

牆外行人

牆裏佳人笑

笑漸不聞聲漸悄

多情却被無情惱

如夢令　秦觀

遙夜沈沈如水
風緊驛亭深閉
夢破鼠窺鐙
霜送曉寒侵被
無寐
無寐
門外馬嘶人起

To the Tune of *Ju meng ling*

The long night is deep like water.
The wind taut, the post station is firmly shut.
My dream cut short, a mouse peeps at the lamp.
The frost sends the morning chill through my
　padded quilt.
No more sleep,
No more sleep,
Outside the horses neigh and men are up and
　about.

Ch'in Kuan (1047-1100)

如夢令　秦觀

遙夜沉沉如水
風緊驛亭深閉
夢破鼠窺燈
霜送曉寒侵被
無寐
無寐
門外馬嘶人起

少年遊　周邦彥

并刀如水
吳鹽勝雪
纖指破新橙
錦幄初溫
獸香不斷
相對坐調笙

低聲問
向誰行宿
城上已三更
馬滑霜濃
不如休去
直是少人行

To the Tune of *Shao-nien yu*

The knife shimmers like water,
The salt is whiter than snow.
The slender fingers cut the new orange.
The curtains of brocade freshly warmed,
The incense from the burner rises unbroken.
Facing each other, they sit playing the pipes.

In a low voice she asks,
'Where are you putting up for the night?
The third watch has sounded on the city walls.
It's slippery for the horse on the thick frost.
I'd rather you didn't go.
The streets are all but deserted outside.'

Chou Pang-yen (1057-1121)

常記溪亭日暮
沈醉不知歸路
興盡晚回舟
誤入藕花深處
爭渡
爭渡
驚起一灘鷗鷺

如夢令　李清照

To the Tune of *Ju meng ling*

I often recall the pavilion by the stream at sunset.
The thought of home never crossed my drunken
    mind.
The mood spent, I turned my boat as night fell
And strayed into the depth of the lotus blossoms.
A scramble for the jetty,
A scramble for the jetty,
Startled a flock of water birds on the sand.

                    Li Ch'ing-chao (1084-?)

如夢令　李清照

常記溪亭日暮
沉醉不知歸路
興盡晚回舟
誤入藕花深處
爭渡
爭渡
驚起一灘鷗鷺

如夢令 李清照

昨夜雨疏風驟
濃睡不消殘酒
試問捲簾人
卻道海棠依舊
知否
知否
應是綠肥紅瘦

To the Tune of *Ju meng ling*

Last night the rain was fitful and the wind abrupt.
A good sleep has not cleared my drunken head.
Asking her who is rolling up the blinds,
I am told the begonias are undisturbed.
'Don't you see?
Don't you see?
The green must have grown fat and the red gone
    thin.'

Li Ch'ing-chao

如夢令

昨夜雨疏風驟
濃睡不消殘酒
試問捲簾人
却道海棠依舊
知否
知否
應是綠肥紅瘦

醜奴兒　辛棄疾

少年不識愁滋味
愛上層樓
愛上層樓
爲賦新詞強說愁

而今識盡愁滋味
欲說還休
欲說還休
却道天涼好箇秋

To the Tune of *Ch'ou nu erh*

In youth, not knowing what grief was about,
I loved to seek a melancholy spot,
I loved to seek a melancholy spot,
And for a new song I would pretend to speak of
    grief.

And now, knowing what grief is all about,
On the point of speaking, I hold back,
On the point of speaking, I hold back,
And say, instead, What a fine autumn, so very cool.

Hsin Ch'i-chi (1140-1207)

醜奴兒　辛棄疾

少年不識愁滋味
愛上層樓
愛上層樓
爲賦新詞強說愁

而今識盡愁滋味
欲說還休
欲說還休
却道天涼好箇秋

虞美人　蔣捷

少年聽雨歌樓上
紅燭昏羅帳
壯年聽雨客舟中
江闊雲低
斷雁叫西風

而今聽雨僧廬下
鬢已星星也
悲歡離合總無情
一任階前滴到明

To the Tune of *Yü mei-jen*

In youth I listened to the rain in houses of song,
The red candle casting a shadow on the bed cur-
      tains.
In my prime I listened to the rain in sojourning
      boats,
The river broad, the clouds low,
A stray bird wailing in the west wind.

And now, I listen to the rain in a monk's hut,
My hair long since bespeckled.
Gaiety and sorrow, meetings and partings, all so
      unfeeling,
I leave the rain to drip on the steps till dawn.

                                        Chiang Chieh (fl. 13th c.)

虞美人　蔣捷

少年聽雨歌樓上
紅燭昏羅帳
壯年聽雨客舟中
江闊雲低
斷雁叫西風

而今聽雨僧廬下
鬢已星星也
悲歡離合總無情
一任階前滴到明

繆鉞：論詞
The Chinese Lyric

By **Miao Yüeh**

Translated by **John Minford**

Origins

CHANG HUI-YEN 張惠言, in the Preface to his *Lyric Anthology* 詞選序, gives a most succinct account of the origins of the lyric: "It originated," he writes, "with the poets of the T'ang dynasty, who made new metres out of popular songs, adding their own words, or 'lyrics'."

T'ang verse, though written in lines of regular length, was sung to irregular tunes, and the singer had to match text with music by adding words as he went along. In time this practice was felt to be too clumsy, and poets, either in response to musicians' requests or on their own initiative, created the new lyric form, which followed the melodic pattern and was easier to sing. The biography of Wen T'ing-yün 溫庭筠 in the *Old T'ang History* 舊唐書, for example, says that "he followed the music of strings and flutes to create his original and captivating lyrics". Such were the beginnings of the lyric as a poetic form.

The new form was at first called "lyrics to music" 曲子詞, then "lyrics" for short. So lyrics are just words to music, and there is no deeper significance in the derivation of the term. It is true that in the ancient dictionary *Shuo Wen* 說文 we find the word *tz'u* 詞 defined as "the Outward Expression of an Inward Idea". But this refers to *tz'u* in the compound *yü-tz'u* 語詞, "verbal expression". Tuan Yü-ts'ai 段玉裁 glosses it as "words with either a descriptive or an expletive function". *Tz'u* as a literary term has a quite separate history. The pregnant nature of lyric verse, which coincided so well with the Inwardness of the *Shuo Wen* definition, may have led writers of a later age to invent this derivation. We come across it for the first time in the Sung dynasty, in Lu Wen-kuei 陸文圭's Preface to the lyrics of Chang Yen 張炎: *White Clouds in the Hills* 山中白雲詞序. Later Chang Hui-yen was particularly fond of the theory, and it became accepted as part of the critical orthodoxy. But the first lyric poets of the Middle and Late T'ang had no such meaning in mind.[1]

---

[1] The lyrics traditionally ascribed to Li Po have been shown in recent times to be forgeries. The first lyrics date from Middle T'ang.

Form

THE LYRICS OF MIDDLE and Late T'ang, of the Five Dynasties and of the early years of Northern Sung were all *hsiao ling* 小令, or Short Snatches, and their prosodic features were still similar to those of regular verse.[2] For example: *Sheng-cha-tzu* 生查子 (The Hawthorn Song) resembles a double five-syllable quatrain in Oblique rhyme; *Yü-lou ch'un* 玉樓春 (Spring in the Jade Pavilion) resembles a double seven-syllable quatrain in Oblique rhyme; *Che-ku t'ien* 鷓鴣天 (Partridge Skies) resembles a double seven-syllable quatrain in Level rhyme, except that the first line of the second quatrain is divided into two three-syllable lines. Other metres, including *Lang t'ao sha* 浪淘沙 (Waves Wash the Sand), *Lin-chiang hsien* 臨江仙 (Fairy at the Riverside), *Yü mei-jen* 虞美人 (Beautiful Lady Yü), *P'u-sa man* 菩薩蠻 (Strangers in Saint's Coif) are all basically five-syllable or seven-syllable metres, with the addition or subtraction of an occasional syllable. In most cases the rules for tonal euphony within the line are similar to and no stricter than those of Regulated Verse.

By the reign of the Sung emperor Jen-tsung 仁宗 (1023-1064), the longer *man tz'u* 慢詞, or Slow Songs, had come into fashion, and in subsequent years musical specialists like Chou Pang-yen, Mo-chi Ya-yen 萬俟雅言 and Chiang K'uei 姜夔 created new metres, and lyric prosody began to acquire a greater complexity. Tonal rules became stricter, and finer distinctions were drawn between both *Yin* and *Yang* tones and Rising and Falling tones. Sometimes lyric poets deliberately created a distorted sound (by the use of irregular tonal sequences), in order to give a feeling of agitation or distress. The later lyrics were moving further and further from the prosody of Regulated Verse and of the earlier Snatches.

An example of the new tonal finesse can be found in the last line of the metre *An hsiang* 暗香 (Faint Fragrance), where the four syllables must be

1. Rising
2. Level
3. Falling
4. Entering

in that order, with no substitution allowed between the three Oblique Tones. e.g.

幾時見得 (Chiang K'uei)

兩隄翠匝 (Wu Wen-ying 吳文英)

In addition to the tones, there were four further subdivisions: Stressed and Unstressed, Voiced and Voiceless. Chang Yen tells how his father, Chang Shu 張樞, when composing a lyric to the metre *Hsi hua ch'un* 惜花春 (Treasuring Spring Blossoms), found the word "deep" 深 in the line "the latticed casement deep" 瑣窗深 unmusical. He changed it to "dark" 幽. He was still not satisfied, however, and only thought the line sufficiently musical (i.e. singable) when he changed the last word again, this time to "bright" 明. All three words are in the old Level Tone, so what was bothering him? The answer is to be found in the phonetic niceties of the Five Sonorities— labial, dental, guttural, lingual and nasal—and in the associated qualities of Stress and Voicing (see Chang Yen's *Origins of the Lyric* 詞源). Distinctions as fine as this had never been observed in Regulated Verse.

---

[2]Prosody is used here as a conventional equivalent of *chü fa* 句法, and refers to pattern of line length.

Flowers and Birds
by Jên Po-nien 任伯年 (1840-1896)

There were also strict rhyming rules in lyric composition. Oblique rhyme usually included all three Oblique Tones. But some metres specified the Entering tone. The *Tz'u-lin cheng-yün* 詞林正韻 by Ko Tsai 戈載 lists more than twenty such metres. If we check them against existing lyrics written in Sung times, we find that not all conform to this rule. But some do, like Chiang K'uei's *An hsiang* (Faint Fragrance), *Shu ying* 疏影 (Scattered Shadows), *P'i-p'a hsien* 琵琶仙 (Fairy with the P'i-pa), and *Ch'i-liang fan* 淒涼犯 (Lonely Song in Parallel Keys). These all have a strong, stirring sonority, and for such "blasts on a muted Tartar pipe", rhymes on the Entering tone were clearly suitable.[3] Rhymes on Rising or Falling tones, while permissible, would somehow alter the effect. *Ch'iu hsiao yin* 秋宵吟 (Autumn Nocturne) and *Ch'ing shang yüan* 清商怨 (Elegy in the Key of Ch'ing-shang) should have a Rising rhyme throughout; *Ts'ui lou yin* 翠樓吟 (Song of the Blue Pavilion) and *Chü-hua hsin* 菊花新 (Fresh Chrysanthemums) should have a Falling rhyme throughout; while some metres have a Rising rhyme in some lines and a Falling rhyme in others, or have set rhyming tones only at the beginning and end of the stanza. It has been said that overstrictness in the rules of regular verse is akin to hardness of heart; but the rules of lyric verse are even stricter—sometimes indeed as rigorous as the proverbial laws of Shen Pu-hai 申不害 and Han Fei-tzu 韓非子.

So, although the lyric was at first only an offshoot of regular verse (as evidenced by another of its early names, Ends of Verse—詩餘), it subsequently flourished in its own right. Like a satellite state, that grows into an independent nation, the lyric grew to maturity, acquired its own unique forms and with the passing of time underwent a more and more complex transformation.

Content

WE SHOULD NOT HOWEVER give the impression that the lyric differs from regular verse only in its outward form, its prosodic structure and tonal rules. There is also a marked difference in its content, in the moods it evokes and the worlds it creates.[4] Outward form may be more crudely tangible than inner content, and in a superficial way easier to differentiate. But at a deeper level content is cause and form only effect. In other words, difference of content precedes difference of form, and if we wish to understand how lyric verse differs from regular verse, and how it grew out of the regular mould and established its own separate identity, its own world, we

[3]C.N. Tay, in his article "From Snow to Plum Blossoms", *Journal of Asian Studies*, 25 no. 2, 1966, compares the "abrupt Entering tone" to a "thud on a muffled drum". Level, Rising and Falling tones he compares respectively to a "dong" (the drum struck at the centre), a "drone" (near the periphery) and a "tom" (forcefully at the centre). He also observes that the two tone categories (Level and Oblique) perform a function in Chinese verse similar to that played by stress in English verse. They are, he says, analogous respectively to "reverberant bells and drums, and dull rapping on wood and rock".

[4]For a good synopsis of the meaning of "world" in Chinese poetics, see James J. Y. Liu, *The Art of Chinese Poetry*, pp. 81-87.

must examine not the secondary differences of form, but the primary differences of content.

When men commit their inner experiences to paper, they may begin by writing prose. But some of these experiences may be too abstruse and subtle for the medium of prose. It is to express these that poetry comes into being. Prose is explicit statement, poetry veiled innuendo; prose is plainspoken, while poetry abounds in metaphors; prose is full and exhaustive, poetry restrained and suggestive. These two forms differ in accordance with the subtlety of their content. Each has its limitations. Poetry can reach beyond the bounds of prose, but cannot encompass the same range.

Although poetry in general deals with the subtler aspects of human experience, there is a still more elusive and refined level of subtlety, a still greater delicacy of nuance, that cannot find expression in the regular poetic forms, even if these are stretched to their utmost limits. A new form is needed. This is where the lyric comes in. Not as the conscious creation of one or two individuals, but as the natural product of experiment and evolution. We have already described how poets of the Middle T'ang, who had previously written in the regular forms, began to write in lines of varying length, in order to fit the irregular melodic patterns. The very first lyrics were in one sense no more than a solution to a musical problem, and the lyric verse of Po Chü-i 白居易, Liu Yü-hsi 劉禹錫 and their contemporaries was not so very different in mood from their regular verse. But once they had led the way, more and more poets experimented with the form, and as they gradually discovered the wealth of different metres, each with its distinctive pattern of varying line-length and its own rhythmic lilt, they realized that here was a form at once lighter and more supple than regular verse. It was perfectly suited to the expression of those very experiences, those subtle feelings and fugitive melancholy moods, that were beyond the reach of the old regular forms. Once one or two writers of genius had exploited its special qualities and revealed its unique possibilities, the lyric was established as an independent literary form.

Wen Ting-yun and Wei Chuang 韋莊 wrote both regular and lyric verse. Wen's lyrics have a wistful melancholy and a mellifluous beauty. Here is one, to the tune *Keng-lou tzu* 更漏子 (The Water Clock):

> *Embers of incense*   玉爐香
> *In the jade brazier*   紅蠟淚
> *With candle's crimson tears*   偏照畫堂秋思
> *Conspire*   眉翠薄
> *To glow on gilded walls,*   鬢雲殘
> *Autumnal mood,*   夜長衾枕寒
> *Faded make-up, hair awry,*
> *Coverlet and pillow cold,*
> *A long night*
> *Ahead.*

> At midnight the rain　　　　　　　　梧桐樹
> On the wu-t'ung tree　　　　　　　　三更雨
> Not knowing the pain　　　　　　　　不道離情正苦
> Of loneliness　　　　　　　　　　　一葉葉
> Falls leaf to leaf　　　　　　　　　一聲聲
> Dripping　　　　　　　　　　　　　空階滴到明
> On the bare steps
> Till dawn.

Wei Chuang's lyrics have a quiet charm, a subtle enchantment. Here is one, to the tune *Ho-yeh pei* 荷葉杯 (The Lotus Leaf Cup):

> I remember　　　　　　　　　　　　記得那年花下
> That year among the flowers　　　　　深夜
> Deep in the night　　　　　　　　　初識謝娘時
> Meeting my love　　　　　　　　　水堂西面畫簾垂
> For the first time:　　　　　　　　攜手暗相期
> West of the Water Pavilion
> Behind painted curtains,　　　　　　惆悵曉鶯殘月
> Holding hands,　　　　　　　　　　相別
> A secret tryst.　　　　　　　　　　從此隔音塵
> 　　　　　　　　　　　　　　　　如今俱是異鄉人
> Heart-ache　　　　　　　　　　　　相見更無因
> At the morning oriole's cry,
> As the tattered moon went down,
> And we said goodbye!
> Since then,
> Not a word.
> We are both far from home;
> Why should we ever meet again?

Wen T'ing-yün and Wei Chuang have created a new world. Nowhere in their regular verse is such an atmosphere as this to be found. If the lyric form had not existed, they could never have embodied this inner world so fully. Li Shang-yin 李商隱 stretched the regular verse-forms to their limit of subtlety and refinement. Beyond this limit, poets were compelled to strike out and find a fresh form, just as water breaks out of an old course into a new channel. It was a natural process. As so often happens, simple beginnings led to far-reaching consequences. The poets of Middle T'ang, when they first modified regular verse to make it easier to sing, could hardly have foreseen what their simple innovations would lead to.

So although in a loose sense lyric verse is akin to regular verse and distinct from prose, if we look more closely we find that it is also quite distinct from regular verse. Regular verse seems explicit when compared with the even more suggestive and veiled mode of expression found in the lyric; it seems plainspoken and exhaustive, when compared with the even more symbolic and restrained style of the lyric. To quote Wang Kuo-wei 王國維:

> "The lyric form is one of exquisite refinement and sophisticated beauty. While this enables it to deal with subjects that are beyond the scope of regular verse, it also limits its range. Regular verse is broader in scope, the lyric deeper in expression." This is the principal distinction between the two forms. (*Lyric Remarks for the Human World* 人間詞話)

Since the lyric is concerned with the subtlest levels of human experience, its chosen themes, the worlds it creates, its soulds and colours must be correspondingly subtle. We can summarize these under four broad headings.

I. Delicacy of Language

While both the writer of regular verse and the lyric poet embody human experience through imagery, while both use natural scenery and living things—animals, birds, plants and trees of all kinds—to create moods, the lyric poet will always choose the more ethereal and exquisite image. When describing the sky, he will prefer a faint rain, a solitary cloud, scattered stars and a pale moon. His landscape will tend to be one of distant peaks, meandering banks, misty isles and fishermen's shoals. For his creatures he will prefer the petrel, the flitting oriole, the cold cicada or newly-arrived geese. For vegetation, wilting blossoms, floating catkins, fragrant herbs and weeping willows. His buildings will consist of painted ceilings, gilded halls, fretted casements and carved portals. His household objects will be such things as silver lamps, golden censers, phoenix screens and jade goblets. When describing jewelry and clothes, he will imagine iridescent sleeves, gauze apparel, jasper hairpin and kingfisher diadem. His preferred emotions will be groundless grief, sweet musings, quiet enjoyment, and feelings of seclusion. Even the language used to describe the most ordinary setting will be exquisite and delicate. For instance, pavilion and hall are common enough things. But "windswept pavilion, moonlit hall" (from one of Liu Yung 柳永's lyrics) are at once part of a more rarefied world. Again, flowers and willows are common enough. But "willows at dusk, flowers in the twilight" (from a lyric by Shi Ta-tsu 史達祖) evoke a very special atmosphere of quiet seclusion. While this type of language is inappropriate in prose, and even in regular verse can seem precious if not used with discretion, in lyric verse it is perfect. Each form has its own standard of appropriateness.

A lyric poet will use delicate imagery to express even a tragic or heroic sentiment. When Chiang K'uei passed through Yangchou, he wrote in his *Yangchou Man* 楊州慢 (Yangchou Elegy) of his grief at the aftermath of the Jurched incursion led by Wan-yen Liang 完顏亮:

After the raid,	自胡馬窺江去後
The Tartar cavalry have gone,	廢池喬木
Leaving behind	猶厭言兵
Ruined ponds,	………
Withered trees,	
And a people	
Loth to mention war.	

And later in the same poem:

> *The Twenty Four Bridges*   二十四橋仍在
> *Have survived:*   波心蕩
> *A ripple in midstream,*   冷月無聲
> *Cold moon,*
> *Silence.*

Ponds, trees, ripple and moon—all delicate touches. Lamenting the decline of the Southern Sung, Chiang wrote the lines:

> *Alas! a whole nation*   最可惜
> *Made over to cuckoo-song!*   一片江山
>   *Pa Keui* 八歸   總付與啼鴃

Here again, a delicate image, this time of the cuckoo.

Hsin Ch'i-chi's lyrics are powerful and free, and yet, when he wished to express his bitterness at the national decline and at his own personal rejection, he wrote lines such as these: from the end of *Mo yü-erh* 摸魚兒 (Catching Fish):

> *Do not gaze*   休去倚危闌
> *From that high balcony:*   斜陽正在
> *The sunset*   煙柳斷腸處
> *And misty willows*
> *Are a sight to break the heart.*

Images like the "high balcony" and the "misty willows" convey his passionate indignation with a subtlety and delicacy appropriate to the lyric form.

As a final example of delicacy, here is Ch'in Kuan 秦觀's lyric to the tune *Huan hsi sha* 浣溪沙 (Wash Creek Sand):

> *Silently a light chill*   漠漠輕寒上小樓
>   *drifts up to my chamber.*   曉陰無賴似窮秋
> *Dawn shadows loiter*   淡煙流水畫屏幽
>   *like autumn lees.*
> *Pale haze*   自在飛花輕似夢
>   *on the moving stream—*   無邊絲雨細如愁
> *The painted screen*   寶簾閒掛小銀鉤
>   *encloses a sequestered ease.*
>
> *Carefree flying petals*
>   *light as dreams,*
> *Endless silken threads of rain*
>   *fine as care.*
> *Limp,*
>   *from its tiny silver hook*

> *Hangs*
>   *the embroidered portière.*

In this perfect fusion, emotion and setting enhance each other like pearl and jade in a necklace. It is one of Ch'in Kuan's finest poems. Take the setting: a little room, and within it a painted screen; on the screen, a pale haze on the stream; an embroidered portière hangs from a tiny silver hook. The physical details are all exquisite. The time of day is dawn, when shadows loiter and a light chill drifts silently upwards. Not just any shadows, but dawn shadows, not just an ordinary chill, but a light chill. And both further attenuated by the words "loiter" and "silently". Outside, the petals fly, carefree and light as dreams; the rain falls in threads, endless and fine as care; throughout the poem, the choice of images and the way in which they are used show a masterly skill, a wonderfully suggestive and delicate touch.

The five-syllable Regulated Octet has been compared to an élite gathering of cultured gentlemen, to which butchers and wine-merchants could not possibly be admitted. I would compare this lyric of Ch'in Kuan's to a gathering of beautiful ladies and young maidens in a garden pavilion, too select not only for commoners but even for scholars and hermits. Its exclusive quality enables it to capture the subtle fragrance, the ineffable essence of an experience, and in reading it we feel transported to a purer and more mysterious realm, and my heart is filled with an almost unbearable melancholy. Even the regular verse of Li Shang-yin does not have such a haunting and magical effect. This is the peculiar power of the lyric poet, to create with delicate imagery a unique world embodying his intimate personal experience. The words are tangible, but their ultimate meaning is elusive. Though small and delicate in themselves, they have the power to suggest something much larger. At a first reading they strike the ear and eye with a vivid impact. Prolonged recitation brings out their deeper and more abiding fascination.

II. *Lightness of Substance*

Chen Tzu-lung 陳子龍 wrote: "The lyric is a fragile form. Pearls and kingfisher feathers are too heavy for it, let alone dragon and phoenix." It is only natural that with delicacy of language should go lightness of substance. Although regular verse and lyric verse are not material objects, and we cannot actually put them on the scales, if we recite them to ourselves and mull them over, we become aware of a relative difference in weight. That is not to say that the lyric is trivial. In a lyric, a very serious idea would still be expressed in a light and ethereal fashion. This is dictated by the nature of the form. Let me give an example. We all know what it is like to be reunited with family and friends after a long absence. The joy is so intense, we feel almost as if in a dream. Tu Fu, in his poem "Ch'iang village", tells how after the An Lu-shan 安祿山 troubles he returned home, to find

> *Wife and children amazed that I'm alive:*　　妻孥怪我在
> *The first shock over, still they wipe their eyes.*　　驚定還拭淚
> *Through the turmoil of the civil war*　　世亂遭飄蕩
> *Kind fate protected me.*　　生還偶然遂
> *Neighbours come crowding to the fence*　　鄰人滿牆頭

> *With sobs and sighs of disbelief.*   感歎亦歔欷
> . . . .
> *When might falls, we light our candle,*   夜闌更秉燭
> *Gazing at each other as in a dream.*   相對如夢寐

A deep feeling weightly expressed, striking the reader with the force of a rock plunging from a perilous height. Compare it with Yen Chi-tao 晏幾道's lyric to the tune *Che-ku t'ien* 鷓鴣天 (Partridge Skies), describing his reunion with his beloved after a long separation:

> *Since we parted*   從別後
> *I would recall our days together.*   憶相逢
> *How often*   幾回魂夢與君同
> *My dreaming soul joined yours!*   今宵賸把銀釭照
> *Tonight*   猶恐相逢是夢中
> *By the silver taper's light*
> *We'll gaze,*
> *Afraid this meeting*
> *Is just another dream.*

The sentiment is very close to Tu Fu's, but cast in a lyric mould its substance becomes lighter and more ethereal, the lightness giving it a dappled grace, like that of a dragonfly skimming the water and whirling through the air, or of a still lake in which the wind stirs a slight ripple. This grace is the hallmark of the lyric. For weight and strength it cannot compare with regular verse. But it excels in lilt and charm, helped in this by its metrical irregularity.

III. Narrowness of Range

Prose can be philosophical, narrative, lyrical or descriptive. Regular verse is usually either lyrical or descriptive, but can also be philosophical or narrative. Lyric verse can *only* be lyrical or descriptive. It is totally unsuited to both philosophy and narration. This is partly because of its metrical intricacy, but is also caused by the essential nature of the lyric form.

Su Shi 蘇軾 (Tung-p'o) and Hsin Ch'i-chi 辛棄疾, both masters of the lyric form, tried using it for philosophical themes. Here are two examples, the first by Su, to the tune *Man t'ing fang* 滿庭芳 (A Courtyard Full of Fragrance):

> *For Fame as insubstantial as the horn of a snail,*   蝸角虛名
> *For Profit the size of the head of a fly—*   蠅頭微利
> *Why make a fuss,*   算來著甚乾忙
> *When gain and loss*   事前皆定
> *Are fixed before we even try?*   誰弱又誰強
> *While I'm young and have the leisure*   且趁閒身未老
> *Let me have my bit of pleasure,*   儘放我
> *Even if a hundred years from now*   些子疏狂

> *I have nothing more to show*   百年裏
> *Than thirty-six thousand five hundred*   渾敎是醉
> *Drunken fits!*   三萬六千場

The second, by Hsin, is to the tune *Shao pien* 哨遍 (A Slow Chant):

> *Two snails-horn kingdoms fight:*   蝸角鬪爭
> *Buffetland to the left,*   左觸右蠻
> *Mauletania to the right.*   一戰連千里
> *The battlefield stretches*   君試思
> *A thousand miles.*   方寸此心微
> *The little mind,*   總虛空
> *So circumscribed,*   並無包際
> *Though void,*   喻此理
> *Contains the Infinite.*   何言泰山毫末
> *In which light,*   從來天地一稊米
> *What need of parables to prove*   嗟大小相形
> *Mount Tai no bigger than a strand*   鳩鵬自樂
> *Of hair?*   之二蟲又何知
> *The universe has always been*   記跖行仁義孔丘非
> *A grain of sand.*   更殤樂長年老彭悲
> *Size is a relative idea.*   火鼠論寒
> *Dove and eagle are quite content*   冰蠶語熱
> *Each to follow his own bent.*   定誰同異
> *Robber Chi a saint*
> *Makes Confucius a sinner;*
> *Joy for a dead child*
> *Means grief for Methuselah.*
> *Have you ever heard*
> *Fire Rats discussing the cold,*
> *Or Ice Worms debating the heat?*
> *Whose is the last word?*

Both these poems fall flat, and the banal effect they create is sufficient proof that the philosophical experiment has failed.

Quotations too, from the Classics, the Histories, the Philosophers and even from Buddhist literature, while they may be introduced quite happily into regular verse, usually seem out of place in lyric verse; Hsin Ch'i-chi was adept at using other men's lines, and his lyrics are often a patchwork of quotations. His favourite sources are the *Analects*, *Mencius*, the *Tso Chuan* 左傳, *Chuang-tzu* 莊子, the *Songs of the South* 離騷, the *Historical Records* 史記, the *Han History* 漢書, *A New Account of Tales of the World* 世說新語, *Chao-ming Wen Hsüan* 昭明文選 and the poetry of Li Po and Tu Fu. Take lines such as

> *Nothing can be better*   最好五十學易
> *Than to be able*   三百篇詩

> *To devote oneself to the* Changes
> *And the* Odes . . .
> *At the age of fifty*
>
> P'o-lo-men yin 婆羅門引
> (The Brahman Song)

and

> *Success and failure,*   進退存亡
> *Survival and destruction,*   行藏用舍
> *Promotion and rejection*   小人請學樊遲稼
> *Are all the same to me.*   衡門之下可棲遲
> *I'd like to ask Fan Chi*   日之夕矣牛羊下
> *About farming.*
> *A humble cottage can make a resting place,*
> *Cattle and sheep*
> *Coming home at sunset.*
>
> T'a so hsing 踏莎行[5]

Such writing is inappropriate in lyric verse.

Sung dynasty lyric poets often used lines from the regular verse of such poets as Li Ho 李賀, Li Shang-yin and Wen T'ing-yün. But then this was exquisite and sumptous poetry to begin with, and lent itself to such adaptation. Even lines from Six Dynasties literature are sometimes too heavy for lyric verse. When Li Ch'ing-chao 李清照 quotes the lines

> *The light dew falls in the morning,*   清露晨流
> *The young* wu-t'ung *tree begins to sprout*   新桐初引
>
> Nien-nu chiao 念奴嬌
> (The Charms of Nian-nu)

from *A New Account of Tales of the World*, she succeeds because she has chosen two unusually appropriate lines. This gives us some idea of the discrimination required in the use of quotations, the need to exclude all but the light and fine.

The lyric is the most refined of all Chinese literary forms, and the only one capable of articulating a certain kind of restrained and elusive melancholy. But the converse is also true. There are some themes, and some sorts of language, that cannot find a place in it. Its refinement imposes a narrowness of range, which is what Wang Kuo-wei meant when he said that "the lyric can deal with themes beyond the range of regular verse, but cannot encompass that entire range".

---

[5] The whole of the last lyric cited is composed of quotations, four from the *Analects*, two from the *Odes*, one from *Mencius*, one from the *Book of Changes*, and one from the *Book of Ritual*. Such writing is inappropriate in lyric verse.

IV. *Elusiveness of the Lyric World*

Chou Chi 周濟 likened the lyrics of Wu Wen-ying to

> *Shadows of passing clouds on a sunny day,*   天光雲影
> *Shimmering green ripples that repay*   搖蕩綠波
> *Endless contemplation;*   撫翫無斁
> *But try to catch them,*   追尋已遠
> *And they fly away.*

He was referring to their elusive and subtle melancholy. But what he says is true not only of Wu but of all fine lyric poets. For depth of inspiration and subtlety of expression, the lyric stands supreme in Chinese literature.

In regular verse, for all its metaphors and symbols, one can still trace the meaning behind the words. Of Juan Chi 阮籍's verse, for example, it has been said that while the words may be seen and heard, their meaning lies beyond the furthest horizon, their ultimate destination is hard to find. But they do at least have such a destination, even if after all these years it has become impossible to uncover all the relevant facts about the poet's life and times, and therefore "hard to establish the true circumstances" referred to.[6]

Lyric poets, on the other hand, were usually men of an extremely sensitive and sentimental disposition, who freely indulged their predilection for wine and women, and lived in a twilight, bitter-sweet world. They used the exquisite form of the lyric to embody their elusive private melancholy, their personal joys and griefs. Reading a lyric is like standing at the edge of an abyss and catching tantalizing glimpses of the fish darting in the depths; it is like riding the waves of the ocean and seeing a mountain approach and recede with the swell. If the poet himself had more than one person or thing in mind when he wrote his poem, how can the reader hope to pin him down to an unambiguous meaning? The depth of any interpretation will depend entirely on the perceptive powers of the individual reader.

Here, for example, is a lyric by Feng Yen-szu 馮延巳 (attributed by some to Ou-yang Hsiu 歐陽修), to the tune *Tieh lien hua* 蝶戀花 (The Butterfly Loves the Flowers):

> *The cloud that drifted days ago*   幾日行雲何處去
> *Forgot to come home,*   忘了歸來
> *Doesn't know*   不道春將暮
> *Spring's on the wane.*   百草千花寒食路
> *Down in the holiday street*   香車繫在誰家樹
> *Flowers and pretty faces,*
> *And that fancy carriage*   淚眼倚樓頻獨語
> *Parked at someone else's door.*   雙燕來時
> *Up at the window, tears*   陌上相逢否

---

[6] These remarks on Juan Chi's poetry can be found in Chung Jung 鍾嶸's *Shih P'in* 詩品, and in Li Shan 李善's commentary to Juan Chi's *Poems of My Heart*, in the *Chao-ming Wen Hsüan*, *Chüan* 23.

> *and faltering soliloquy:*
> *"Swallows, swallows,*
> *On your way,*
> *By the footpath,*
> *Did you see . . . ?"*
> *Tangled spring-sorrow*
> *Like catkins*
> *Won't let go;*
> *But dreaming*
> *Never finds.*

撩亂春愁如柳絮
依依夢裏無尋處

This poem has been variously interpreted as an allegory of the poet's "unwavering allegiance to his country" (Chang Hui-yen), and as a more generalized "social lament" (Wang Kuo-wei). Interpretations vary from reader to reader, and while the poet need not have had either of these two ideas in his mind, each reader is entitled to come to his own conclusions.

The lyric poet's perceptions and impression arise from the depth of his personal joy and sorrow, and although they may appear far-fetched or confused, they have an aesthetic unity and intricate balance of their own—rounded like a pearl, smooth as jade, and with the translucent clarity of a carved miniature. When approaching such poems, we should appreciate that the poet is echoing in his song his distant vision and innermost yearnings, and we should allow the music of the words to stir us to the heart. Surely it is enough to be transported to a rarefied world, where we may catch a glimpse of life's essence? Why bog ourselves down trying to work out exactly how the poet achieved his effect, and precisely what he meant, when by clinging to such details we may miss the point altogether? Like the man in the boat who, having dropped his sword overboard, marked the place on the side of the boat. . . . . What we must strive for is a sense of intuitive wonder. The world of the lyric is like a mountain viewed through the mist, or a flower seen in the moonlight. Its beauty resides in its elusive ambiguity, and if we insist on bringing it out into the light we are acting contrary to the very nature of the form, and will only end up with something shallow and crude.

Under these four headings I have tried to give a broad characterization of the lyric, and of the ways in which it differs from regular verse.

Delicacy and Inner Strength

SOME MAY ARGUE THAT the late Ch'ing critics stressed weight, rugged spontaneity and grandeur in the lyric, qualities quite at variance with the picture I have drawn. But it should be remembered that their purpose (that of the Ch'ing critics) was to counteract the decadent tendencies of their time towards superficial and fussy writing. They were concerned with correcting stylistic habits. I am discussing the fundamental nature of the lyric. Our ideas are in fact complementary.

Take Hsin Ch'i-chi's lines quoted earlier:

> *Do not gaze*
> *From that high balcony:*
> *The sunset*
> *And misty willows*
> *Are a sight to break the heart.*

The language is delicate, but the sentiment and overall effect are forceful and grand. Or take Yen Chi-tao's lines:

> *Since we parted*
> *I would recall our days together.*
> *How often*
> *My dreaming soul joined yours!*
> *Tonight*
> *By the silver taper's light*
> *We'll gaze,*
> *Afraid this meeting*
> *Is just another dream.*

The substance is light, but the feeling is deep and sincere. . . . This complementary tension (between delicacy and strength, lightness and depth) is an acquired taste, and it takes a true connoisseur to appreciate its beauty.

Another objection that may be raised is that I have made the lyric appear to be a vehicle exclusively suited to the expression of love and sentiment in their subtler and sadder aspects, and have ruled out the more heroic and passionate themes such as patriotism and protest. But I am not being so dogmatic. I have tried to elucidate the special qualities of the lyric by tracing its origins as a form. Its transformations will reflect the artistry of the individual poet.

Take Yueh Fei 岳飛, for example. His determination to pursue the Jurched invaders, his outspoken opposition to the appeasers, his indignation that a petty-minded clique was betraying China while his own counsels went unheeded—all these emotions found expression in lyrics such as this one, to the tune *Hsiao ch'ung shan* 小重山 (Little Chung-shan):

> *I rise and pace the steps alone.* 起來獨自遶階行
> *A silent night,* 人悄悄
> *And through the curtain* 簾外月朧明
> *Brilliant moonlight.* ⋯⋯⋯⋯
> *. . . .* 欲將心事付瑤琴
> *I'd let my grief sing on the lute,* 知音少
> *But why—* 絃斷有誰聽
> *In a deaf world,*
> *Where a broken string would pass unheard!*

There is something heroic and dashing about the lyrics of Hsin Ch'i-chi. He succeeds in expressing his brilliant wit, his burning ambition to restore the North, and his bitterness at the court for leaving his talents unused and denying him an opportunity to hunt down the Jurched troops and strike a blow for his country.

The Empress never won her assignation;	長門事
Feeling against her was too strong.	準擬佳期又誤
Even a eulogy that cost a thousand pounds	蛾眉曾有人妒
Could not buy ears	千金縱買相如賦
To hear her heartfelt yearnings.	脈脈此情誰訴
But don't crow too soon!	君莫舞
Have you not seen	君不見
Beauties of old	玉環飛燕皆塵土
Turned to dust?	閒愁最苦
O bitter and most futile grief!	休去倚危闌
Do not gaze	斜陽正在
From that perilous balcony:	煙柳斷腸處
The sunset	
And misty willows	
Are a sight to break the heart.	

Mo yü erh 摸魚兒
(Catching Fish)

Wen T'ien-hsiang 文天祥 was a man of unswerving loyalty who refused to compromise with the Mongols, a man of indomitable courage who faced many hardships and dangers, preferring death to dishonour.

The world veers from side to side	世態便如翻覆雨
like rain.	妾身元是分明月
I have always been pure	
as the shining moon.	

Man chiang hung 滿江紅
(Red River)

The glory and grandeur of these three great men have lived on through the ages. They expressed their patriotic fervour and their single-minded dedication—indirectly, in that most elusive and exquisite of literary forms, the lyric, and as a result their poems are not marred by strident overstatement, but have a profound sincerity and beauty.

If this is still not enough, let me add that the lyric is also capable of expressing the most vehement sentiments. Take this lyric by Chang Yüan-kan 張元幹, to the tune *shih-chou man* 石州慢 (Shih-chou Adagio):

Broken-hearted!	心折
Mars glowers	長庚光怒
At brigand hordes run amuck,	羣盜縱橫
Rebel tartars on the rampage.	逆胡猖獗
I'd pull down the Milky Way	欲挽天河
To wipe this blood and scum	一洗中原膏血

From our land!
Where have they taken
Our King and Prince?
Why are we pinned
To the Yangtze Line?
My heart is in the distant North,
While I must sit in the South—
Like a helpless old general
Beating a cracked spittoon—
To accompany my futile lament.

兩宮何處
塞垣祇隔長江
唾壺空擊悲歌缺
萬里想龍沙
泣孤臣吳越

Or Chang Hsiao-hsiang 張孝祥's lyric to the tune *Shui tiao ko t'ou* 水調歌頭 (Water Song):

Ghosts of monkeys
Wail in the bamboo grove.
In the bivouac at midnight
Distribution of bows.
Young heroes from Ching and Ch'u
In the red embroidered jackets
Of the Light Brigade.
For a thousand miles
Wind blows
And thunder crashes.
Troops sweep
Like meteors
And shooting stars.
Chopping shallots with an axe;
Talking and laughing under canvas;
Every day
New victory despatches are sent off.

猩鬼嘯篁竹
玉帳夜分弓
少年荊楚劍客
突騎錦襜紅
千里風飛雷厲
四校星流彗掃
蕭斧挫春蔥
談笑青油幕
日奏捷書同

Or Lu Yu 陸游's lyric to the tune *Hsieh ch'ih ch'un* 謝池春 (Spring at the Hsieh Pool):

As a young soldier
I had the courage to gobble up
The last of the tartars!
High serried clouds,
Beacons burning in the night.
Ruddy cheeks and flashing locks,
Bow and spear in hand
On the western frontier.
Laughing at how
The old fogeys
In their scholar's caps

壯歲從戎
曾是氣吞殘虜
陣雲高
狼烽夜舉
朱顏青鬢
擁雕戈西戍
笑儒冠自來多誤

> *Had been wrong*
> *All along.*

These last three poems all have a loud, reverberant sonority and create a vivid effect. But in their mood and in the poetic world that they create, they fall short of the first three. Yueh, Hsin and Wen excelled in the qualities most prized by the lyric poet. Stirring, heroic sentiments are appropriate to oratory, where the purpose is to rouse a crowd to immediate action. In regular verse, which is written to be intoned and enjoyed at leisure, to be mulled over several times, and in lyric verse, where sophistication, refinement and restraint are prized above all, passion and vehemence must be tempered with tenderness and deep sincerity. Passion is aroused by momentary moral indignation, whereas deep sincerity is the product of daily cultivation. Passion resembles the bravery of the common soldier, whereas deep sincerity is the higher courage that stems from love towards humanity. Since the days of old, the great exemplars of loyalty and chivalry, who in their love for motherland and people braved danger and remained unflinching to the end, always drew on the strength of their deep self-cultivation. They never relied solely on their exuberance and animal spirits. It is the achievement of the greatest literary creations that they are able by the skilful use of subtly beautiful language to express this deep inner sincerity. Literature that is noisy, self-publicizing, superficial and propagandist cannot be held in high esteem.

Many of the finest lyrics are soft and yielding on the surface, but contain a hard inner core. Critics have always praised Wen T'ien-hsiang's *Song of an Upright Soul* 正氣歌, but I would single out those last two lines from his "Red River":

> *The world veers from side to side*
>   *like rain.*
> *I have always been pure*
>   *as the shining moon.*

They combine verbal beauty with spirited content, and suggest a whole world of single-minded loyalty and integrity. To lay emphasis on the excitement generated by a lyric to the exclusion of all else, and therefore to condemn some of the finest lyrics as effete, is to betray not only a shallowness of aesthetic judgement, but also a coarseness of feeling, a lack of cultivation and a spirit capable only of the outward manifestations of passion and incapable of inner sincerity.

The Lyric Spirit in Life

The lyric came into being and flourished because it corresponded to a part of the natural world and to a realm of human feeling. So long as this world and these feelings exist, there will always be people who appreciate lyric poetry and try to write it. Slanting wind, fine rain, pale moon and scattered stars characterize the lyric sky. Lonely valleys and crystal streams, unrippled lakes and meandering banks shape the lyric landscape. Sensitive feelings and transcendant thoughts, deep aspirations and intimate yearnings are the pulse of the lyric soul. All true lyric poets, all men with a character cultivated in the lyric mould, manifest this lyric quality in their life and thought. They are gentle and sincere, pure of mind, idealistic and free from contrived or petty thoughts.

Such a man was Yen Chi-tao: "though repeatedly a failure in his career, he refused to pay court to the influential. He had his own literary style, and refused to ape the fashonable scholars' language. Though he was wildly extravagant and though his family went cold and hungry, his complexion remained like that of a child. When men betrayed him a hundred times he took no offence, and always had faith in others, never suspecting that they might be trying to take advantage of him." (From Huang T'ing-chien 黃庭堅's "Preface to The Lyrics of Little Hill 小山詞序")

Another was Chiang K'uei "of pure and shining countenance, like an immortal. Even if he was down to his last bean, he would still manage somehow to feed several guests at every meal. His was an eccentric nature. Sometimes, on finding some beautiful spot in the countryside, he would be so enchanted by it that he would disappear, and no one could find him. Or late at night, he would stroll out by the light of moon and stars, reciting his poems in a loud voice. He was in his element even in a cruel northerly wind, when lesser mortals huddled inside to keep warm." (from Chang Yü 張羽's *Biographical Account of White Stone the Taoist* 白石道人傳)

From these two men we can form an idea of the lyric spirit in action. In the realm of ideas and scholarship, the signs of the lyric spirit are wit, perspicacity and profundity of interpretation, and an intuitive understanding of inner truth as opposed to an obsession with literal meaning. A fine example is to be found in Wang Kuo-wei's widely respected work in the field of literary and historical research. His interpretations, while they may seem novel, are in fact quite natural. He unravels age-old mysteries in the most logical and plausible way, and by the liveliness and precision of his argument and the freshness and clarity of his style succeeds in bringing his subjects to life. Learned dissertations are as a rule tedious to read. But Kuo-wei's scholarly works (*Kuan-t'ang ji-lin* 觀堂集林) are like a work of fiction. To read them is a pleasure and a refreshing experience.

Wang was himself originally a lyric poet, and a very good one. Here is one of his lyrics, to the tune *T'ieh lien hua* (The Butterfly Loves the Flowers):

By the road stands a mansion	百尺朱樓臨大道
a hundred feet high;	樓外輕雷
Light thunder in the sky	不間昏和曉
in the half-light of dusk	獨欄干人窈窕
or dawn.	閒中數盡行人小
At a balcony,	
alone,	一霎車塵生樹杪
a maiden idly counts	陌上樓頭
the tiny passers-by.	都向塵中老
A momentary shower reveals	薄晚西風吹雨到
tree-tops	明朝又是傷流潦
above the dust	
of carriage-wheels.	

> *In mansion and lane*
> > *age turns to dust again.*
> *Toward evening,*
> > *west wind blows in the rain.*
> *Tomorrow will bring*
> > *more puddles, more pain.*

It was because Wang approached scholarly criticism in a lyric spirit that he was able to write with such profound understanding and clarity. He was indeed one of the greatest writers of his age. Nowadays, while there is considerable admiration for his *Lyric Remarks for the Human World*, there are few that appreciate his *Lyrics for the Human World*. And yet the intensely alive quality of his scholarship, its almost magical brilliance, are precisely manifestations of his fundamentally lyric talent. This is basic to an understanding of the man. (There are men whose genius is creative and not scholarly, and I am not claiming that all lyric poets make good scholars. But in Wang Kuo-wei we have a particular case of lyric genius employed to brilliant effect in scholarly research.)

The Chinese Lyric and Western Poetry

A comparison with Western literature may help to bring out the nature of Chinese lyric verse, and shed some light on its position within literature as a whole. The origins and course of development of Western poetry are quite different from those of Chinese poetry. Western poetry traces its origins back to Classical Greece, where the most important genres were epic poetry and drama (especially tragedy). Indeed Aristotle in his *Poetics* only discusses epic poetry and tragedy, and makes no mention of lyric poetry. There was lyric poetry in Greece, but its development was negligible. It was not until the Italian poet Petrarch in the fourteenth century that lyric poetry began to flourish, reaching its heyday with the rise of the Romantic Movement in the eighteenth and nineteenth centuries. Chinese poetry, on the other hand, had been lyric, or rather lyrical, from its earliest days. Many of the finest poems in *The Book of Odes* are lyrical in this broader sense. The works of Ch'ü Yüan 屈原 and Sung Yü 宋玉, though cast in a different form, were also lyrical in essence. The Han *fu* was a departure in the direction of purely descriptive verse. It proved shortlived, however, and from Wei 魏 and Chin 晋 times the *fu* reverted to being a lyrical form. The five-syllable verse of the Six Dynasties, the old-style and new-style verse of the T'ang dynasty, the lyrics proper of the Five Dynasties and Sung, the extended lyric forms of the Yüan and Ming—all these forms were lyrical in character. Even the early *tsa-chü* drama of the Yüan and Ming, and the later *ch'uan-ch'i* 傳奇 drama of the Ming and Ch'ing were essentially lyric dramas. While China lacks an epic or tragic tradition, the unique development of "lyrical" poetry has led to a great diversity of forms to suit many varieties of feeling.

The same variety of mood is to be found in Western poetry, although it never underwent such a detailed formal division. In English poetry, for instance, Milton's "L'Allegro" and "Il Penseroso" can be compared to some of the shorter *fu* 賦 of the

Six Dynasties. Shelley's "Ode to the West Wind" can be compared to seven-syllable old-style verse. Wordsworth's Sonnets to Regulated Octets; Browning's verse dramas to the verse passages in our own dramas of the Yüan, Ming and Ch'ing dynasties; and when we come to Keats and the Rossettis, we find a true counterpart to our own lyric verse. The hundred and one poems in Dante Gabriel Rossetti's *The House of Life*, with their subtle melancholy and fragrance, their plaintive and slender charm, all read like short lyrics by Ch'in Kuan or Yen Chi-tao. After all, impressions and emotions are alike the world over. That realm of veiled tenderness and dreamy melancholy exists everywhere. In China it led to the creation of the lyric, in the West to the verse of poets such as Keats and the Rossettis. The only difference is that in China it became a separate form, with its own ramifications and its own golden age. If Keats and the Rossettis had been born in China, they would surely have been lyric poets to rank with Ch'in Kuan, Yen Chi-tao and Li Ch'ing-chao.

Conclusion

I am not trying to publicize or make a case for the lyric; only to point out some of its distinctive qualities, and its relation to other literary forms. I am not claiming all the world's beauty for the lyric, nor am I urging everyone to read or write lyrics. I only wish to say that lyric verse has its value in Chinese literature. Men's natures differ just as their appearances do. To those born with a sensitive spirit and an appreciation of subtle beauty, lyric verse can bring delight and release, it can be a source of peace and strength. And this aesthetic sensitivity, if coupled with a sincere cultivation of character, can greatly enhance the quality of a man's everyday life and of his literary and scholarly pursuits. Many human activities co-exist, many paths lead to the same goal. The lyric, an expression of the human heart and mind, and of human perceptions of the world, is one path leading to an understanding of beauty and goodness.

韋莊詞

Eleven Tz'u by Wei Chuang

Translated by C. Y. Hsu

To the Tune of *P'u-sa man*

Everyone has praise for Chiang-nan fair;
A traveler may well get old there.
The spring water is bluer than the unclouded sky.
In a painted barge listening to the rain I lie.

The tavern maid by the stove is fair like the moon
With arms white as frost and snow strewn.
Do not go home before you get old;
If you do, your heart'll get stone-cold.

菩薩蠻

人人盡說江南好
遊人只合江南老
春水碧於天
畫船聽雨眠

爐邊人似月
皓腕凝雙雪
未老莫還鄉
還鄉須斷腸

還鄉須斷腸　未老莫還鄉　皓腕凝雙雪　爐邊人似月　畫船聽雨眠　春水碧於天　遊人只合江南老　人人盡說江南好　菩薩蠻

45

荷葉杯

記得那年花下
深夜
初識謝娘時
水堂西面畫簾垂
攜手暗相期

惆悵曉鶯殘月
相別
從此隔音塵
如今俱是異鄉人
相見更無因

To the Tune of *Ho-yeh pei*

I recall that year under flowers blooming
Late at night
The fair one and I had the first meeting.
In the water pavilion behind the west screen hang-
    ing low
Hand in hand we secretly pledged our vow.

At the orioles' first warbling under a waning moon
We lamentably parted.
Since then, we haven't met again, late or soon.
Now we are both strangers in different regions;
Far less pretense is there for reunions.

荷葉盃

記得那年花下
深夜
初識謝娘時
水堂西面畫簾垂
攜手暗相期

惆悵曉鶯殘月
相別
從此隔音塵
如今俱是異鄉人
相見更無因

女冠子

昨夜夜半
枕上分明夢見
語多時
依舊桃花面
頻低柳葉眉

半羞還半喜
欲去又依依
覺來知是夢
不勝悲

To the Tune of *Nü kuan tzu*

At midnight last night
I distinctly saw you in a dream
And talked with you in delight.

You've the same peach-blossom face,
Lowering your eyebrows like willow leaves,
Showing both coyness and happy grace,

Starting to go and yet lingering.
On waking up I realized it was a dream.
Deep sorrow keeps me agonizing.

女冠子

昨夜々半
枕上分明夢見
語多時
依舊桃花面
頻低柳葉眉

半羞還半喜
欲去又依々
覺來知是夢
不勝悲

菩薩蠻

如今却憶江南樂
當時年少春衫薄
騎馬倚斜橋
滿樓紅袖招

翠屏金屈曲
醉入花叢宿
此度見花枝
白頭誓不歸

To the Tune of *P'u-sa man*

I now recall Chiang-nan's days of delight:
Young I was, wearing a spring dress light.
On an arched bridge I was on horse back resting
When I saw on a tower red sleeves beckoning.

Behind a kingfisher blue screen with golden
Hinges in a flowery boudoir I slumbered drunken.
This time if flower-like beauties come in sight,
I won't go home till my hair turns white.

白頭誓不歸　此度見花枝　醉入花叢宿　翠屏金屈曲　滿樓紅袖招　騎馬倚斜橋　當昔年少春衫薄　如今却憶江南樂　菩薩蠻

菩薩蠻

紅樓別夜堪惆悵
香燈半捲流蘇帳
殘月出門時
美人和淚辭

琵琶金翠羽
絃上黃鶯語
勸我早歸家
綠窗人似花

To the Tune of *P'u-sa man*

Parting at night in the red chamber evoked melancholy
With lamplight upon the half-lifted tasseled canopy.
As I sadly stepped outdoors under a moon waning,
The fair lady bade me farewell with tears streaming.

The *pi-pa* with a kingfisher feather plectrum
Issued on its strings an oriole's warble blithesome,
Urging me to come home without delaying an hour
For at the green casement she waits, beautiful like a flower.

綠窗人似花
勸我早歸家
絃上黃鶯語
琵琶金翠羽
美人和淚辭
殘月出門時
香鐙半捲流蘇帳
紅樓別夜堪惆悵
菩薩蠻

浣溪沙

夜夜相思更漏殘
傷心明月凭欄干
想君思我錦衾寒

咫尺畫堂深似海
憶來唯把舊書看
幾時攜手入長安

To the Tune of *Huan hsi sha*

Night after night I pine till the watches wane.
In grief I stand at the balustrade under moonlight
And think you imagine me freezing in my quilt of
    brocade.

The small painted hall is deep as the main.
When I think of you I take out your letters to
    recite.
When may we hand in hand into Ch'ang-an pro-
    menade?

幾時攜手入長安　憶来惟把舊書看　咫尺畫堂深侶海　想君思我錦衾寒　傷心明月凭欄干　夜夜相思更漏殘　浣溪沙

浣溪沙

欲上鞦韆四體慵
擬敎人送又心忪
畫堂簾幕月明風

此夜有情誰不極
隔墻梨雪又玲瓏
玉容憔悴惹微紅

To the Tune of *Huan hsi sha*

I wish to mount the swing but my limbs are
    languid.
To ask someone to give me a push I'm too timid.
'Twas windy and moonlit outside the hall, painted
    and tapestried.

On such a night what lover wouldn't yearn deeply?
O'er the wall the snowy pear blossoms are lovely.
My pallid comely face blushes slightly.

玉容憔悴惹微紅
隔墻梨雪又玲瓏
此夜有情誰不極
畫堂簾幕月明風
擬敎人送又心忪
欲上鞦韆四體慵
浣溪沙

荷葉杯

絕代佳人難得
傾國
花下見無期
一雙愁黛遠山眉
不忍更思惟

閒掩翠屏金鳳
殘夢
羅幕畫堂空
碧天無路信難通
惆悵舊房櫳

To the Tune of *Ho-yeh pei*

Rare indeed is a supreme beauty,
State-toppling,
Dateless for a tryst under flowers comely.
Her twin eyebrows like distant hills
Are too sad to bear more musings on ills.

Behind a blue screen with golden phoenixes un-
    folded
A dream wanes.
The silk-curtained painted hall is deserted.
No message can reach the trackless azure skies.
In the old chamber sorrow ever lies.

荷葉盃

絕代佳人難得
傾國
花下見無期
一雙愁黛遠山眉
不忍更思維

閒掩翠屏金鳳
殘夢
羅幕畫堂空
碧天無路信難通
惆悵舊房櫳

女冠子

四月十七
正是去年今日
別君時
忍淚佯低面
含羞半斂眉

不知魂已斷
空有夢相隨
除却天邊月
沒人知

To the Tune of Nü kuan tzu

'Twas exactly a year ago today
—The seventeenth of the fourth moon—
When I saw you off on a long way.

I held back tears, bowing my head
And looked shy and half-frowning.
Not knowing my soul already dead,

I vainly followed you in dream.
Nobody knew the secret in my heart
Save the moon on the horizon agleam.

女冠子
四月十七
正是去年今日
別君時
忍淚佯低面
含羞半斂眉
不知魂已斷
空有夢相隨
除却天邊月
沒人知

菩薩蠻

勸君今夜須沉醉
樽前莫話明朝事
珍重主人心
酒深情亦深

須愁春漏短
莫訴金杯滿
遇酒且呵呵
人生能幾何

To the Tune of *P'u-sa man*

Friend, drink tonight till aglow;
With a jug in hand talk not about tomorrow.
Cherish the host's hearty generosity;
Equally deep are his wine and hospitality.

Mind the brevity of the spring night;
Complain not about the fullness of the goblet
      bright.
With wine in hand laugh and cavort
For life is after all short.

菩薩蠻

勸君今夜須沈醉
尊前莫話明朝事
珍重主人心
酒深情亦深
須愁春漏短
莫訴金杯滿
遇酒且呵呵
人生能幾何

菩薩蠻

洛陽城裏春光好
洛陽才子他鄉老
柳暗魏王堤
此時心轉迷

桃花春水綠
水上鴛鴦浴
凝恨對殘暉
憶君君不知

To the Tune of *P'u-sa man*

Spring in Lo-yang is bright and fair
But the scholar of Lo-yang is aging elsewhere.
The shady willows on Prince Wei's embankment
Charm my palpitating heart to utter bewilderment.

Peach blossoms on the green waters of spring
Float with mandarin ducks bathing and frolicking.
I gaze at the evening glow
And think of you but you won't know.

憶君〻不知
凝恨對殘暉
水上鴛鴦浴
桃花春水綠
此時心轉迷
柳暗魏王堤
洛陽才子他鄉老
洛陽城裏春光好
菩薩蠻

Wei Chuang

As one of the pioneering *tz'u* poets, Wei Chuang 韋莊 (836?-910) set the pace for this literary genre, which flowered in the Sung dynasty (960-1279). His *tz'u* poems, some 53 in number, are noted for simplicity and beauty of diction, naturalness and elegance of style, and poignancy in the expression of love, separation and remembrance of the past.

Wei, born in Tu-ling near Ch'ang-an, came from a poor family but he was very studious and intelligent when young. In 880 he went to Ch'ang-an to take the Imperial examinations. But he was trapped there when the rebel Huang Ch'ao 黃巢 (died 884) took the capital and devastated the country. In 882 when Huang Ch'ao was defeated he escaped from Ch'ang-an to Lo-yang.

In 883 while in Lo-yang he wrote *Ch'in-fu-yin* 秦婦吟 (Ballad of the Lady of Ch'in), numbering 1,666 characters, one of the longest Chinese poems. It is a realistic poem describing the disturbance and devastation of the time through the lips of a woman refugee. Wei gained such popularity for this poem that he was nicknamed *Ch'in-fu-yin hsiu-tsai* 秦婦吟秀才. But because of certain remarks in the poem critical of the nobility he later suppressed it and it was not included in his collection of poems *Huan-hua-chi* 浣花集 compiled by his brother in 903. It had been lost for more than a thousand years until it was rediscovered among the manuscripts at a Tun-huang grotto in 1899.

In the same year when he wrote *Ch'in-fu-yin* Wei traveled to Chiang-nan or south of the Yangtze River. In 893 he returned to Ch'ang-an to take the examinations and in the following year he won the *hsiu-tsai* degree and served in the court of the T'ang Emperor Chao Tsung 昭宗. In 897 he was sent as an emissary to the principality of Shu (now Szechwan) and in 901 he went there a second time to become the secretary of Prince Wang Chien 王建 (died 918). An admirer of the earlier T'ang poet Tu Fu 杜甫 (712-770), he found in 902 the site of his dilapidated house in Cheng-tu and built a cottage on it. After the fall of T'ang in 907, Prince Wang Chien established an independent kingdom in Shu 蜀 and ascended the throne as Emperor of the Earlier Shu State. Wei assisted in the enactment of laws, statutes and institutions and rose to become the Prime Minister. He passed away in Cheng-tu in 910.

張宗橚：詞林紀事

Behind the Lines:
Tz'u Poets and Their Private Selves

By **Chang Tsung-su**

Translated by **Frederick C. Tsai**

TZ'U LIN CHI SHIH 詞林紀事 (*Anecdotes of Tz'u Poets*), as the title suggests, is concerned exclusively with *tz'u*. In this collection are to be found amusing stories about *tz'u* poets, pithy sayings, and critical remarks by *tz'u* poets, and studies of authorship and textual differences. The work was edited by Chang Tsung-su 張宗橚, a poet himself, well known in the eighteenth century. Also included in the book are perceptive comments by the editor. Entries about more than four hundred *tz'u* poets from the T'ang to the Yüan dynasties (618-1368) make it comprehensive enough to be regarded as an indispensable work of reference in the study of *tz'u* and *tz'u* poets.

The following is a selection of a few anecdotes which, perhaps no less than the lyrical grace and perfection shown by poets in their *tz'u*, helped to perpetuate their fame.

Yueh-fu Chi-wen 樂府紀聞:

In his middle age, as Chief Administrator of the Prefecture of Ying 潁州[1] Ou-yang Yung-shu 歐陽永叔 (courtesy name of Ou-yang Hsiu 歐陽修) styled himself Recluse Liu-i (Six-one), which, according to him, was derived from the fact that he had collected *one* thousand *chüan* 卷[2] of rubbings of ancient bronze and stone inscriptions, *one wan* (ten thousand) *chüan* of books, was in possession of *one ch'in* 琴,[3] *one* set of chess, *one* bottle of wine, together with himself, *one* old man, growing old amidst the five things.

His works include a collection of his *tz'u* poems entitled *Liu-i Tz'u* 六一詞.

---

[1] In modern Anhuei 安徽 Province.

[2] In ancient China books were copied on silk or paper to be rolled up for storage. Hence the classifier *chüan*. A modern volume may contain several *chüan*, that is, several parts or divisions.

[3] A seven-stringed zither.

Yao Shan T'ang Wai Chi 堯山堂外記:

One day, when His Excellency Ch'ien Wen Hsi (the Errant) 錢文僖[4] entertained his guests in his garden, a state-owned courtesan and Ou-yang Yung-shu were late in arriving. Asked for the reason, the girl said, "I was suffering from the heat, so I went to sleep it off in a cool chamber. There I lost my gold hairpin which I haven't as yet found."

"If you can ask His Excellency Ou-yang, Assistant to the Governor-general, to write a *tz'u*," said Ch'ien, "you'll be compensated for it."

Thereupon Ou-yang composed impromptu a *tz'u* to the tune of *Lin-chiang hsien* 臨江仙.[5] All those present applauded. The courtesan was told to pour Ou-yang a cup of wine. A sum of money was drawn from the public coffers to pay her in compensation for her lost gold hairpin.

I-yüan Tz'u-huang 藝苑雌黃:

Liu San-pien 柳三變 (Three Changes, courtesy name of Liu Yung 柳永) given to philandering, was fond of writing *tz'u* poetry. Some recommended him to the Emperor for his talent.

"Isn't he the *tz'u* poet, Liu San-pien?"

"Yes, your Majesty."

"Then leave him to write *tz'u*!" said the Emperor.

This put paid to Liu's hopes of preferment. From then on he spent his days in the company of rakes in brothels and public houses, leading a life of total abandon.

"Here is Liu San-pien," he often declared, "who writes *tz'u* by Imperial command."

"While he was a candidate for the imperial examination," wrote Yeh Shao-yün 葉少蘊, "Liu Ch'i-ch'ing 柳耆卿 (another courtesy name of Liu Yung) used to frequent brothels and was good at writing songs. Whenever court musicians came across a new tune, they would not release it until they had got Liu to compose the lyrics. Consequently, his fame spread far and wide. When I was the magistrate of Tan-t'u 丹徒[6] I met a government official returning from Western Hsia 西夏,[7] who told me that 'wherever there is well-water there are people able to sing Liu's *tz'u*.' "

[4] Ch'ien Wai Yen 錢惟演, a noted man of letters as well as a minister in the Sung dynasty, with the posthumous title "The Errant", for his inglorious manipulations in politics.

[5] Please refer to the original of this *tz'u* poem and its translation by Teresa Yee-wha Yü on p. 116.

[6] The old name of Chenkiang, the capital of Kiangsu Province.

[7] State on the borders of China, destroyed by the Yüan dynasty in 1227.

Ch'ing-ni Lien-hua Chi 青泥蓮花記:

Liu Ch'i-ch'ing and his Excellency Sun Ho 孫何[8] were friends when they were still living in obscurity. Later, when Sun became Chief Administrator of the Prefecture of Hangchow, the entrance of his official residence was so heavily guarded that Liu found it impossible to see him. Then having composed a *tz'u* poem to the tune of *Wang Hai-ch'ao* 望海潮, he went and called on a famous courtesan named Ch'u-ch'u 楚楚.

"I want," he said to her, "to see the Prefect, but I have no access. When there is festivity at his Excellency's would you do me the favour of singing this song with your beautiful voice in his presence? Should he ask who the author was, just say, 'A scholar named Liu.' "

At the celebrations on the evening of the Mid-autumn Festival, Ch'u-ch'u sang the song melodiously. Immediately Sun sent for Liu to join the party.

Ch'ui-chien Lu 吹劍錄:

When Su Tung P'o 蘇東坡 was a member of the Imperial Academy, one of the assistants there was a skilful singer.

"What do you think of my *tz'u* in comparison with that of Liu (Yung)?" asked Su.

"As far as the *tz'u* poems of Liu Lang-chung[9] are concerned his line 'On the willow-fringed bank in the morning breeze under the setting moon' is fit only to be sung by a young lady of seventeen or eighteen, holding a pair of red ivory clappers. However, as for your Excellency's *tz'u* poems, your line 'Eastward flows the Great River' must be sung by a burly fellow from the west of the Han-ku Pass 函谷關 accompanied by a brass pipa and a pair of iron clappers."

On hearing these remarks, Su was immensely amused.

Kui Erh Lu[10] 貴耳錄:

The Superior Taoist,[11] Emperor Huei 徽宗 of the Sung dynasty, once went to see Li Shih Shih 李師師. It happened that Chou Pang-yen 周邦彥 arrived there before the Emperor. On learning of the arrival of

[8] A famous scholar as well as a capable statesman in the reigns of the emperors Chen 眞宗 and Jen 仁宗 (998-1063) of the Sung dynasty.

[9] Liu had been *t'un-t'ien yüan-wai-lang* 屯田員外郎, an official supervising frontier guards raising crops on the border. By this title he was referred to as *lang-chung* 郎中.

[10] By Chang Tuan-i 張端義 of the Sung dynasty.

[11] The Emperor Huei of the Sung dynasty was a devout Taoist, and styled himself the Superior Taoist.

the Emperor, he hid under the bed. The Emperor brought a fresh orange with him, saying that it had just arrived as tribute from the south of the Yangtze River. He joked and flirted with Shih Shih, and every word was overheard by Pang-yen.

Subsequently, the poet turned what he had heard into a *tz'u* to the tune of *Shao Nien Yu* 少年游. Then one day Shih Shih sang this song to the Emperor.

"Who is the author?" asked the Emperor.

"It is a *tz'u* by Chou Pang-yen."

The Emperor flew into a rage and instructed Ts'ai Ching 蔡京, the Prime Minister, to expel Chou Pang-yen forthwith from the Forbidden City under escort for neglect of duty.

A couple of days later the Emperor went to see Shih Shih again, and did not find her at home. Upon inquiry he was told by her family that she had gone to see Chou[12] off. The Emperor waited and waited until the last watch. When Shih Shih came back, she looked distressed, her eyelashes wet with tears, pathetically wan and sallow.

"Where have you been?" the Emperor demanded angrily.

"Your maid-servant deserves to die ten thousand times." said Shih Shih. "I learned that Chou had incurred your Majesty's wrath and was to be expelled under escort. I could not but go and offer him a farewell cup. I didn't know your Majesty were coming."

The Emperor asked if Chou had written any *tz'u*. Shih Shih told him that Chou had written a *tz'u* to the tune of *Lan-ling wang* 蘭陵王. (This is the poem that begins with the line "The shadow of willows was straight . . . ".)

"Sing it and let us see what it's like."

"Allow me to offer your Majesty a cup of wine, and sing this *tz'u* to wish your Majesty health."

When Shih Shih finished the song the Emperor was greatly pleased, and ordered Chou to be restored to the post of Chief Musician of the Ta Ch'eng Imperial Conservatoire.

Random Jottings in Kuei-hsin[13] 癸辛雜識:

Lu Wu-kuan 陸務觀 (courtesy name of Lu Yu 陸游, 1125-1210) first married the daughter of T'ang Hung, who was his maternal uncle. In spite of their mutual affection the young lady did not find favour with her mother-in-law. When on account of this she was sent away, Lu Wu-kuan could not bear severing their relationship totally, so he housed her in a secret place where they could continue to meet. His mother, on discovering it, made a surprise raid on the hide-out. Although he got wind of it and had his wife taken away before his mother arrived, they could not continue to meet after their secret

---

[12] In the original, Chou is referred to as a revenue officer.

[13] Kuei-hsin, the name of a street in Hangchow, where this book by Chou Mi 周密 (1232-1298), poet, anthologist, and historian, was written.

became known. As a result, their separation became final. Later, Lu's ex-wife was married again, this time to Chao Shi-ch'eng of the same Prefecture, who was the eldest son in the family.

One spring day she met Lu during an outing at Shen's Garden 沈氏園, south of Yu-chi Szu 禹跡寺 (The Empire Temple). She told Chao of their former relations, and had wine and meat delivered to Lu. This left him in a pensive mood for quite a long time. Thereupon he composed a song to the tune of *Ch'ai-t'ou-feng* 釵頭鳳, which he wrote on the wall of the garden. It was in the year 1155.

In his later years living in Sanshan 三山 or The Three Hills, on Chien Lake 鑑湖, Lu made a point of visiting the temple each time he entered the city for sightseeing. In 1199, he wrote two *chüeh-chü* 絕句:[14]

> *Since you disappeared from my dream forty years ago,*
> *The willows of Shen's Garden have grown too old to*
> *   have catkins adrift.*
> *Albeit my body will soon become earth on Mount*
> *   Chi,*[15]
> *With heart-ache I still search for the footprints you left*
> *   behind.*
>
> *The sun is setting over the city-wall when bugles wail.*
> *In Shen's Garden the ponds and towers have gone.*
> *O how the green spring ripples under the bridge*
> *Once reflected your graceful but too transient image!*

Soon after the poems were written Lu's ex-wife died.

"Pai-shi Tao-jen 白石道人 (White-stone, the Taoist),"[16] wrote Ch'en Ts'ang I 陳藏一, "looked as if he could not support the weight of his clothes, whereas his pen is so Herculean as to be able to raise a cooking vessel with a capacity of 100 *hu* 斛.[17] He didn't have a speck of land, yet not a meal at his home was served without guests. His collection of books, historical records, paintings and masterpieces of calligraphy was so large as 'to weigh down the oxen transporting it and to fill a house to the rafter'. Generous and expansive, he was more of a man from the Chin and Sung dynasties (265-479), with his philosophical attitude to life. His speech was always meticulous and to the point. He is a man of noble character without consciously aspiring to nobility.

---

[14]A poem of four lines each containing five or seven characters, with a strict tonal pattern and rhyme scheme.

[15]That is, Mount Huei-chi 會稽山, in Chekiang Province.

[16]An alias taken by Chiang K'uei 姜夔 (c. 1155-c.1221).

[17]Equivalent to 1,000 decalitres.

柳永詞

Thirteen Tz'u *by Liu Yung*

Translated by Winnie Lai-fong Leung

甘草子

愁暮
亂灑衰荷
顆顆眞珠雨
雨過月華生
冷徹鴛鴦浦

池上憑欄愁無侶
奈此箇
單棲情緒
卻傍金籠共鸚鵡
念粉郎言語

甘草子

秋暮

亂灑衰荷

顆顆眞珠雨

雨過月華生

冷徹鴛鴦浦

池上憑闌愁無侶

奈此箇

單棲情緒

卻傍金籠共鸚鵡

念粉郎言語

To the Tune of *Kan-ts'ao tzu*

Autumn evening,
Rain splashes on wilted lotus, each drop a pearl.
After the rain the moon appears,
And coolness fills the mandarin-duck bank.

I lean against the railing by the pond,
Sad for a companion.
How can I bear this loneliness?
I approach the golden cage
And with the parrot repeat the words of my be-
loved.

菊花新

欲掩香幃論繾綣
先斂雙蛾愁夜短
催促少年郎
先去睡
鴛衾圖暖

須臾放了殘鍼線
脫羅裳
恣情無限
留取帳前燈
時時待
看伊嬌面

To the Tune of *Chü-hua hsin*

When I am about to close the perfumed curtain to
    indulge in love,
She knits her eyebrows and complains that the
    night is short.
She urges me to go to bed first.
To get warm under the mandarin-duck quilt.

After a while, she puts down her unfinished needle-
    work,
And removes her silk skirt,
Exhibiting her passion with abandon.
In front of the curtain, I leave the lamp on,
So that I can look at her face
Time and time again.

重湖疊巘清嘉
有三秋桂子
十里荷花
羌管弄晴
菱歌泛夜
嬉嬉釣叟蓮娃
千騎擁高牙
乘醉聽簫鼓
吟賞煙霞
異日圖將好景
歸去鳳池誇

望海潮

東南形勝
三吳都會
錢塘自古繁華
煙柳畫橋
風簾翠幕
參差十萬人家
雲樹繞堤沙
怒濤卷霜雪
天塹無涯
市列珠璣
戶盈羅綺競豪奢

To the Tune of *Wang hai-ch'ao*

A scenic spot in the South-East,
The capital city of the Three-wu region,
Ch'ien-t'ang has been bustling since ancient days.
There are misty willows and painted bridges;
There are swaying blinds and green jade curtains
Amidst a hundred thousand households in rows.
Trees soar into the sky around the dykes and the
　　　　sands.
Furious billows hurl up frost and snow.
The river stretches endlessly.
In the markets, pearls and gems are displayed.
Houses are full of people in silk,
Vying with each other in showing off their wealth.

望海潮

東南形勝
三吳都會
錢塘自古繁華
煙柳畫橋
風簾翠幕
參差十萬人家
雲樹繞堤沙
怒濤卷霜雪
天塹無涯
市列珠璣
戶盈羅綺
競豪奢

重湖疊巘清嘉
有三秋桂子
十里荷花
羌管弄晴
菱歌泛夜
嬉嬉釣叟蓮娃
千騎擁高牙
乘醉聽簫鼓
吟賞煙霞
異日圖將好景
歸去鳳池誇

Lakes adjoining lakes and peaks upon peaks are
    clear and beautiful,
With autumn cassia
And miles of lotus flowers.
On sunny days, Ch'iang flutes pipe.
At night, water-caltrop songs are heard everywhere.
Happy are the old fishermen and the lotus girls.
Thousands of cavalrymen escort the lofty banners.
Tipsy, I listen to the lutes and the drums,
Chanting poetry and admiring the mist and clouds.
Some day, I will go back to the capital
And proudly describe this beautiful scene to my
    colleagues.

為憶
芳容別後
水遙山遠
何計憑鱗翼
想繡閣深沈
爭知憔悴損
天涯行客
楚峽雲歸
寂寞狂蹤迹
望京國
空目斷
遠峯凝碧

傾杯

鶩落霜洲
雁橫煙渚
分明畫出秋色
暮雨乍歇
小楫夜泊
宿葦村山驛
何人月下臨風處
起一聲羌笛
離愁萬緒
聞岸草
切切蛩吟如織

To the Tune of *Ch'ing pei*

The wild ducks descending on the frosty isles
And the wild-geese flying across the misty sand-
    bank
Clearly delineate an autumn scene.
The evening rain has just stopped.
At nightfall, I moor my small boat by the riverside,
And lodge in a post-house up the hill in the reeded
    village.
Facing the wind in the moonlight
Who is there playing the Ch'iang flute?
Hearing the crickets in the shore grass
I am filled with the sorrow of parting.

傾盃　柳永

鶩落霜洲
鴈横煙渚
分明畫出秋色
暮雨乍歇
小檝夜泊
宿葦村山驛
何人月下臨風處
起一聲羌笛
離愁萬緒
聞岸草
切切蛩吟如織

為憶
芳容別後
水遙山遠
何計憑鱗翼
想繡閣深沈
爭知憔悴損
天涯行客
楚峽雲歸
高陽人散
寂寞狂蹤迹
望京國
空目斷
遠峯凝碧

I recall that, since I left her,
Separated by rivers and mountains,
I have had no means to send her messages.
In her secluded chamber, how would she know
That a traveller is wasting away
At the end of the world?
Where are my former lovers
And passionate companions?
Not a trace of their revelling to be found.
I gaze at the capital, but in vain.
In the distance, the peaks are silent in a limpid
　　blue.

幾許
秦樓永晝
謝閣連宵奇遇
算贈笑千金
酬歌百琲
盡成輕負
南顧
念吳邦越國
風煙蕭索在何處
獨自箇
千山萬水
指天涯去

引駕行

虹收殘雨
蟬嘶敗柳長堤暮
背都門
動消黯
西風片帆輕舉
愁覩
泛畫鷁翩翩
靈鼉隱隱下前浦
忍回首
佳人漸遠
想高城
隔煙樹

To the Tune of *Yin chia hsing*

The rainbow has gathered up the rain.
As evening descends upon the long dyke,
Cicadas chirp in the withered willows.
In sorrowful mood I turn my back
Upon the capital and start my journey.
My light sail is hoisted in the west wind.
In sorrow,
I see the painted boat moving gracefully
With the faint rumbling of its drums heading down-
     stream.
I cannot bear to look back,
For my love is left farther and farther behind.
Though the capital is in my thoughts,
It is blocked by the trees in the mist.

引駕行

虹收殘雨
蟬嘶敗柳長堤暮
背都門
動消黯
西風片帆輕舉
愁覩
泛畫鷁翩翩
靈鼉隱隱下前浦
忍回首
佳人漸遠
想高城
隔煙樹

幾許
秦樓永晝
謝閣連宵奇遇
算贈笑千金
酬歌百琲
盡成輕負
南顧
念吳邦越國
風煙蕭索在何處
獨自箇
千山萬水
指天涯去

How many times

Have I spent the whole day in the house of courtesans?

How many nights have I had amorous encounters in their mansions?

Even though I gave away a thousand pieces of gold to buy her smile,

Even though I paid a hundred strings of pearls for her song,

All for nothing but fickleness

As I look south:

In winds and mist forlorn,

The States of Wu and Yüeh are nowhere to be found.

Alone, amidst endless mountains and rivers

I make for the end of the sky.

綺綃袖舉
雲鬟風顫
半遮檀口含羞
背人偷顧
競鬥草
金釵笑爭賭

對此嘉景
頓覺消凝
慈成愁緒
念解佩
輕盈在何處
忍良時
孤負少年等閒度
空望極
回首斜陽暮
歎浪萍風梗知何去

夜半樂

豔陽天氣
煙細風暖
芳郊澄朗閒凝佇
漸妝點亭臺
參差佳樹
舞腰困力
垂楊綠映
淺桃穠李夭夭
嫩紅無數
度綺燕
流鶯鬥雙語

翠娥南陌簇簇
躡影紅陰
緩移嬌步
擡粉面
韶容花光相妒

To the Tune of *Yeh-pan yüeh*

On such a sunny day,
When the mist is light, the breeze warm,
I meditate in the clear, fragrant countryside.
Beautiful trees, short and tall,
Are decking the pavilions and terraces.
Weeping willows, languorous from dancing,
Are dazzling in green.
Light peaches and luxuriant plums are flourishing,
With myriads of pink flowers.
Lovely flying swallows and orioles
Are trying to outdo each other in song.

On the southern path are bevies of beautiful girls
Leisurely moving their elegant steps
Under the flower shades.
When they raise their powdered faces,
Even the flower envy them.

夜半樂

艷陽天氣
煙細風暖
芳郊晴朗閑凝竚
漸妝點亭臺
參差佳對
舞腰綠映
垂楊禮李天：
淺桃禮李天：
嫩紅無數
度綺燕
流鶯鬥雙語

翠娥南陌簇：
蹴影紅陰
緩移嬌步
檯粉面
韶容花光相妒

絳綃袖舉
雲鬟風顫
半遮檀口含羞
背人偷顧
競鬥草
金釵笑爭賭

They raise their red silk sleeves,
Their cloud-like hair quivering gently in the breeze.
Half covering their red lips with their sleeves,
They shyly turn their head and steal a look at the
    passers-by.
Laughing, they play the "grass game" and bet with
    their golden pins.

對此嘉景
頓覺消凝
惹成愁緒
念解佩
輕盈在何處
忍良時
孤負少年等閒度
空望極
回首斜陽暮
歎浪萍風梗知何去

Facing such a beautiful scene,
I suddenly feel lost,
With sorrow gradually aroused in me.
Where is the beautiful one who undid her pen-
    dants?
How could one bear to waste the happy hours of
    youth?
In vain, I look back and gaze at the setting sun as
    dusk falls,
I ask, like a drifting duckweed and the stem in the
    wind,
Whither shall I be going?

憶帝京　柳永

薄衾小枕天氣
乍覺別離滋味
展轉數寒更
起了還重睡
畢竟不成眠
一夜長如歲

也擬待
卻回征轡
又爭奈
已成行計
萬種思量
多方開解
只恁寂寞厭厭地
繫我一生心
負你千行淚

憶帝京

薄衾小枕天氣
乍覺別離滋味
展轉數寒更
起了還重睡
畢竟不成眠
一夜長如歲

也擬待
卻回征轡
又爭奈
已成行計
萬種思量
多方開解
只恁寂寞厭厭地
繫我一生心
負你千行淚

To the Tune of *Yi ti ching*

In weather such as this, with a light coverlet and a
    small pillow,
I suddenly realize what it feels like to be parted.
Tossing about in bed, I count the sounds of the
    watch in the cold night.
I get up and go back to bed again,
But still I'm unable to go to sleep,
For the night is long as a year.

I have thought of turning back my horse,
Only I have already made up my mind to travel.
I ponder over this many times,
Trying to cheer myself in many ways.
In this manner, I am overwhelmed by loneliness
    and languor.
All my life my heart is tied to you,
Which you shed a thousand tears in vain.

迎春樂

近來憔悴人驚怪
為別後
相思煞
我前生
負你愁煩債
便苦恁難開解

良夜永
牽情無計奈
錦被裏
餘香猶在
怎得依前燈下
恣意憐嬌態

To the Tune of *Ying-ch'un yüeh*

Recently people are surprised at my haggard looks.
This is all because after our parting
I have been pining for her.
In my previous life
I must have owed you a debt of sorrow.
Thus it is so difficult to cheer myself.

The beautiful night is long;
Distracted by love, what can I do with it?
Inside the brocade quilt her fragrance still remains.
How can I have her here as before
And feast my eyes on her loveliness under the lamp?

惨黛蛾
盈盈無緒
共黯然消黯
重攜纖手
話別臨行
猶自再三
問道君須去
頻耳畔低語
知多少
他日深盟
平生丹素
從今盡把憑鱗羽

傾杯

離宴殷勤
蘭舟凝滯
看看送行南浦
情知道世上
難使皓月長圓
彩雲鎮聚
算人生
悲莫悲於輕別
最苦正歡娛
便分鴛侶
淚流瓊臉
梨花一枝春帶雨

To the Tune of *Ch'ing pei*

She is busy preparing a farewell drink
While the magnolia boat is waiting.
It is time to bid farewell on the southern bank.
Now I realize that in this world
It is not possible for the moon to be always full,
Or for the colorful clouds to stay together.
In one's life,
Nothing could be more grievous
Than allowing ourselves to be parted too lightly,
And the most painful thing is to separate during
    happy hours.
With tears trickling down her jade-like face,
She is like a branch of pear-flowers in the spring
    rain.

傾杯

離宴殷勤
蘭舟凝滯
看、送行南浦
情知道天上
難使皓月長圓
彩雲鎮聚
算人生
悲莫悲於輕別
最苦正歡娛
便分鴛侶
淚流瓊臉
梨花一枝春帶雨

惨黛蛾
盈盈無緒
共黯然消魂
重攜纖手
話別臨行
猶自再三
問道君須去
頻耳畔低語
知多少
他日深盟
平生丹素
從今盡把憑鱗羽

Her forlorn, black eyebrows are beautiful and cheerless.
Together our souls waste in gloom.
When I hold her delicate hands again to bid farewell,
She asks again and again,
"Must you go?"
She keeps whispering in my ear,
"Do you know how much of
The deep vow you made in the past,
Together with my love in this life,
Is entrusted on the fish-and-bird messenger."

空牀展轉重追想
雲雨夢 任攲枕難計
寸心萬緒
咫尺千里
好景良天
彼此
空有相憐意
未有相憐計

婆羅門令

昨宵裏
恁和衣睡
今宵裏
又恁和衣睡
小飲歸來
初更過
醺醺醉
中夜後
何事還驚起
霜天冷
風細細
觸疏窗
閃閃燈搖曳

To the Tune of *P'o-lo-men ling*

Last night, in this manner,
I slept with my clothes on.
Tonight I will, again, sleep with my clothes on.
When I returned from a brief drinking-bout,
The first watch being over, and I dead drunk.
Why did I wake up after midnight?
In the cold and frosty sky,
A gentle wind was blowing.
As it brushed past the window,
The lamp flickered.

婆羅門令

昨宵裏恁和衣睡
今宵裏又恁和衣睡
小飲還來
初更過
醺醺醉
中夜後何事還驚起
霜天冷
風細細
觸疏窗閃閃燈搖曳

空牀展轉重追想
雲雨夢
任敧枕難繼
寸心萬緒
咫尺千里
好景良天
彼此空有相憐意
未有相憐計

Tossing about in my empty bed,
I try again to recall our intimacy.
Yet, leaning on my pillow, I cannot recapture it.
My heart is filled with myriad thoughts.
She is so near and yet so far.
On fine days with beautiful scenery,
Without the means to realize our love,
We love each other in vain.

早知恁麼
悔當初不把雕鞍鎖
向雞窗
只與蠻牋象管
拘束教吟課
鎮相隨
莫拋躲
針線閑拈伴伊坐
和我
免使年少
光陰虛過

定風波

自春來
慘綠愁紅
芳心是事可可
日上花梢
鶯穿柳帶
猶壓香衾臥
暖酥消
膩雲嚲
終日厭厭倦梳裹
無那
恨薄情一去
音書無箇

To the Tune of *Ting feng-po*

Ever since spring came with its grieving green and
　　sad red,
I have lost interest in doing anything.
The sun has risen to the tip of the flowers;
The orioles are flying through the willow branches.
Still I lie on the perfumed quilt,
The warm cream on my face having faded,
My hair hanging down.
All day long I feel too languorous to do my make-
　　up.
What else can I do?
I hate the fickle one, who, once gone,
Sends me not a word.

定風波

自春來慘綠愁紅
芳心是事可可
日上花梢
鶯穿柳帶
猶壓香衾臥
暖酥消
膩雲嚲
終日厭厭倦疏裹
無那
恨薄情一去
音書無箇

早知恁麼
悔當初
不把雕鞍鎖
向雞窗
只與蠻箋象管
拘束教吟課
鎮相隨
莫拋躲
針綫閒拈伴伊坐
和我
免使年少
光陰虛過

Had I foreseen this, I would have locked his carved-saddle.
Forcing him to sit in his study,
I would give him only Szuch'üan paper and an ivory brush,
And make him recite his lessons.
I would follow him closely, never leaving him alone.
Idly holding a needle and thread,
I would sit by him,
And he would be with me alone.
Thus, my youth would not be spent in vain.

乍入霓裳促徧
遲盈盈漸催檀板
慢垂霞袖
急趨蓮步
進退奇容千變
算何止傾城傾國
暫回眸萬人腸斷

柳腰輕

英英妙舞腰肢軟
章臺柳
昭陽燕
錦衣冠蓋
綺堂筵會
是處千金爭選
顧香砌
絲管初調
倚輕風
佩環微顫

To the Tune of *Liu yao ch'ing*

Ying-ying is lithe in her wonderful dancing,
Like Green Willow and Flying Swallow[1]
Feasting in magnificent halls,
High-ranking officials in brocade gowns
Compete with one another in bidding for her,
Offering a thousand pieces of gold.
She casts a glance upon the perfumed stone steps,
To the sound of musical instrument freshly tuned,
Her pendants trembling faintly in the gentle breeze.

柳腰輕

英々妙舞腰肢軟
章臺柳　昭陽燕
錦衣冠蓋
綺堂筵會
是處千金爭選
倚輕風
顧香砌絲管初調
佩環微顫

乍入霓裳促徧
逞盈盈
漸催檀板
慢垂霞袖
急趨蓮步
進退奇容千變
算何止
傾國傾城
暫回眸
萬人腸斷

As she starts the quick beat of the Ni-shang dance,
With grace she speeds up the castanets.
Slowly letting fall her cloud-like sleeves,
She hastens her lotus steps.
Back and forth she shows myriad variations in her
　　wondrous postures,
Quite capable of overturning cities and states,
But, with only one brief backward glance,
Teases to death ten thousand men.

[1]Miss Liu ("Green Willow") a famous courtesan of the T'ang dynasty; Chao Fei-yen (Flying Swallow), consort of Emperor Ch'eng of the Han dynasty, noted for her lightness and lithesome beauty.

木蘭花令

有箇人人真攀羨
問著洋洋回卻面
你若無意向他人
為甚夢中頻相見

不如聞早還卻願
免使牽人虛魂亂
風流腸肚不堅牢
祇恐被伊牽引斷

To the Tune of *Mu-lan-hua ling*

There is a maiden of great beauty
Yet when I talk to her she turns her face away
    repeatedly.
If you do not care for me,
Why then do you often appear in my dream?

You had better grant me my wish sooner,
Lest you should disturb my empty soul.
My amorous heart is weak,
I fear it will break for being attached to you.

葉嘉瑩：大晏詞的欣賞

An Appreciation of the *Tz'u* of Yen Shu

By **Chia-ying Yeh Chao**

Translated by **James R. Hightower**

THE JUDGMENT OF A WORK of literature is to some extent a subjective matter, much as an individual's enjoyment of food depends on his own palate and experience; tastes notoriously differ, and there is no need to insist that everyone share one's own preferences. But, like the old peasant who recommended the flavor of fresh celery and the warmth of the spring sun on the back to the Emperor, I will pass on my honest opinion about the value of Yen Shu 晏殊's songs.

Among song writers at the beginning of the Northern Sung, Yen Shu (991-1055), his son Yen Chi-tao 晏幾道, and Ou-yang Hsiu 歐陽修 are commonly mentioned together. Most readers consider Yen Chi-tao the best of the three, fewer would choose Ou-yang Hsiu, while Yen Shu has the fewest admirers. There are two reasons why Yen Shu's songs are not easily appreciated: first, his style is smooth and unruffled: there is no strong emotion, no striking language—neither colors to dazzle nor vigor to impress. His songs are like the title under which they are collected, "Pearls and Jade" *Chu yü tz'u* 珠玉詞, smooth and polished as jade and pearls; they may be pure and refined and crystalline, but in the eyes of most readers they are not so splendid or interesting as a multi-colored piece of jasper.

Another impediment to the appreciation of Yen Shu's songs is the fact that he was highly successful in his public career. Many people feel that great poetry can only be written by a poet who has experienced hardship and poverty, and Yen Shu fails to fulfill their expectations. In Wan Min-hao's book on the *tz'u* of Yen Shu and Yen Chi-tao, Yen Shu's songs are dismissed as the groans of a rich man who has nothing wrong with him.[1] Mr. Wan's study is a thorough one, and while he is unstinting in his praise of the son, he finds little to appreciate in the father. As Chiang Jo-liu 蔣弱六 once remarked in another context,[2] to be overlooked by someone who is not looking for you is nothing to complain of, but to be rejected after careful scrutiny is truly distressing. Mr. Wan's remark makes me sigh at Yen Shu's misfortune in being so fortunate.

[1] Wan Min-hao 宛敏灝, *Erh Yen chi ch'i tz'u* 二晏及其詞 (Shanghai: 1934, Commercial Press), p. 166.

[2] Chiang Jo-liu 蔣弱六, commenting on the third of Tu Fu's poems 遊何將軍山林十首, *Tu-shi ching-ch'üan* 杜詩鏡銓 (Taiwan: 1970, Hsin-tien Shu-chü) 2.8a.

To appreciate Yen Shu's songs one must first of all recognize that he is an intellectual poet, a rational poet. It is not necessarily true that "Poetry is incompatible with success in life"[3] or that "Talent and luck do not go together,"[4] but a man's character does have something to do with shaping his career, and we can divide poets into two large groups, those who were successful in their extra-poetic lives and those who failed. In terms of temperament, among the successful will be found the rational, intellectual poets, while the failures will include the poets of pure feeling. Wang Kuo-wei 王國維 said of Li Yü 李煜, "He was a poet who never lost his child-heart. That he was born in the seclusion of the palace and raised by women was a handicap to him as the ruler of a state, but it was his great advantage as a poet. . . . The subjective poet needs no wide experience of the world. The less his experience, the more genuine his own nature."[5] This is certainly true of the poet of pure feeling. The emotions of such a poet are like the unimpeded flow of water. He reacts emotionally to circumstances, unreflecting, without control or afterthought, uncritically. Of such poets it is not enough to say that they never lost their child-heart, in the world of practical affairs they simply remain children. Li Yü is an excellent example, and "kingdom ruined, family finished" is the classic end of this kind of poet. "Heaven takes a hundred disasters to make one poet"—for poets like this the disasters that are his lot and the pure feeling of his poetry are but two sides of the same coin.

It is otherwise with the intellectual poet. His emotions are more like a placid pool than flowing water; the wind may raise thousands of ripples; cast a stone in and it will sink in a little whirlpool, but nothing will make it lose its essential stillness, its limpid beauty. The intellectual poet is always reflecting on his experience, trying to understand it, or examining his own feelings and keeping them under control. He has developed an adult's standards of behavior while preserving a poet's sensitivity. Yen Shu is representative of this kind of poet.

When the Emperor Jen-tsung 仁宗 (1023-1063) came to the throne as a child of thirteen the government was left in the hands of his adoptive mother, the Empress Chang-hsien. The Minister Ting Wei and the Commissioner of Military Affairs Ts'ao Li-yung both wanted exclusive access to the Empress to present their memorials. The situation called for tact and a thorough grasp of the intricacies of court politics. When no one ventured to decide the matter, Yen Shu proposed that the Empress listen to all memorials from behind a screen, so that no one would get to see her individually.[6]

On another occasion he had to deal with a military crisis. The Hsi Hsia under the leadership of Yuan Hao 元昊 (Li Hsiang-hsiao) were making incursions along the Shensi border. Yen Shu requested that the generals be allowed to operate without interference by the Palace Commissars and that tactics not be prescribed from the

[3]Tu Fu, 天末懷李白, (*Tu Fu yin-te* 杜甫引得, v. 2) 20/25.

[4]Li Shang-yin 李商隱, 有感, *Li I-shan shih chi* 李義山詩集 (*Ssu-pu ts'ung-k'an* ed.) 6.18b.

[5]Wang Kuo-wei 王國維, *Jen-chien tz'u-hua* 人間詞 話 (Hongkong: 1961, Commercial Press, 蕙風詞話及 人間詞話合刊本) p. 197-198.

[6]*Sung shih* (Taiwan: Yi-wen Yin-shu-kuan reprint of Wu-ying-tien ed.) 70.1b-2a.

court, so they would be free to respond to the movements of the enemy. He proposed that bowmen be conscripted and trained, that palace luxuries be curtailed to aid those defending the borders, and that other government agencies apply directly to the treasury for all their income.[7]

These proposals show Yen Shu to have had a clear, incisive mind and a good grasp of the situation. The measures he proposed were those of a statesman and a general—certainly he was not just a ladies' man, nor was he a child with no experience of the world. Yet his songs show a real poetic talent. Practical accomplishments did not keep him from writing good poetry, nor was the value of his poetry diminished by the fact that he was successful and well-off.

Some may object to the label "intellectual" or "rational" for a poet, since poetry is supposed to rouse feeling, and feeling is diametrically opposed to intellect. This may be true if you think of intellect as the rationally calculating part of the mind, when it stands as the antithesis of feeling. But this is not a poet's rationality. For the poet, reason serves only as a restraint exercised over feeling, a controlling force that both refines and enhances feeling. It is not a matter of ratiocination, but of education and experience of life. Far from being antithetical to feeling, it is in fact steeped in feeling; the two are perfectly compatible, indistinguishable even as they arise simultaneously in the heart. Poetry may well be an emotional creation, but a poet may be a rational, intellectual writer.

YEN SHU'S SONGS, as the product of an intellectual poet, have several characteristic features. The first is feeling that holds a thought. It is a mixture of two perfectly blended elements. There is no lack of poems and songs by other writers which convey an idea; what makes Yen Shu's different is that theirs give the impression of being done deliberately, where in his songs it seems to be quite unconscious. If you take a cup of water from the sea, it is all salty without your intervention; or you can make a cup of salt water by adding salt to water. In Yen Shu's songs the reader is not confronted with an Idea, something the poet holds up for his consideration and approval. For instance, the lines in his famous song to the tune *Huan hsi sha* 浣溪沙 (Sands of the Washing Stream) (No. 17, p. 90)[8]

> *Hills and rivers fill the eyes: vain to think of what*　　滿目山河空念遠
> 　*is far away.*　　　　　　　　　　　　　　　　　　落花風雨更傷春
> *When flowers fall in wind and rain we grieve the*　　不如憐取眼前人
> 　*more for spring—*
> *Best love the one that's here right now.*

On the surface these lines are an emotional response to the passing of spring in a place far from home, with no intellectual content whatever, and it seems certain that Yen Shu was not consciously trying to express a thought. But the reader gets something in addition to the feeling, a stimulus or an invitation to a thought. In the

---

[7]*Ibid.*

[8]All references to Sung *tz'u* are to T'ang Kuei-chang 唐圭璋, *Ch'üan Sung tz'u* 全宋詞 (Peking: Chung-hua Shu-chü). The No. refers to the number in sequence of any author's *tz'u* in that collection, followed by a page reference.

first line, besides the emotion roused by "vain to think of what is far away," the words lead the reader to reflect on the things in life that lie out of reach which we long for in vain. The second line stirs feelings of regret at the passing of spring and at the same time invites us to think of all loveliness irrevocably gone. And the last line makes us think not only of "the one that's here right now," but of the precious fleeting moment we should cling to. Yen Shu uses the same line in another song to the tune *Mu-lan-hua* 木蘭花 (Magnolia Flower) (No. 56, p. 95)

> *Best love the one that's here right now*   不如憐取眼前人
> *And not ask too much of your soul in dreams.*[9]   免使勞魂兼役夢

We can take this repeated line "the one that's here right now" (*yen ch'ien jen*, 眼前人 "the person before your eyes") as representing Yen Shu's awareness of the necessity of facing reality.

Associations and inferences of this sort demand no profound reflection. The reader is aware of the implication at the same time he is moved by the emotional content of the poem. As suggested earlier, this intellectual content derives from Yen Shu's experience of life, it is not produced deliberately by reflective thought; it originates in the feelings and is not something tacked on. It follows that this intellectual content can appropriately only be felt and savored, it does not really lend itself to analysis and elucidation. My sort of exegesis is open to the objection that it is forced and trumped up, but Yen Shu's *tz'u* undeniably do suggest reflections about the human condition. Wang Kuo-wei, for instance,[10] remarked that the poet showed weariness of life in the lines, from the song *Ch'üeh t'a chih* 鵲踏枝 (Magpie Treads the Branch) (No. 23, p. 91)

> *Last night the west wind withered the green trees.*   昨夜西風凋碧樹
> *Alone I climb the high stairs*   獨上高樓
> *And gaze down the world's-end road.*   望盡天涯路

Of the same passage he said elsewhere,[11] "This is the first experience of one who has done great things, who is greatly learned." I shall not stop to elucidate Wang Kuo-wei's comment here,[12] having quoted it only to show that I am not the first to find an element of philosophy in Yen Shu's *tz'u*. That his songs owe their characteristic depth and significance to this factor is apparent when we compare them with those written by his son Yen Chi-tao, who surpasses him certainly in the qualities praised by Huang T'ing-chien 黃庭堅:[13] "refined strength of phrasing" that "agitates the heart," as in the lines

[9]In a dream one's soul is supposed to make journeys to a distance to see another person; such dream trips are considered dangerous or fatiguing. For example, see Tu Fu's "Dreaming of Li Po," *Tu Fu yin-te* 2.

[10]*Jen-chien tz'u-hua* p. 202.

[11]*Ibid.*, p. 203.

[12]The author has discussed Wang Kuo-wei's *tz'u* criticism in her 談詩歌的欣賞與人間詞話的三種境界 *Chia-ling t'an tz'u* 迦陵談詞. (Taiwan: 1970, Ch'un-wen-hsüeh Ch'u-pan-she) p. 1-11.

[13]Huang T'ing-chien 黃庭堅, Preface to *Hsiao-shan tz'u* 小山詞 (Taiwan: 1962, Shih-chieh Shu-chü), p. 1.

The moon of that night is there still
Which once shone on the Bright Cloud going home.　　當時明月在
　　曾照彩雲歸
To the tune *Lin-chiang hsien* 臨江仙
(Immortal by the River), No. 7, p. 222

Tonight I keep shining the silver lamp on her
Fearful lest this encounter might be a dream.　　今宵剩把銀釭照
　　猶恐相逢是夢中
To the tune *Che-ku t'ien* 鷓鴣天
(Partridge in the Sky), No. 24, p. 225

We danced the moon down from the peak of the
　　willow house
And sang the air to the end under the peach
　　blossom fan.　　舞低楊葉樓心月
　　歌盡桃花扇影風

(Ibid.)

But the son's verse is both narrower and shallower, lacking the intellectual component found in Yen Shu. For Yen Chi-tao's songs are preoccupied with "song, wine, and dalliance," "grief and joy, then and now;" they present only one aspect of human life, and appeal only to the reader's feelings. It is because Yen Shu's songs involve the reader's whole philosophy of life that they go beyond the limits of a given situation and suggest the entire human predicament.

Wan Min-hao argued that Yen Chi-tao had a better command of diction than Yen Shu, quoting these lines in support of his view, first by Yen Shu,

I remember the red candle in Orchid Hall
The heart was long, the flame short
Shedding tears for someone.　　念蘭堂紅燭
　　心長焰短
　　向人垂淚
To the tune *Han t'ing ch'iu* 撼庭秋
(Moved by Autumn in the Courtyard), No. 48, p. 94

and by Yen Chi-tao,

The crimson candle joins me in idle tears　　絳蠟等閒陪淚
To the tune *P'o-chen tzu* 破陣子
(Break the Ranks), No. 173, p. 246

The red candle is sorry but has nothing to suggest
And through the cold night drips futile tears for
　　me.　　紅燭自憐無好計
　　夜寒空替人垂淚
To the tune *Tieh lien hua* 蝶戀花
(Butterfly Loves Flowers), No. 15, p. 224

He claims that the word *hsiang* (in 向人 "for someone") is less effective than *p'ei* (in 陪淚, lit., "accompanies my tears"), and especially is weaker than *t'i* (in 替人 "for me"). That is all very well, as far as these two words are concerned, but it overlooks the fact that in Yen Chi-tao's poems what sheds tears is nothing more than a candle, while the figurative language of Yen Shu's "The heart was long, the flame short" leads the reader by a process of association from the burning candle to human life where "the heart is ready for more, but the strength is lacking." Yen Shu may have had no intention of rousing such an association, yet it is his peculiar characteristic to make such reverberations accessible to his reader. So we may grant Yen Chi-tao the greater emotional content, while insisting that Yen Shu is a more profound and a more intellectual poet.

Precisely here lies the difference between the poet of feeling and the poet of intellect. The one responds passively to life, registering experience as pure feeling; the other does not simply experience reality, he contributes a ray of understanding to his experience. The response of the former suffers from its narrowness, where the latter has the advantage of breadth. Where the response is purely emotional, the poetry conveys emotion but lacks thought, making for superficiality, while the one who can illuminate his subject will include thought with his feelings, and the result is greater depth. Consider these lines by Yen Shu:

> *The flowers will fall for all you can do*   無可奈何花落去
> *And the swallows that look familiar return.*   似曾相識燕歸來
>   To the tune *Huan hsi sha* 浣溪沙
>   (Sands of the Washing Stream), No. 9, p. 89

> *The flowers don't give out*   花不盡
> *The willow lasts forever—*   柳無窮
> *They should be just like my feelings.*   應與我情同
>   To the tune *Hsi ch'ien ying* 喜遷鶯
>   (The Oriole Flies for Joy), No. 45, p. 94

In both passages the observation of seasonal change is not just the occasion for an emotional response. The poet perceives a pattern, a contrast or a repetition, that gives a rational basis for the emotion. Or the following, which suggests rational control of the feelings:

> *Don't share these carnelian blossoms casually,*   莫將瓊蕚等閒分
> *Keep them for the one you love.*   留贈意中人
>   To the tune *Shao-nien yu* 少年游
>   (Youthful Diversions), No. 49, p. 94

It is this combination of feeling and idea which is Yen Shu's trademark, and it must be recognized for a true appreciation of his poetry. If you fail to see it, you will find no treasure in his "Pearls and Jade".

THE NEXT SPECIAL quality of his poetry is a certain quiet elegance of tone, the sort of thing the provincials admired in Ssu-ma Hsiang-ju 司馬相如's demeanor, an aristocratic bearing. It is something that seldom finds expression in Chinese poetry, chiefly no doubt because few poets lived the life of refined luxury that Yen Shu enjoyed, and men who did live such a life lacked his talent for poetry. Yen Shu lived under the peaceful reigns of Chen-tsung 眞宗 (998-1022) and Jen-tsung. The chronicle of his promotions, from the time he passed his examinations as a child prodigy of fourteen and received the post of Collator in the Chancellery until he became Prime Minister thirty years later, is recorded in his biography and does not need to be reviewed here. His poetic talent is attested by the sensitivity and insight of his songs. He portrays a girl's psychology:

> *You might suspect she had a nice spring dream* 疑怪昨宵春夢好
> *last night,*
> *But it was winning the flower competition this* 元是今朝鬪草贏
> *morning* 笑從雙臉生
> *That spread the smile on her cheeks.*
>> To the tune *P'o-chen tzu* 破陣子
>> (Break the Ranks), No. 135, p. 108

On the yellow hollyhock:

> *The autumn scene is late under the phoenix tree* 高梧葉下秋光晚
> *leaves—* 珍叢化出黃金盞
> *The rare plant transformed into golden cups.*
>> To the tune *P'u-sa man* 菩薩蠻
>> (Bodhisattva Barbarian), No. 117, p. 105

> *You can pick a blossom for a golden winecup* 摘承金盞酒
> *When you wish me a long long life,* 勸我千長壽
> *Or I can hold it up as a Taoist nun's cap* 擎作女眞冠
> *And try it on you to see how pretty you look.* 試伊嬌面看
>> To the tune *P'u-sa man* 菩薩蠻
>> (Bodhisattva Barbarian), No. 116, p. 105

There is a fresh vision in these lines which conveys something of the poet's delight in the flower (and the occasion), a sensitive perception effectively translated into verse.

He has an ear and an eye for nature and can write as though it were capable of human feeling:

> *From the Lung-t'ou the water voices gurgle* 壟頭嗚咽水聲繁
> *Behind the leaves soon the orioles will be chatter-* 葉下間關鶯語近
> *ing.*
>> To the tune *Mu-lan-hua* 木蘭花
>> (Magnolia Flower), No. 64, p. 96

> The spring breeze has not learned to keep the
>   willow fluff
> From pelting the pedestrians in the face.
>   To the tune *T'a so hsing* 踏莎行
>   (Treading the Sedge), No. 82, p. 99

春風不解禁楊花
濛濛亂撲行人面

Anyone with such sensitivity and insight is a poet, whether a failure or success in everyday life, though his experience of life will naturally affect the tone and style of his poetry. Yen Shu enjoyed a successful career, and there are no themes of banishment and frustrated ambition in his songs. If you are committed to the belief that to be a poet one must first be a failure, you will be disappointed at not finding such themes in his poetry, but their absence does not diminish his poetic endowments. The quiet elegance characteristic of his poetry is precisely a product of his experience and of his temperament. It is best illustrated by one of his songs to the tune *Ch'ing-p'ing yüeh* 清平樂 (Ch'ing-p'ing Music) (No. 32, p. 92):

> The autumn wind stirs
> And one by one the leaves fall from the phoenix
>   tree.
> It's easy to get drunk on the green wine
> And nap soundly by the little window.
>
> Blue myrtle and rose of Sharon both are faded
> The setting sun shines on the railing
> The pair of swallows are ready to leave.
> It was a bit chill last night inside the silver screen.

金風細細
葉葉梧桐墜
綠酒初嘗人易醉
一枕小窗濃睡

紫薇朱槿花殘
斜陽却照闌干
雙燕欲歸時節
銀屏昨夜微寒

We look in vain here for the usual stereotypes of Chinese poetry—sorrow in parting or grief at separation, lament on growing old or complaint about poverty,—nor is there the effect peculiar to Yen Shu of an idea conveyed through feeling. All we have is a poet's subtle aesthetic perceptions. In poetry of this sort we should not seek either emotion or idea, but only attempt to savor the unadulterated poetic impulse. As Chuang Tzu 莊子 put it, "Great is the usefulness of the useless!" Fair warning to readers who are determined to find emotion and idea in poetry, this is no place to look. It is like a vintage wine: you do not drink it to quench your thirst. The excellence of a poem like this is the aesthetic experience itself, unmixed with any of the more substantial ingredients of other poetry.

THE THIRD CHARACTERISTIC OF Yen Shu's songs could be described as an embracing perspective. Lu Chi 陸機 said of the poet,[14] "He sighs at the passing of the seasons, and is pensive as he regards the complexity of Nature." Everyman to some degree feels the approach of old age when he is made aware of the flight of time, of the evanescence of happiness, of the decline of human affairs, and the poet is more responsive than everyman. The poet also puts his feelings into verse. Where Wan

---

[14]Lu Chi, *Wen fu* 文賦, *Wen hsüan* 文選 (Taiwan: Yi-wen Yin-shu-kuan), 17.1b.

Min-hao dismissed Yen Shu's poems of feeling as "moaning when he was not sick," I would understand them differently. What moves one emotionally need not be some great human tragedy; even the natural sequence of flourishing and decay will suffice to make one feel the sadness of impermanence. And in human terms, the threat of transience makes no distinction between the rich and the poor, the successful and the failures. Likewise the intensity of the poet's reaction to that threat has nothing to do with his station in life, but depends on his sensitivity. Yen Shu's response can be every bit as intense as that of a poet who did not enjoy his privileged position in society. Poets may react similarly, but the tone of their reaction will vary. If you compare Yen Shu's songs with those of Feng Yen-szu 馮延巳 and Ou-yang Hsiu, the two poets most nearly like him in style, the difference is apparent. Feng Yen-szu responds to grief with stoical resolution. Ou-yang Hsiu is exuberant and refuses to be depressed by it, and Yen Shu brings a broad view that puts the unhappiness in perspective.

Let us take a look at a few songs by Yen Shu.

To the tune *Ts'ai-sang tzu* 采桑子 (Picking Mulberry Leaves), (No. 41, p. 93)

All the spring is good for is to make us old.	時光只解催人老
I don't think I'm so very sensitive,	不信多情
But still I always grieve at the parting place	長恨離亭
When tears fall on the spring gown and wine has no effect.	滴淚春衫酒易醒
	梧桐昨夜西風急
Last night the west wind was sharp in the phoenix tree,	淡月朧明
The pale moon shone clear.	好夢頻驚
I kept waking up from a dream of her:	何處高樓雁一聲
Above a tall building somewhere, the call of a wild goose.	

To the tune *Yeh chin men* 謁金門 (Visiting the Golden Gate), (No. 1, p. 87)

Autumn dew falls	秋露墜
Dripping out the red tears of the southern orchid.	滴盡楚蘭紅淚
Past affairs, the old joys—	往事舊歡何限意
All like a dream.	思量如夢寐
One's face has aged since last year	人貌老于前歲
But breeze and moonlight are just as they were.	風月宛然無異
A guest at the table, cinnamon wine in the glass	座有嘉賓樽有桂
We must not fail to get drunk tonight.	莫辭終夕醉

To the tune *P'o-chen tzu* 破陣子 (Break the Ranks), (No. 5, p. 88)

On the lake the west wind and slanting sun　　　湖上西風斜日
The lotus have dropped all their pink petals.　　荷花落盡紅英
Tiny pearl-buds in the bed of golden chrysan-　　金菊滿叢珠顆細
*   themum.*　　　　　　　　　　　　　　　　　海燕辭巢翅羽輕
The sea swallow leaves its nest on light wings—　年年歲歲情
Every year, the same feelings.

A cup of the new wine,　　　　　　　　　　　　美酒一杯新熟
A few stanzas of a wild song to listen to.　　　　高歌數闋堪聽
If we don't get drunk together on this bottle,　　不向尊前同一醉
Whatever shall we do about time like water　　　可奈光陰似水聲
Slipping off into the distance without stopping?　迢迢去未停

Some of these lines ("All the spring is good for is to make us old", "When tears fall on the spring gown and wine has no effect", "Past affairs, the old joys,—/All like a dream") express feeling. Others invoke something high and far-off ("Above a tall building somewhere, the call of a wild goose") or invite to uninhibited abandonment ("A guest at the table, cinamon wine in the glass,/We must not fail to get drunk tonight"). On the other hand, there are lines that show acute sensitivity to the transience of things:

On the lake the west wind and slanting sun
The lotus have dropped all their pink petals.

Whatever shall we do about time like water
Slipping off into the distance without stopping?

But the sadness is tempered by "A cup of the new wine,/A few stanzas of a wild song to listen to." From these lines we can see that though he was sensitive to the fact of impermanence, he had the courage to face reality and the perspective to accept it.

Feng Yen-szu's attitude toward suffering was simply to bear it with fortitude.

For long she leans on the rail, but he does not　一晌凭闌人不見
*   appear.*　　　　　　　　　　　　　　　　　鮫綃掩淚思量遍
With a bit of silk she wipes her tears, and keeps
*   on thinking.*

To the tune *Ch'üen t'a chih* 鵲踏枝
(Magpie on the Branch), No. 1, p. 234[15]

Watching the flowers every day, I drink too much;　舊日花前常病酒
It's all the same to me the mirrored face is thin.　敢辭鏡裏朱顏瘦

(same tune), No. 2, p. 234

[15]References for Feng Yen-szu are to Lin Ta-ch'un　　hsüeh ku-chi, 1956).
林大椿, *T'ang Wu-tai tz'u* 唐五代詞 (Peking: Wen-

Ou-yang Hsiu's unconcern in the face of painful reality is only playful high spirits:

> *After all your drinking and scheming you've got* 尊前百計得春歸
> *spring back—* 莫爲傷春歌黛蹙
> *Don't knit your brows now lamenting spring.*
> To the tune *Yü lou-ch'un* 玉樓春
> (Spring in the House of Jade), No. 86, p. 134

> *Watch until all of Loyang's blossoms fall,* 直須看盡洛城花
> *Then you can easily bid spring farewell.* 始共春風容易別
> (same tune, No. 75, p. 132)

We can see how Yen Shu finds in his broad perspective a way of coping; it is a perfect demonstration of the character and self-discipline of an intellectual poet. There are no shrill cries in his songs, no despair. Emotion in the *Chu-yü tz'u* is only a delicate shading on the smooth surface of the pearls and jade, a nuance of color that adds to the viewer's appreciation and enjoyment, a special beauty that is part of Yen Shu's poetry.

THE FOURTH CHARACTERISTIC OF Yen Shu's songs involves something generally appreciated by his readers, his ability to describe luxury without being vulgar and to write about love affairs without seeming either coarse or frivolous. Critics have frequently remarked on these qualities. For example, Wu Ch'u-hou 吳處厚 (late 11th century) wrote,[16]

> Although His Excellency Yen Yuan-hsien (Yen Shu) came from
> the country, he was a natural aristocrat in letters. On reading the lines
> in Li Ch'ing-sun 李慶孫's "Song of the Rich Man"
>
> > *Fine bound songbooks written in letters of gold*
> > *Trees and flowers named on plaques of jade,*
>
> he commented, "This is the beggar's view, someone with no firsthand
> knowledge of upper class life. When I write on such subjects, I never
> directly mention gold or jade, brocade or embroidery. I just speak of
> their effects. For instance,
>
> > *On the path by the pavilion the willow flowers are past,*
> > *Between the curtains the swallows fly.*[17]
>
> > *In the pear blossom park the spreading moonlight*
> > *Across the willow-fluff pond the flowing wind*[18]

[16]Wu Ch'u-hou 吳處厚, *Ch'ing-hsiang tsa-chi* 青箱雜記 (*Pai hai* 稗海, Taiwan: 1968, Hsin-huan Shu-chü photoreprint of Chen-lu-t'ang 振鷺堂 ed.) 5.1b-2a.

[17]This couplet is not in any of the poems collected in *Yen Yuan-hsien i-wen* 晏元獻遺文 (v. 17 of *Sung erh-shih chia chi* 宋二十家集)

[18]*Ibid.* 7b "Untitled Poem" 無題.

Do you think such scenes exist for the poor?"

Chang Shun-min 張舜民 (late 11th century) tells the following anecdote:[19]

> When Liu San-pien (Liu Yung 柳永) had offended the Emperor
> Jen-tsung by one of his songs, the Ministry of Civil Appointments
> would not give him a promotion. Dissatisfied, San-pien went to the
> office to complain. Minister Yen said, "Sir, you write songs?" San-pien
> said, "Like your Excellency, I too write songs." The Minister said, "I
> may write songs, but I never wrote such a line as 'Languidly holding
> her needlework she nestles close to him'." Whereupon Liu withdrew.

These anecdotes show Yen Shu's dislike of both vulgarity and impropriety. These
he avoided by describing the spirit, not external appearance.

Generally speaking, there are two ways of reacting to experience, one simply
registers the perceptions of the senses and is content with external appearances,
the other, reacting through the mind, penetrates through superficial appearances
to the underlying essentials of a situation. If someone enters a rich man's house and
simply records what his senses tell him, then it will be the gold and jade, the brocade
and embroidery that he sets down. But if he reacts through his mind, then what he
perceives will be the aura of wealth, and this will have to be conveyed more indirect-
ly. In the matter of sensuality, two people going hand in hand can be reported in
terms of their physical contact, or, to the other kind of perception, the feeling of
closeness is what matters. Of course, the feeling of affluence and luxury in the first
case comes initially from the visible objects of luxury and in the second it is the
evidence of physical contact that lets one conceive the intimacy between the couple.
But for the one who perceives essences, the evidence of the senses is unimportant
except as intermediary. Like Chuang Tzu, when you catch the fish you can forget
the net, and when you have the idea you can forget the words. Once you have
grasped the essence of a situation, you are no longer aware of the evidence provided
by the senses; it is a spontaneous process, not something deliberately contrived. Yen
Shu avoided the words "gold" and "jade," not as a matter of policy, as the anecdote
would seem to suggest, but because his reaction was of the mind and led him to the
essentials underlying appearance.

Here are some examples of how he presented a setting of luxury in his songs:

> *A swallow passes by the double curtains of the*　　　小閣重簾有燕過
> 　　*little hall,*　　　　　　　　　　　　　　　　　晚花紅片落庭莎
> *Late pink petals fall on the courtyard grass;*　　　曲欄干影入涼波
> *Reflection of a curving bannister in the cool water.*
> 　　　　　　To the tune *Huan hsi sha* 浣溪沙
> 　　　　(Sands of the Washing Stream), No. 12, p. 88

> *Green leaves hide the orioles*　　　翠葉藏鶯
> *Red curtains keep out the swallows*　朱簾隔燕

---

[19]Chang Shun-min 張舜民, *Hua-man lu* 畫墁錄 (vol. 2 of Pai-hai) 1.30b.

> *Incense from the burner slowly pursues twisting*
> *gossamer.*
>
> To the tune *T'a so hsing* 踏莎行
> (Treading on the Sedge), No. 82, p. 99

爐香靜逐遊絲轉

> *The red curtain half lowered, incense burned out.*
> *A second-month east wind brings an urgent*
> *message to the willow.*
> *Beside her lute, lost in thought—*
> *Don't ask in front of the parrot.*
>
> To the tune *Mu-lan-hua* 木蘭花
> (Magnolia Flower), No. 60, p. 96

朱簾半下香銷印
二月東風催柳信
琵琶旁半且尋思
鸚鵡前頭休借問

In all of these passages Yen Shu manages to suggest a setting of luxury without flaunting the appurtenances of wealth. "You know this is not someone living in a three-family village," as Ch'ao Pu-chih 晁補之 put it.[20]

> *Right now I would like to be*
> *A thousand-foot strand of gossamer*
> *To hold fast the Moving Cloud.*
>
> To the tune *Su chung-ch'ing* 訴衷情
> (Telling How I feel), No. 66, p. 97

此時拚作
千尺游絲
惹住朝雲

> *Green liquor in the cup, and someone she loves*
> *Always together beneath the flowers, in the moon-*
> *light.*
>
> To the tune *T'a so hsing* 踏莎行
> (Treading the Sedge), No. 81, p. 96

樽中綠醑意中人
花朝月下長相見

> *So much love beyond telling*
> *Is written into the words of the song—*
> *This feeling a thousand thousand times.*
>
> To the tune *P'o-chen tzu* 破陣子
> (Breaks the Ranks), No. 3, p. 88

多少襟懷言不盡
寫向蠻牋曲調中
此情千萬重

It is lines like these which create the feeling of sensuality without the impropriety of Liu Yung's "languidly holding her needlework she nestles close to him" or "She wants to draw the fragrant curtain and talk of love." This is because the feelings Yen Shu evokes are those of real love, not simply erotic dalliance. Obviously his verse is never indecent, and although his worldly position and circumstances undoubtedly played some part in determining his standards of taste, his natural delicacy and refinement kept him from writing vulgar or obscene verse. Wan Min-hao was surely less than generous in asserting that he was only inhibited by what others might say.

---

[20]Ch'ao Pu-chih 晁補之, quoted in Wu Ts'eng　*ts'ung-pien* 詞話叢編, vol. 1) 16.1a.
吳曾, *Neng-kai-chai man lu* 能改齋漫錄 (*Tz'u hua*

In Yen Shu's "Pearls and Jade" are a certain number of congratulatory songs which provide good material for readers who are looking for something to criticize. It is a kind of verse which easily becomes empty and fatuous. As a minister of state, Yen Shu naturally had to write poems to order on social occasions, and these are certainly not among his best poems. However, compared with the congratulatory songs written by his contemporaries, Yen Shu's have some redeeming features. As in his other songs, he does not descend to the obvious; he manages to introduce some subtlety, and conveys a feeling rather than just presenting the subject's excellencies for our admiration. He offers his congratulations soberly and with restraint, most often against a background of natural description, about which he retains his poet's sensitivity. The result is congratulatory poetry that is refined and graceful, but which still manages to be fresh and original. For example, to the tune *Tieh lien hua* 蝶戀花 (Butterfly Loves Flowers) (No. 107, p. 103)

Purple chrysanthemums begin to bloom when Rose of Sharon declines.	紫菊初生朱槿墜
The moon is nice, the breeze fresh.	月好風清
Gradually the feel of full autumn—	漸有中秋意
The nightwatches grow longer, the sky is like water.	更漏乍長天似水
The silver screen is spread to show the green of far-off hills.	銀屏展盡遙山翠
The embroidered curtain rolled in waves, the incense ash grows,	繡幕卷波香引穗
Quick pipes, massed strings.	急管繁絃
Everyone loves this old man.	共愛人間瑞
Fill the jade cups full, whirl dancing sleeves.	滿酌玉盃縈舞袂
The southern spring congratulates his long, long life.	南春祝壽千千歲

Or one celebrating the Emperor, to the tune *Fu ni-shang* 拂霓裳 (Brushing the Rainbow Robe) (No. 114, p. 105)

We smile to see the autumn sky	笑秋天
Evening lotus with round strung dew-pearls,	晚荷花綴露珠圓
The breeze, the sun are nice.	風日好
Several rows of new geese stuck onto the cold mist cloud.	數行新雁貼寒烟
On silver reeds blow crisp woodwind notes,	銀簧調脆管
On jasper frets pluck clear strings.	瓊柱撥清絃
We offer a flowing bowl,	捧觥船
With one voice sing of this age of peace.	一聲聲齊唱太平年

Neither of these songs is particularly profound or subtle, but they are not wholly without merit in rousing a response in the reader. When one thinks how many happy occasions in a lifetime need celebrating, one can hardly disparage all such songs as vulgar or common.

ONE FINAL POINT I WOULD LIKE to make. There is one song in the "Pearls and Jade" that stands out as being in a different style from the others. It is to the tune *Shan t'ing liu* 山亭柳 (Mountain Pavilion Willow) and carries the subtitle "To a Singer 贈歌者" (No. 123, p. 106):

> She hails from Ch'in in the west
> And takes her chances with the skills she has.
> In the entertainment world
> She ranked with the best.
> Sometimes she equaled Nien-nu's virtuosity
> And on occasion could stop the marching clouds.
> Her reward—any amount of Shu brocade;
> Her efforts were not wasted.

家住西秦
賭博藝隨身
花柳上
鬪尖新
偶學念奴聲調
有時高遏行雲
蜀錦纏頭無數
不負辛勤

> For some years now she's worked the capital road
> Wearing out her soul for heeltaps and poor fare.
> To whom can she confide
> Her heart's pain?
> If a real connoisseur would choose her
> She would willingly sing the Spring Song to the end.
> A song at the banquet, and her tears fall
> She keeps wiping her eyes on a silken kerchief.

數年來往咸京道
殘盃冷炙謾消魂
衷腸事
託何人
若有知音見採
不辭徧唱陽春
一曲當筵落淚
重掩羅巾

In all his other songs Yen Shu's style is smooth and placid, but this one throughout is written with strong feeling. None of his songs has a subtitle, except this one, which is carefully labeled "To a Singer." It is interesting that one song should be exceptional in two different ways, and some explanation seems called for. First we need to amplify a bit what has already been said about Yen Shu's disposition and his career. The quiet elegance and the balanced perspective that appear in his songs show clearly the rationality which he cultivated: everything tranquil and under control. But his biographer mentions another side of his character: "He was forceful and incisive, and in his assignments as prefectural governor the officers and people were somewhat fearful of his temper and impatience."[21] Ou-yang Hsiu uses the same terms "forceful and incisive" *kang chien* 剛簡 to characterize him,[22] and the Ssu-k'u 四庫 editors[23] echo it with "Yen Shu was endowed with a forceful and rugged disposition, but his written style was particularly graceful and lovely." To keep a forceful and rugged disposition in check, Yen Shu certainly must have exercised self-control, and the "graceful and lovely" language of his songs is the result of a forceful

---

[21] *Sung shih* 6.3b.   p. 74.

[22] Ou-yang Hsiu 歐陽修, *Ou-yang Wen-chung-kung chi* 歐陽文忠公集. (*Kuo-hsüeh chi-pen ts'ung-shu* ed.)

[23] *Sus-k'u tsung-mu t'i-yao* (Liao-hai Shu-she ed.) 113.1a.

nature showing through the rational control, conflicting elements held in balance, a complex amalgam. Consequently they can be limpid without being monotonous, smooth without being insipid.

Let me suggest an analogy: White sunlight contains the seven colors of the spectrum, and when it passes through a prism, the colors appear. The complexity of Yen Shu's character likewise was revealed only under special circumstances. When he was involved in difficulties, he could be provoked to the point where the forceful, rugged component of his nature appeared. His biography tells a story[24] about the time he was Assistant Court Commissar of Military Affairs. He had memorialized against making Chang Ch'i 張耆 Commissar, against the wishes of the Empress Dowager. He was ordered to follow her to the palace. His servant was late in bringing his ivory tablet of office, and Yen Shu struck the servant with the tablet, breaking his teeth. Another anecdote[25] tells how Chang Hsien 張先, a fellow poet-official, insisted on discussing business in Yen Shu's home. Yen Shu would not respond to his remarks and finally flushed and said in his southern accent, "I got you an appointment because you could write 'There's nothing so strong as love',[26] but now you come here to talk business."

Once we have recognized these elements of forcefulness and irritability in Yen Shu's character, we can see that there is nothing to be surprised at in the passionate complaint of the "Mountain Pavilion Willow" song. Although the subtitle specifically says, "For a Singer," Cheng Ch'ien suggested that with it Yen Shu is "Borrowing a winecup from someone else to drown his own sorrows."[27] He also comments, "Since the song mentions 'Ch'in in the west' and the 'capital at Hsien,' it should date from the time he was in charge of the Yung-hsing District, when he was over sixty and had long been out of the court and found it hard not to be depressed." This is very perceptive. From the time Yen Shu was recommended as a child prodigy at age fourteen and was appointed Collator by Shen-tsung until he was dismissed as minister when he was fifty-four, his career was as successful as one could wish. But during the nearly ten years after his dismissal until his death in 1055 he was given provincial assignments, of which the one in Yung-hsing was the farthest away from the court. The reason for his dismissal, according to the *Sung History*[28] was an accusation that he failed to mention in the grave inscription he was ordered to write for the Imperial Concubine Li the fact that she was the real mother of the Emperor Jen-tsung. Further, that he had used conscripts to repair a building for his personal profit. But, in the words of the *Sung History*, "Since the Empress Dowager Chang-hsien was ruling, Shu did not dare state the truth (that she was not the Emperor's real mother), and it was one of the perquisites of a Minister to make use of conscript labor for private purposes. Contemporaries felt that Shu was not at fault."

Having been dismissed for offences for which he was not to blame and then to be left in exile for such a long time were frustrations which prompted him to reveal the forceful, irritable side of his character in a song. But this song has another

---

[24] *Sung shih* 6.3b, 6.2a.

[25] *Hua-man lu* 1.33a-b.

[26] A line from Chang Hsien's song to the tune "A

Clump of Flowers," No. 22, p. 61.

[27] Cheng Ch'ien 鄭騫, *Tz'u hsüan* 詞選, p. 24.

[28] *Sung shih* 6.3a.

peculiarity already noted: it is "For a Singer." If, as seems likely, the song expresses his own feelings during his later years of exile, why did he "borrow someone else's winecup to drown his own sorrows" and give the song this subtitle? It seems to me that this can be accounted for as another sign of Yen Shu's rational self-control. Wang Kuo-wei quoted Nietsche, "The literature I love is all written in blood."[29] Some authors, having written in their own fresh blood, want to show you the still dripping wound. Others prefer to keep the wound out of sight and make up a story to account for the painful event. This is the characteristic method of the intellectual poet. He prefers to maintain a distance from his emotion, and that is why Yen Shu chose to write "For a Singer," separating himself from his feelings by attributing them to someone else, so that he could write without inhibition.

At the same time, I do not believe that this subtitle is a convention, something concocted for the purpose; there must have been a singer. The singer's situation elicited a response in the poet, and his long-harbored feelings were released by it.

This sort of encounter is not something that can be arranged, and so it is not easy to find in Yen Shu's songs another that is comparably unrestrained in expression, for such a perfect occasion may never have happened again. And since he was not one to flaunt his wounds without such a disguise, the fact that this uncharacteristic poem is unique in his collection is further confirmation that he was indeed an intellectual poet.

In conclusion I would like to imitate Wang Kuo-wei by quoting a *tz'u* poet's own verse as a critical evaluation of his poetry. Yen Shu's songs have a touch of melancholy under the placid surface, the sharp clarity of the autumn sun along with the spring sun's mild warmth; this and the freshness and appropriateness of his images make one think of his lines:

> *In the frost, under the moon* 霜前月下
> *The slanting pinks, pale petals* 斜紅淡蕊
> *Fresh and charming enough to bring back spring.* 明媚欲回春
> To the tune *Shao nien yu* 少年游
> (Youthful Pleasures), No. 50, p. 94

[29]*Jen-chien tz'u-hua*, p. 198.

歐陽修詞

Twenty-one Tz'u *by Ou-yang Hsiu*

Translated by Teresa Yee-wha Yü

採桑子

歐陽修

羣芳過後西湖好狼籍殘紅飛絮濛濛垂
柳闌干盡日風 笙歌散盡游人去始
覺春空垂下簾櫳雙燕歸來細雨中

採桑子

羣芳過後西湖好
狼籍殘紅
飛絮濛濛
垂柳闌干盡日風

笙歌散盡遊人去
始覺春空
垂下簾櫳
雙燕歸來細雨中

To the Tune of *Ts'ai-sang tzu*

The West Lake is lovely
After the passing away of the
Many splendors of spring.
Heaps of red scattered,
Flying catkins like delicate rain.
Over the railings,
Hanging willows sway all day in the breeze.

The musicians have left,
Pleasure-seekers are gone, before I realize
The emptiness of spring.
The window curtain let down,
In the gentle rain
A pair of swallows come flying home.

蝶戀花

面旋落花風蕩漾
柳重烟深
雪絮飛來往
雨後輕寒猶未放
春愁酒病成惆悵

枕畔屏山圍碧浪
翠被華燈
夜夜空相向
寂寞起來褰繡幌
月明正在梨花上

To the Tune of *Tieh lien hua*

蝶戀花

Falling petals waft
And whirl in the wind
In the face.

面旋落花風蕩漾

柳重烟深

The willows are heavy,
The mist deep and dense,

雪絮飛來往

Snowy white catkins fly around.

雨後輕寒猶未放

As the touch of cold after rain lingers on,
I feel depressed,

春愁酒病成惆悵

Wrapped in spring sorrow and the ill-effects of
wine.

枕畔屏山圍碧浪

Beside the pillow,
The bedscreen encloses like blue waves.

翠被華燈

A green quilt, an ornate lamp,

夜夜空相向

Night after night these things I face
In vain emptiness.

寂寞起來褰繡幌

Lonely, I rise
To lift the embroidered curtain.

月明正在梨花上

The moon is right above
The pear blossoms, so bright.

漁家傲

暖日遲遲花裊裊
人將紅粉爭花好
花不能言惟解笑
金壺倒
花開未老人年少

車馬九門來擾擾
行人莫羨長安道
丹禁漏聲衢鼓報
催昏曉
長安城裏人先老

To the Tune of *Yü-chia ao*

The warm sun moves slowly, flowers gracefully
    sway.
Girls with their rouge and powder compete with
    the flower for beauty.
Flowers cannot speak, they can only smile.
Let's empty the golden jug.
Flowers, not yet past their prime,
Are blossoming, and we are still young.

In front of the city gates,
Horses and carriages throng the thoroughfares.
Travellers, don't you long for the roads of Ch'ang-
    an.
From the palace, the sound of the water-clock—
The street drum announces the hour,
Hastening the dusk and the dawn.
Men are the first to grow old in the city of Ch'ang-
    an.

漁家傲

十月小春梅蕊綻
紅爐畫閣新妝遍
鴛帳美人貪睡暖
梳洗懶
玉壺一夜輕澌滿

樓上四垂簾不卷
天寒山色偏宜遠
風急雁行吹字斷
紅日晚
江天雪意雲撩亂

漁家傲

十月小春梅蕊綻
紅爐畫閣新妝遍
鴛帳美人貪睡暖
梳洗懶
玉壺一夜輕澌滿

樓上四垂簾不卷
天寒山色偏宜遠
風急雁行吹字斷
紅日晚
江天雪意雲撩亂

To the Tune of *Yü-chia ao*

The tenth month—month of the Little Spring.
Plum trees are starting to send out blossoms.
A red stove, a painted chamber refurbished
Behind the bed-curtain, she who is beautiful snuggles in the warm bed,
Too lazy to wash and comb her hair.
Over the night, the jade water-clock is covered lightly with ice.

Upstairs, on all four sides, curtains are left hanging.
The cold mountain looks its best from afar.
The wind blows urgently, breaking off
The line of migrating birds.
The red sun sets,
Over the river, confused clouds signal the coming of snow.

漁家傲

四月園林春去後
深深密幄陰初茂
折得花枝猶在手
香滿袖
葉間梅子青如豆

風雨時時添氣候
成行新筍霜筠厚
題就送春詩幾首
聊對酒
櫻桃色照銀盤溜

To the Tune of *Yü-chia ao*

The fourth month—spring has gone from the
woods.
Deep and dense, like a heavy curtain the trees give
leafy shade.
With the flower twig I've plucked still in my hand,
My sleeves were full of scent.
Among the leaves, the plums are green like peas.

Often, rain and wind season the weather.
Rows of new bamboo-shoots sprout—
Their frosty skin thickening.
I dash off a few poems on the departure of spring,
Simply to go with the drinking.
The color of the cherries reflect brightly on the
silver plates.

漁家傲
七夕

喜鵲塡河仙浪淺
雲軿早在星橋畔
街鼓黃昏霞尾暗
炎光歛
金鈎側倒天西面

一別經年今始見
新歡往恨知何限
天上佳期貪眷戀
良宵短
人間不合催銀箭

To the Tune of *Yü-chia ao*

*Evening of the Seventh Day of the Seventh
Month of the Year*

The magpies fill the Milky Way, the fairy waves
　　are shallow.
The cloud-chariot is already by the Star Bridge.
With the fading end of the twilight glow
The street drum announces the hour.
The bright daylight shrinks.
To the west of the sky a golden crescent hangs
　　tiltedly.

Parted for a whole year, they now meet again.
Where do old woes and new joy end?
Treasure this joyful period in Heaven,
The good night is short.
On earth, the silver-marker of the water-clock
　　should not be urging time on men!

蝶戀花

水浸秋天風皺浪
縹緲仙舟
只似秋天上
和露採蓮愁一餉
看花却是啼妝樣

折得蓮莖絲未放
蓮斷絲牽
特地成惆悵
歸棹莫隨花蕩漾
江頭有箇人相望

蝶戀花

水浸秋天風皺浪
縹緲仙舟
只似秋天上
和露採蓮愁一餉
看花却是啼妝樣

折得蓮莖絲未放
蓮斷絲牽
特地成惆悵
歸棹莫隨花蕩漾
江頭有箇人相望

To the Tune of *Tieh lien hua*

The water mirrors an autumn sky;
The wind makes wrinkles of wavelets.
Dim and distant, the fairy boat seems to float in an
    autumn sky.
Gathering lotus blossoms covered with dew—
For one moment she is plunged into sadness.
The flowers, too, look like a tear covered face.

She plucks a lotus stem, but the threads would not
    let go.
The stem is broken, but the threads remain un-
    severed—
How sad!
On your way home, do not let your boat float with
    the flowers.
Somewhere, on the bank of the river,
Someone is waiting for you!

採桑子

十年前是尊前客
月白風清
憂患凋零
老去光陰速可驚

鬢華雖改心無改
試把金觥
舊曲重聽
猶似當年醉裏聲

採桑子

十年前是尊前客
月白風清
憂患凋零
老去光陰速可驚

鬢華雖改心無改
試把金觥
舊曲重聽
猶似當年醉裏聲

To the Tune of *Ts'ai-sang tzu*

Ten years ago I was a winebibber,
Beneath a bright moon, a wind clear and cool
And so I withered and waned,
As sorrow and worries grew.
Relentless time flashes by.

My hair has changed, but not my heart.
Let me hold on to this golden goblet,
And listen to the old songs again—
Songs that remind me of those good old drunken
    days.

採桑子

平生為愛西湖好
來擁朱輪
富貴浮雲
俯仰流年二十春

歸來恰似遼東鶴
城郭人民
觸目皆新
誰識當年舊主人

To the Tune of *Ts'ai-sang tzu*

採桑子

平生為愛西湖好　　　All my life I have loved the West Lake,
來擁朱輪　　　　　　Where I once arrived with a retinue of vermilion
　　　　　　　　　　　　wheels.
富貴浮雲　　　　　　But riches and honor are like floating clouds.
俯仰流年二十春　　　In a moment, twenty springs have slipped by.

歸來恰似遼東鶴　　　Coming back, I feel like the crane of Liao-tung.
城郭人民　　　　　　The city and its people,
觸目皆新　　　　　　All have changed wherever I turned.
誰識當年舊主人　　　Who is there to recognize the governor of long ago?

長相思

蘋滿溪
柳繞堤
相送行人溪水西
回時隴月低

煙霏霏
風淒淒
重倚朱門聽馬嘶
寒鷗相對飛

長相思

蘋滿溪
柳繞堤
相送行人溪水西
回時隴月低

煙霏霏
風淒淒
重倚朱門聽馬嘶
寒鷗相對飛

To the Tune of *Ch'ang hsiang-ssu*

Floating duckweed covers the stream,
Willows wind along the embankment.
I saw the wayfarer off, to the west of the stream.
As I return, the moon is low over the fields.

The mist is heavy, the wind chills.
Once more, leaning against the vermilion gate,
I listen for the sound of his horse neighing—
In the freezing cold, a pair of gulls fly together.

長相思

花似伊
柳似伊
花柳青春人別離
低頭雙淚垂

長江東
長江西
兩岸鴛鴦兩處飛
相逢知幾時

長相思

花似伊
柳似伊
花柳青春人別離
低頭雙淚垂

長江東
長江西
兩岸鴛鴦兩處飛
相逢知幾時

To the Tune of *Ch'ang hsiang-ssu*

The flowers are like you,
The willows are like you,
Flowers and willows are in their youth as we part.
You hang your head while tears fall.

East of the Yangtze River,
West of the Yangtze River,
On the two shores of the river two mandarin ducks
      fly their separate ways—
When will they ever meet again?

玉樓春

燕鴻過後春歸去
細算浮生千萬緒
來如春夢幾多時
去似朝雲無覓處

聞琴解珮神仙侶
挽斷羅衣留不住
勸君莫作獨醒人
爛醉花間應有數

To the Tune of *Yü-lou ch'un*

With the wildgoose and the swallow gone,
Spring too takes its leave.
I try to figure out the endless, straggling threads
Of this floating life on earth—
Like a spring dream each comes, who knows for
  how long?
Like the morning cloud each disappears,
Nowhere to be found.

For the sound of my zither,
She gives me a girdle-gem,
Kindred spirit of immortals.
Though I hold on to her silken dress which tears,
I cannot induce her to stay.
Don't alone be the sober one, my friend.
There aren't many times
You can be dead drunk among the flowers.

浪淘沙

把酒祝東風
且共從容
垂楊紫陌洛城東
總是當時携手處
遊遍芳叢

聚散苦怱怱
此恨無窮
今年花勝去年紅
可惜明年花更好
知與誰同

浪淘沙

把酒祝東風
且共從容
垂楊紫陌洛城東
總是當時携手處
遊遍芳叢

聚散苦怱怱
此恨無窮
今年花勝去年紅
可惜明年花更好
知與誰同

To the Tune of *Lang t'ao sha*

With a glass of wine in hand
I drink to the east wind:
Pray tarry a little!—
East of Loyang,
Along the streets of the capital
Where the willows hang,
There, we used to stroll hand in hand,
Rambling past every flower shrub.

Meeting and parting,
All is too hasty.
This sorrow has no end.
Flowers bloom redder this year than last.
Next year, they will blossom even finer.
But who will be
There to share them
With me?

玉樓春

離歌且莫翻新闋
一曲能教腸寸結
直須看盡洛城花
始共春風容易別

尊前擬把歸期說
未語春容先慘咽
人生自是有情癡
此恨不關風與月

玉樓春

尊前擬把歸期說
未語春容先慘咽
人生自是有情癡
此恨不關風與月

離歌且莫翻新闋
一曲能教腸寸結
直須看盡洛城花
始共春風容易別

To the Tune of *Yü-lou ch'un*

With a jug of wine before me, I try to announce
    the day of my departure.
Before I can utter a word, the face of spring dis-
    solves into choking tears.
Some men are born with dedicated love.
This sorrow has nothing to do with the moon, nor
    the wind.

Please do not set the parting-song to a new tune,
One is enough to tie the heart in knots.
Until I have seen the last of Loyang's flowers,
It'll not be easy for me to bid the spring wind
    goodbye.

玉樓春

殘春一夜狂風雨
斷送紅飛花落樹
人心花意待留春
春色無情容易去

高樓把酒愁獨語
借問春歸何處所
暮雲空闊不知音
惟有綠楊芳草路

玉樓春

殘春一夜狂風雨
斷送紅飛花落樹
人心花意待留春
春色無情容易去

高樓把酒愁獨語
借問春歸何處所
暮雲空闊不知音
惟有綠楊芳草路

To the Tune of *Yü-lou ch'un*

A night of blustering storm and wind
In the last days of spring
Sends red petals
Falling and flying from the trees.
Men and flowers alike would love spring to stay on.
Having no feeling, spring leaves with no qualms.

Alone and sad, with wine in hand,
Upon this high tower I murmur to myself—
"May I ask where Spring has gone to?"
Wide and empty,
The evening clouds do not understand me.
There are only the green willows and the grassy
        road.

玉樓春

洛陽正值芳菲節
穠艷清香相間發
游絲有意苦相縈
垂柳無端爭贈別

杏花紅處青山缺
山畔行人山下歇
今宵誰肯遠相隨
惟有寂寥孤館月

玉樓春

洛陽正值芳菲節
穠艷清香相間發
游絲有意苦相縈
垂柳無端爭贈別

杏花紅處青山缺
山畔行人山下歇
今宵誰肯遠相隨
惟有寂寥孤館月

To the Tune of *Yü-lou ch'un*

Loyang is perfect in the flowering season.
Rich fragrance and gentle scent
Fill the air in turn.
The gossamer deliberately entwines me,
The willows, for no reason, vie to bid farewell.

Where the apricots blossom pink
The green of the hills is dented.
At the foot of the hill,
A traveller takes his rest.
Tonight, who would follow me over such a distance?
None but the lonely moon above the solitary inn.

臨江仙

柳外輕雷池上雨
雨聲滴碎荷聲
小樓西角斷虹明
闌干倚處
待得月華生

燕子飛來窺畫棟
玉鈎垂下簾旌
涼波不動簟紋平
水精雙枕
傍有墮釵橫

臨江仙

柳外輕雷池上雨
雨聲滴碎荷聲
小樓西角斷虹明
闌干倚處
待得月華生

燕子飛來窺畫棟
玉鈎垂下簾旌
涼波不動簟紋平
水精雙枕
傍有墮釵橫

To the Tune of *Lin-chiang hsien*

A light peal of thunder
From beyond the willow trees.
Rain on the pond,
Falling,
Scatters and patters,
Upon the lotus leaves.
Across the western corner of the
Small house, a broken rainbow hangs
Brightly, as I rest on the balcony,
Awaiting moonrise.

A swallow comes flying,
Taking a peek under the painted beam.
Jade hooks let the curtain hang loose.
The cool waves remain still,
A bamboo mat spreads unruffled.
Beside the twin crystal pillows
Lies a fallen hairpin.

玉樓春

一任西樓低曉月
大家金盞倒垂蓮
老去風情尤惜別
人生聚散如弦筈
莫對新花羞白髮
便須豪飲敵青春
正值柳綿飛似雪
兩翁相遇逢佳節

玉樓春

兩翁相遇逢佳節
正值柳綿飛似雪
便須豪飲敵青春
莫對新花羞白髮

人生聚散如弦筈
老去風情尤惜別
大家金盞倒垂蓮
一任西樓低曉月

To the Tune of *Yü-lou ch'un*

Two old men happen to meet on this festive day
When the willow catkins are flying like snow.
Against youth let's drink, to the very last cup!
Faced with the young blossoms, don't let us
Feel ashamed of our white hair.

Like an arrow on the bowstring
Are life's meetings and partings.
A feeling for separation grows intense with old age.
Let's pour from our golden lotus cups,
And leave the morning moon
To sink behind the Western tower!

南歌子

鳳髻金泥帶
龍紋玉掌梳
走來窗下笑相扶
愛道畫眉深淺
入時無

弄筆偎人久
描花試手初
等閒妨了繡功夫
笑問雙鴛鴦字
怎生書

南歌子 | ## To the Tune of *Nan-ko tzu*

鳳髻金泥帶
龍紋玉掌梳
走來窗下笑相扶
愛道畫眉深淺
入時無

A phoenix-shaped bun in a gold-splashed ribbon.
A palm-like comb of jade carved with dragons.
She comes over under the window,
Laughing and putting her arms under mine,
Keeps asking,
"Are my brows painted in the right shade
To be in fashion?"

弄筆偎人久
描花試手初
等閒妨了繡功夫
笑問雙鴛鴦字
怎生書

She leans on me
And plays long with her brush.
Drawing flowers, trying her first sketch.
Lightly idling away all those sewing hours!
With a smile she asks,
"Those words for mandarin drake and duck,
How do you write them?"

訴衷情
眉意

清晨簾幕卷輕霜
呵手試梅妝
都緣自有離恨
故畫作遠山長

思往事
惜流芳
易成傷
擬歌先斂
欲笑還顰
最斷人腸

訴衷情
眉意

To the Tune of *Su chung-ch'ing*

The Eloquent Brows

清晨簾幕卷輕霜
呵手試梅妝
都緣自有離恨
故畫作遠山長

Rolling up gently a curtain in the clear morning
    frost,
She blows on her hands and applies a beauty mark.
All because of this parting-sorrow,
Deliberately, she draws her eyebrows long,
Like the distant hills.

思往事
惜流芳
易成傷
擬歌先斂
欲笑還顰
最斷人腸

Thinking of the past,
Lamenting the flight of youth—
So easy to be grieved!
She tries to sing,
But first composes her features;
Just about to smile,
She knits her brows again.
Most heart-rending!

望江南

江南柳
葉小未成陰
人為絲輕那忍折
鶯嫌枝嫩不勝吟
留著待春深

十四五
閒抱琵琶尋
階上簸錢階下走
恁時相見早留心
何況到如今

望江南

江南柳
葉小未成陰
人為絲輕那忍折
鶯嫌枝嫩不勝吟
留著待春深

十四五
閒抱琵琶尋
階上簸錢階下走
恁時相見早留心
何況到如今

To the Tune of *Wang chiang-nan*

A willow South of the River,
With leaves so small it gives yet no shade.
No one would have the heart to pluck its boughs,
Boughs so soft and frail.
The warbler fears that its branches are too delicate
     to support a song,
Branches so tender and young.
They are best left till spring is farther along.

Fourteen years of age, or fifteen,
Leisurely, with a *p'i-p'a* in her arms
She looked around—
As we gambled on the steps and she ran past down
     below,
Then had I already noticed her,
How could I fail to see her now?

Confucian Gentleman and Lyric Poet:
Romanticism and Eroticism in the *Tz'u* of Ou-yang Hsiu

By **Ruth W. Adler**

> Mencius said to Wan Chang: "The best Gentleman of a village is in a position to make friends with the best Gentlemen in other villages; the best Gentleman in a state, with the best Gentlemen in other states; and the best Gentleman in the Empire, with the best Gentlemen in the Empire. And not content with making friends with the best Gentlemen in the Empire, he goes back in time and communes with the ancients. When one reads the poems and writings of the ancients, can it be right not to know something about them as men? Hence one tries to understand the age in which they lived. This can be described as 'looking for friends in history' ".[1]

THESE WORDS EXPRESSED a major function of literature as conceived by the Confucian ideal—that of forming a link between the "superior men" of all ages, a link of common understanding and sympathy which would serve to fortify, inspire and perpetuate all that was noblest in the thought and conduct of man. Implicit in this statement also is the ancient concept of the great statesman and the literary genius as two facets of one man—a tradition which dates back to the time of the Duke of Chou (ca. 1000 B.C.) and which has extended even into the present century.

In a country which has produced many such men, there are yet those special few who stand out above the others among the unforgettable names in the history of Chinese culture. Ou-yang Hsiu 歐陽修[2] is one of these. He was statesman, historian, classical scholar, antiquarian, essayist and poet. Born nearly a millennium and a half after Mencius, he might have served as a model for that "best Gentleman" of whom Mencius spoke. He did indeed make friends with all the "best Gentlemen" of his day—scholars, talented statesmen and fellow writers. Beyond that, he befriended and became the mentor of many of the outstanding and brilliant elites of

---

[1] Translated by D. C. Lau. *Mencius* (Penguin Classics, 1970), VB, 8, p. 158.

[2] Ou-yang Hsiu (*tz'u* 字 Yung-shu 永叔; *hao* 號 Tsui-weng 醉翁 and Liu-i Chü-shih 六一居士; posthumous title, Wen-chung Kung 文忠公) was born in A.D. 1007 in Mienchow (present day Szechuan). According to custom, however, he is considered a native of Lu-ling 廬陵 in present day Kiangsi, the ancestral home of his father, and was often referred to as Lu-ling Hsien-sheng 廬陵先生.

the younger generation. And he did, further, "commune with the ancients" as evidenced by his appreciation of the Confucian classics and of the works of later prose writers who followed the ancient style. Deriving inspiration from these, he was eventually to become a major influence in the revival and perpetuation of that style, particularly as exemplified in the writings of the 9th century statesman, Han Yü 韓愈.

Ou-yang Hsiu was only ten when he came across an incomplete set of Han Yü's works stored in an old basket at the home of friends. Having few books of his own, he persuaded them to let him have the discarded volumes which he took home and read eagerly, though comprehending but a part of the old text. The writings of Han Yü were clear and unadorned, concerned more with thought and content than with mere cleverness of style. Contrasting sharply with the ornate parallel prose and sentimentality which characterized late T'ang and early Sung literature, Han's writings were not at all popular during this time and were almost entirely neglected by most scholars. But the impact on Ou-yang Hsiu was profound and lasting. As he himself described his impressions some thirty years afterward:

> "On studying the words of Han, I was struck by their profundity, richness, boldness and breadth. Although young and as yet unable to understand their full meaning, I was already attracted by their tremendous, almost boundless spirit . . . "[3]

Though required by the expedience of the examination system to perfect the current parallel prose style of writing, Ou-yang Hsiu continued to study the classical style of prose on his own. After passing the examinations in 1030, he was appointed to serve at Loyang, the so-called West Capital and leading cultural metropolis of Northern China. Here he continued his literary studies guided by the outstanding writers of the day, particularly the historian Yin Shu 尹洙, another enthusiast of the style of early *ku-wen* 古文 writers.

It was at this time that Ou-yang Hsiu established his great friendship with Mei Yao-ch'en 梅堯臣, one of the most talented poets of that era. Under the stimulation of this friendship, he turned his efforts to the composition of poetry, attempting to perfect his style in the traditional *shih* 詩 form and becoming interested in the writing of the currently popular *tz'u* 詞 as well. The writing of *tz'u*, considered at the time not only popular but even frivolous, was perhaps an unusual departure for a Confucian scholar such as Ou-yang Hsiu, even more so because of his firm devotion to the ancient style of writing. However, scholar and official though he may have been, with wide-ranging interests in literature, the classics, the decipherment of archaic bronzes, and the like, Ou-yang Hsiu was also very much a man of his day. He possessed a certain *joie de vivre* and he took pleasure in the conviviality of informal gatherings with other scholars and poets—often in the company of the gay and talented courtesans who charmed these men with their knowledge of classical poetry and their virtuosity as singers and players of the newest poetic and musical creations of the day. Not to have been inspired to accept the challenge of

---

[3]Translated by James T. C. Liu. *Ou-yang Hsiu:*   p. 26.
An 11th Century Neo-Confucianist. (Stanford, 1967)

creating in the new genre would have been far more unusual.

This time at Loyang was one of the happiest periods in his life and one to which Ou-yang Hsiu often alluded with great nostalgia in *tz'u* such as the following composed during his later years:

To the Tune of *Yeh hsing ch'uan* 夜行船

Memories of carefree pleasures in the West Capital. 憶昔西都歡縱
Since we parted, 自別後
Who can share them with me? 有誰能共
Scenic beauty of the Yi; flowers along the Lo. 伊川山水洛川花
I strain my memory. 細尋思
The old ramblings seem but a dream. 舊遊如夢

To see it now is even more poignant. 今日相逢情愈重
Wistfully I hear the songs, 愁聞唱
And bells tolling in painted towers. 畫樓鐘動
Returning, white-haired, from distant shores 白髮天涯逢此景
I drain the golden goblet. 倒金尊
Who is left to see me off? 殢誰相送

That there was an even lighter side to these early years of officialdom and literary pursuits is clearly revealed in the following *tz'u* which recaptures the charm and spirit of this period in his life:

To the Tune of *Yü-lou ch'un* 玉樓春

Often I recall the charm of Loyang— 常憶洛陽風景媚
Warm mists, gentle breezes adding pleasure to wine; 煙暖風和添酒味
Orioles' songs at banquets seemed invitations to linger, 鶯啼宴席似留人
While blossoms peeped atop the walls as by design. 花出牆頭如有意

Parted now by the blue of a thousand hills, 別來已隔千山翠
I gaze 'til slanting rays sink below the tower . . . 望斷危樓斜日墜
Memories stir just seeing peonies turn red. 關心只爲牡丹紅
A flood of spring sadness fills my dreams. 一片春愁來夢裏

In the tradition of the poetic diction of the time, warm mists, breezes, orioles and flowers were delicately veiled descriptions of pleasures among the courtesans in the drinking houses of the gay metropolis. Because Ou-yang Hsiu was known to have been devoted to the pleasures of wine and women, this and other of his *tz'u* were interpreted as having erotic implications. But even beyond this, it is lovely even considered as nothing more than an evocation of a natural setting once known and long remembered.

Indeed, the writings of Ou-yang Hsiu very much reflect his awareness and love of nature, as well as a wide knowledge of plants and flowers. Among his prose writings, for example, there is a remarkable treatise on the peony of Loyang (*Feng-su chi ti san* 風俗記第三). In the third chapter of this, he describes the delight the residents of the city take in their springtime flowers:

> "According to the custom of Loyang, almost everybody is fond of flowers. When spring comes, everyone in the city, whether rich or poor, wears flowers—even the peddlars. When the flowers bloom, the scholars and populace alike, all turn out for a stroll...."

洛陽之俗。大抵好花。春時。城中無貴賤。皆插花。雖負擔者亦然。
花開時。士庶競爲遊遨。

And so, when he exclaims, "Memories stir just seeing peonies turn red," this may really be nothing more than fond recollections of those spring strolls in Loyang. In the context of the poem, however, it does seem quite clear that remembrance of peonies triggers a host of other memories and sensual pleasures as well, so that it may be closer to actuality to consider this and similar *tz'u* a blend of both nostalgia and eroticism.

These carefree years were soon interrupted by political controversy, power struggles at court, foreign invasions, clashes between the newly-arisen progressive thinkers and the older conservatives. More than once, Ou-yang Hsiu became embroiled in these controversies and was intermittently exiled, for a total of about ten years, to posts remote from the court. When the time came for him to leave the pleasures and beauties of Loyang, he voiced his sorrow in a beautiful lyric which, like the preceding ones, suggests beneath its surface charm, once again the charming world of courtesans:

To the Tune of *Yü-lou ch'un*　　玉樓春

Now is Loyang's season of fragrant beauty.　　洛陽正值芳菲節
Perfumes, now heady, now faint, float forth.　　穠艷清香相間發
Floating gossamer tendrils mean to entwine us fast,　　遊絲有意苦相縈
Low bending willows, on impulse, vie to say farewell.　　垂柳無端爭贈別

Rosy apricot blossoms obscure the verdant hills.　　杏花紅處靑山缺
Travelling toward the mountain paths, I rest in the foothills.　　山畔行人山下歇
Tonight, who will roam afar with me?　　今宵誰肯遠相隨
None but the moon beyond the silent, lonely inn.　　惟有寂寥孤館月

These banishments took him to I-ling 夷陵 in 1036 as district magistrate (nearly two thousand miles from the capital where the Yangtze emerges from the grandeur of the Three Gorges and not far from his childhood home in Suichow 隨州); then from 1045 to 1048 to Ch'uchow 滁州 in Anhwei where he served as governor, and finally, after a brief sojourn in Yangchow 揚州, to the beautiful lake country of Yingchow 穎州 (modern Fu-yang). It was during these periods of comparative retirement that Ou-yang Hsiu was able to devote many hours to work on the *New History of the Five Dynasties* which he had begun with Yen Shu 晏殊[4] and to the writing of essays and poetry, creating in particular the great prose masterpieces which have earned him his enduring fame.

HE CONSIDERED WRITING TO BE a natural and integral part of the personality of the ideal Confucian gentleman, rather than something to be viewed independently as an art in itself. It was a belief to which he attached considerable significance as this advice to a fellow writer makes clear:

> "It is not that scholars do not try to seek the Way, it is rather that only a few succeed in attaining it. Not that the Way is beyond reach, but scholars are often diverted by other goals. Although it is difficult to acquire mastery and felicity in the art of writing, it is all too easy to be pleased with oneself and scholars frequently succumb to the attractions of this art. Having achieved some degree of mastery, they conclude: 'I have attained genuine knowledge.' Some even go so far as to discard all other matters, concerning themselves with nothing else and justifying their behavior by stating: 'I am a writer and my sole job is to write well.' This is why those who succeed in attaining the Way are so few. In his old age, Confucius returned to the State of Lu and completed the *Six Classics* in a matter of only a few years. Yet students of *The Book of Changes* cannot spare any time for *The Spring and Autumn Annals*, nor can students of *The Book of History* spare any time for *The Book of Songs*. How slight was the added effort on the part of Confucius! And yet what a supreme achievement! Though it is impossible to emulate the Sage's writings, if a person attains the Way, maturity will manifest itself spontaneously in his writings."[5]

Always outspoken and frank, even during his early years at court, Ou-yang Hsiu frequently offended those in power, yet never feared to defend what he thought was right though it might provoke Imperial wrath and demotion or banishment from court. He put into practice what he wrote and stood firmly by his ideals and his friends. When political controversies arose, he did not hesitate to voice his beliefs, siding with his friend, Fan Chung-yen 范仲淹, author of the famous quote that a scholar should be "first in worrying about the troubles of the world and last in enjoying its pleasures." It was this that led to his first banishment to I-ling in the wake of Fan's similar dismissal from court. Nevertheless, upon his recall some years

[4]The project had been begun during his younger days as a joint venture with his friend, Yen Shu. Unfortunately, Yen died after having written only about 4,000 words. Ou-yang Hsiu decided to continue the project alone during his exile and, on his return to political prominence in 1060, was asked as an honor to present his manuscript to the court. He declined, saying it was not yet satisfactory or complete because of the lack of reference material in the remote places where he had been. He withheld the manuscript for political reasons during his lifetime and it was not until after his death that it became available.

[5]Translated by Huang Kuo-pin. *"Ta Wu Ch'ung hsiu-ts'ai shu"* (答吳充秀才書), *Ou-yang Wen-chung-kung ch'üan-chi* 歐陽文忠公全集.

later to catalogue the Imperial Library and then to serve as critic-advisor on policy, Ou-yang Hsiu again unhesitatingly defended the close alliance between himself and his coterie, including Fan, in his celebrated essay, "On the Partisanship of Friends 朋黨論." In defense against these charges, he argued for the rights of superior men to form political groups as long as these were founded on moral and ideological principles:

> "Your subject has heard that the partisanship of friends is traceable to ancient times but it is expected of the ruler to distinguish between gentlemen and unworthy men. The friendship between gentleman and gentleman is based on the Way, and that among unworthy men, on profit. This is a matter of course."
>
> "Not so with the gentleman. What he adheres to is honor and righteousness; what he practices is loyalty and honesty; and what he prizes is a good name and integrity. When gentlemen cultivate themselves on such a basis, they share the Way and help improve one another. When they serve the country on this basis, they are of one mind and cooperate from beginning to end. Such is the friendship of gentlemen.
>
> "He therefore who is the ruler should merely rid himself of false parties consisting of unworthy men and employ the true associations of gentlemen; then he can bring peace and order to his land."[6]

No less trenchant were his advisory memorials to the throne, as illustrated by these excerpts from a work entitled, "On the Difficulty of Being a Ruler":

> "Alas, the difficulty of selecting personnel is great indeed! But it is not so great as that of judging advice. This is varied in nature. Some, being brilliantly eloquent and presenting all sides of each question, gives delight. Some of it, being faithful counsel, is straightforward and plain but mostly deliberate. It is not difficult to judge either, but it depends on the enlightenment, or lack of it, on the part of the listener. Flattering advice complies with the wishes of the man to whom it is offered and thus is disposed to please. On the other hand, frank advice, which is displeasing to the listener, can provoke anger. It is not difficult to judge either, but it depends on the wisdom or stupidity of the listener."
>
> "In the selection of personnel, a mistake visible to the whole country but not to the ruler is the greatest danger. There are innumerable instances in history where disorder, disaster, defeat and downfall have resulted from such an error."[7]

His persuasive prose writings, produced during his terms at court, as well as the historical writings and reflective essays written during his intermittent periods of banishment, not only revived the ancient classical style in brilliant form, but were

[6]Translated by S.S. Liu. *Chinese Classical Prose*, A *RENDITIONS* book, (The Chinese University Press, 1979) p. 141.

[7]*Ibid*. pp. 159 and 163.

to shape the character of Chinese prose for centuries to come. As a man to whom writing was the visible expression of his inner world, the tangible essence of his emotions and ideals, Ou-yang Hsiu instinctively sought emotional satisfaction and spiritual sublimation during these turbulent times through the medium of his writing, perhaps especially through poetry. And here, too, his influence was felt as he laid the groundwork for the new type of *shih* which came to be regarded as typical of the Sung.

At this time poetry was undergoing a transition from the passion of the T'ang to a more subtle mood of unadorned simplicity (*p'ing-tan* 平淡) and incorporated a broader range of subject matter, notably social problems and the human scene. There was an attempt to transcend the artificial elegance and flowery diction of much of T'ang poetry and to replace it with a diction that was plain, concrete and even colloquial—a diction which included the frequent use of "raw words" (*ying yü* 硬語), another instance of stylistic inspiration from the poetry of Han Yü.

In sharp contrast to these innovations, the *tz'u* which had developed earlier during the late T'ang and Five Dynasties, now began to flourish. It was a poetry of elegance, languor and sentimentality. Taking as its central motif feminine loveliness and the exquisite melancholia of separation and love denied, this poetry was written in a new style, intimately dependent upon music for its structure, from which derived the term, *"tz'u"* 詞, literally, "words" (for music).

With music as an integral part of the *tz'u* form, the lyric and emotional qualities of poetry inevitably gained ascendancy over the moral and didactic aspects. The "world" was largely that of love—neglected, lost or denied—in settings of extravagant beauty and peopled by women of exquisite loveliness. But if the themes of love, beauty and loneliness were ever-recurring, the words for narrating them were even more rigidly fixed. The physical attributes of this world were, *de rigeur*, storied towers, carved balustrades, fragrant boudoirs, a slender curve of moon, fine mists and rain, drooping willows, clouds of incense or cold, dead ashes in a golden censer, utensils of jade, golden wells, crystal curtains, fallen flowers, the lonely drip of the water clock. Delicate hands and soft flesh were "jade;" luxuriant masses of hair were "black clouds;" "pearls" of dew sparkled on the grass; golden phoenixes danced on embroidered screens. A typical example is this poem by Wen T'ing-yün 溫庭筠 (ca. 820-870), from the *Hua-chien chi* 花間集, flowery, sensuous and almost completely delineated by the highly selective diction mentioned above:

To the Tune of *Keng-lou tzu*　　　　　　　　　更漏子

Willows droop softly　　　　　　　　　　　柳絲長
In the fine spring rain.　　　　　　　　　　春雨細
Past the flowers, sounds of distant dripping.　　花外漏聲迢遞
Cries of wild geese from beyond the passes　　驚塞雁
Wake the crows on the city walls.　　　　　起城烏
On my painted screen—golden partridges.　　畫屏金鷓鴣

Mist—fragrant, gossamer,　　　　　　　　香霧薄
Drifts past the screen.　　　　　　　　　　透簾幕
Deep is my sorrow in this cage of gold.　　　惆悵謝家池閣

> *Red candles shaded,*   紅燭背
> *Silken curtains drawn,*   綉簾垂
> *Long, long I dream. If you but knew!*   夢長君不知

The scene is one of fragile beauty and the mood of gentle sadness is suggested subtly: willows, symbols of parting, accentuating a lonely hour as they droop in the fine, cold mist; the melancholy sound of dripping from accumulations of rain somewhere off in the garden; the pre-dawn quiet shattered by cries of crows startled into wakefulness. With the economy of a single metaphor, "lakes and pavilions of the Hsieh," (the literal reading of the phrase in the third line of the second verse), Wen T'ing-yün further delineates the setting—an elegant house of courtesans—recalling at the same time, in the origin of the metaphor, another courtesan, the beautiful Hsieh Ch'iu-niang. Unlike the wild geese flying free from the remotest reaches of the land, or even the homely city crows, the speaker feels caged, destined to remain, like the golden partridges on her screen, confined to this place of luxury and love, but without the one of whom she dreams and for whom she longs.

The attitude of Ou-yang Hsiu toward the ornate parallel prose of his time was reflected in his feeling about the poetry of his age as well. He deplored the over-refinement of the *Hsi-kun* 西崑 school with its elaborate allusions and fanciful imagery and urged, in its place, a return to greater simplicity and realism. With respect to the new genre, the *tz'u*, however, he did not entirely escape the influence of the *Hua-chien* poets, as can be seen from many of his own *tz'u*. This may have been both because of the peculiar nature of the *tz'u* itself, particularly because it was intended to be sung, and also because of the social milieu in which it flourished.

THE NORTHERN SUNG CAPITAL of Pien-ching 汴京, to which Ou-yang Hsiu returned in later years, was a busy, thriving metropolis. After the chaotic period of the Five Dynasties, times were relatively stable. All manner of small trades flourished; artisans of all sorts produced a wide variety of wares; shops, restaurants, places of entertainment, wine shops and brothels abounded. Musical entertainment was a major source of enjoyment and relaxation for all classes,—men of leisure, intellectuals, officials of all ranks, as well as the common people. It became a challenge for literati to compose lyrics for the popular tunes of the day, often embodying in these the tunes of the common people, the world of the leisured class as well as that of the courtesan. In the gay and carefree milieu which gave rise to these poems, it is scarcely to be wondered at that the themes were frivolous, romantic and frequently erotic. Yet, in these times, it was not considered amiss even for men of distinction and stature, such as Ou-yang Hsiu himself, to write such poetry as a diversion, nor did these men consider the writing of *tz'u* beneath their dignity. Such notable *tz'u* writers as K'ou Chun 寇準, Yen Shu, Han Ch'i 韓琦, Fan Chung-yen, Sung Ch'i 宋祁, Ch'ien Wei-yen 錢帷演, Ssu-ma Kuang 司馬光 and Chen Yao-tso 陳堯佐 constitute a veritable roster of prominent statemen of the early Sung. Because most of these were not as prolific as Yen Shu or Ou-yang Hsiu, their romantic and even erotic lyrics attracted less attention. Nor were great statesmen the only contributors to this genre. The ranks were swelled by the creations of married women, Taoist priests and Buddhist monks. Of some forty-six *tz'u* which remain today out of the voluminous output of the Buddhist monk, Chung Shu 仲殊 for example, a signifi-cant number are more overtly erotic than those of many popularly recognized writers of romantic *tz'u*. Many deal quite openly with illicit love affairs and the betrayal of young woman, as in the following:

To the Tune of *T'a so hsing*   踏莎行

Thick moisture penetrates her garments;   濃潤侵衣
A hidden fragrance drifts over the steps.   暗香飄砌
Flowers in the rain heighten her grief-worn looks.   雨中花色添憔悴
Phoenix slippers sodden, she lingers long,   鳳鞋溼透立多時
Silent, wordless, and languorous.   不言不語厭厭地

On her brow, fresh sorrows;   眉上新愁
In her hand, the written word—   手中文字
Why not ask a courier to dispatch the letter?   因何不倩鱗鴻寄
Her grievance must be only against her fickle love.   想伊只訴薄情人
But who at court would care about lovers' com-   官中誰管閑公事
   plaints?[8]

Though Ou-yang Hsiu was not immune to the frivolity of trying his hand at the popular new genre, and even of adopting much of its conventionalized language, he did bring a special dimension to this poetry with his unusually perceptive under-standing of the feminine psyche and his keen awareness of a woman's emotions. Two *tz'u* on the theme of parting lovers illustrate this sensitivity as well as his skill-ful use of natural symbols to achieve a sense of realism and universal appeal:

To the Tune of *Tieh lien hua*   蝶戀花

A Yüeh maiden gathers lotus by autumn waters.   越女採蓮秋水畔
Golden bracelets gleam dimly   窄袖輕羅
Through narrow sleeves of gauze.   暗露雙金釧
Shimmering reflection gathering flowers—flowers   照影摘花花似面
   fair as she.   芳心只共絲爭亂
Her tender heart, more tangled than fibrous lotus
   root.   鸂鶒灘頭風浪晚
                                                      霧重煙輕
Purple mallards on the bank, wind-tossed waves at   不見來時伴
   evening.   隱隱歌聲歸棹遠
Through heavy mists, floating vapors—   離愁引著江南岸
No sign of earlier companion.
Faint singing floats from distant boats homeward
   bound,
But parting grief reaches the far shores of Chiang-
   nan.

[8]Translated by Frederick C. Tsai.

Here the poet presents a beautiful young girl kneeling by the water. It is a scene of freshness far removed from the cloying artificiality of the boudoir. Her face is reflected, not in a jewelled mirror, but in the coolness of rippling water. Even mention of her simple gold bracelets is muted, seen as they are veiled through gauze. There is no need for elaborate adornments and appurtenances for us to know she is extraordinarily lovely. The simple appelation "Yüeh maiden" brings to mind Hsi Shih 西施, the legendary beauty of Yüeh, whose charms were deployed to bring about the downfall of the Prince of Wu in the 5th century B.C. The feeling of intense sorrow is expressed through natural phenomena: autumn waters, windtossed waves at day's end, the curtain of mists screening her last view of her departing lover. Her state of mind is likened to the tangle of fibrous lotus, confused and in turmoil. Added significance is given to this metaphor, as pointed out by Liu[9], by the use of *ssu* 絲, threads or fibres (of the lotus) to evoke its homonym 思, meaning thoughts. The feeling of aloneness is intensified by the sound of singing from boats whose happy occupants are going home *together* after a day's outing. It is a feeling that anyone who has ever been alone in a crowd of merrymakers can well understand. Similar devices are used in the following poem:

To the Tune of *Ch'ang hsiang-ssu*   長相思

Duckweed blankets the stream   蘋滿溪
Willows ring the bank.   柳繞堤
I see him off west of the river.   相送行人溪水西
When I return, the moon hangs low on the shore.   回時隴月低

Heavy, heavy the mists   煙霏霏
Chill, chill the wind.   風淒淒
Again I lean on the vermilion gate and hear the   重倚朱門聽馬嘶
   horses neigh.   寒鷗相對飛
So cold . . . a pair of gulls fly by.

Having said farewell, the girl returns alone as the day is ending and the cool moon is just rising. It is damp and cold and the only sound—hardly companionable— is a distant neighing of horses, perhaps the very ones bearing her lover away. As in the previous poem, aloneness is underscored by a solitary pair of gulls flying by in the cold. But even they are a pair and have each other. Even more poignant are those lyrics which describe the heartbreak of a woman who has been abandoned. Some of these, as for example, *Ying t'ien ch'ang* below, retain the conventional boudoir setting with its appointments of phoenix hairpins, pearl curtains, fallen blossoms and the mirror decorated with fabulous *luan* birds, and are highly reminiscent of the *Hua-chien* poets. The final line, however, instead of fading away in gossamer melancholia, ends harshly with the perceptive observation: "Spring grief—crueller than any other ill!"

[9]James J.Y. Liu. *Major Lyricists of the Northern   Sung.* (Princeton, 1974) p. 52.

To the Tune of *Ying t'ien ch'ang*   應天長

Slim crescent moon. She is before her luan *mirror.*   一彎初月臨鸞鏡
Tresses and phoenix hairpins in careless disarray.   雲鬢鳳釵慵不整
Pearl curtains sparkle.   珠簾淨
Remote, her two-storied tower.   重樓迥
Forlorn. Fallen blossoms scattered by a fickle   惆悵落花風不定
   wind.

Green mists hang low on the willow lane.   綠煙低柳徑
Whence comes the sound of the windlass in the   何處轆轤金井
   golden well?   昨夜更闌酒醒
Near dawn, recovered from last night's wine.   春愁勝卻病
Spring grief—crueller than any other ill!

In other *tz'u* on this theme, Ou-yang Hsiu frequently returns to nature for metaphors to convey emotions. Viewed after a sleepless and desolate night, a lonely scene at the shore of a lake becomes the setting in *Yü chia ao*:

To the Tune of *Yü chia ao*   漁家傲

Waters reflect the green of patterned lotus leaves.   荷葉田田青照水
Shaded by flowers, a solitary boat is moored.   孤舟挽在花陰底
Last night the rain fell, thin and cold.   昨夜蕭蕭疏雨墜
Sleepless, I grieved.   愁不寐
At dawn, I felt again the stirring of the west wind.   朝來又覺西風起

Rain-tossed, wind-pounded, golden pistils scattered   雨擺風搖金蕊碎
   —   合歡枝上香房翠
Only the green pods remain on the double stems.   蓮子與人長廝類
Lotus seeds and I—how much alike!   無好意
Ill-favored our fate.   年年苦在中心裏
Year after year, bitterness deep in the heart.

The lake is deserted, a lone boat anchored quietly at the shore, and only the orderly array of lotus leaves is reflected in the mirror of the waters. Against this scene of solitude, the poet explores the woman's feelings: grief has destroyed her sleep with a relentless persistence like that of the cold rain which has shattered the blossoms, leaving to each nothing but a shell filled with the bitter seeds of sorrow.

    Sometimes, both conventional *tz'u* imagery and ordinary activities are combined in the same poem. In *Tieh lien hua* below, interwoven with images of golden censer, embroidered coverlet and silken curtains, is the homely touch of small paper cutouts which the woman has fashioned for the New Year's decorations and to help while away the lonely hours. Thinking of her lover, she has cut out a pair of swallows to perch together on the bare branches. Perhaps she is also thinking of the flight of swallows as symbols of farewell. The time, early spring and the beginning of a New Year, should be a time of anticipation and hope, but for her there is only a brief dulling of sorrow with wine and the long wait for the respite of sleep through the cold night.

To the Tune of *Tieh lien hua*   蝶戀花

Through the screen, the cold East wind.   簾幕東風寒料峭
Amid snow, sweet plum blossoms   雪裏香梅
Herald early Spring.   先報春來早
On branches of wintersweet, a pair of tiny   紅蠟枝頭雙燕小
    swallows—   金刀剪綵呈纖巧
Papercuts artfully fashioned with golden scissors.

Hastily she kindles the golden censer, orchid-   旋暖金爐薰蕙藻
    fragrant.   酒入橫波
Her lovely eyes, bright with wine.   困不禁煩惱
Troubled and distraught.   繡被五更春睡好
Beneath embroidered coverlets, Spring's sleep   羅幃不覺紗窗曉
    comes but with dawn.
Beyond the gauze window—unsensed within
    silken cutains—daybreak.

The use of elements of nature and the external world as counterpoint to the inner world of emotions is indicative not so much of originality in his handling of the *tz'u* form, as it is in revealing the depth of Ou-yang Hsiu's own intuitive perception of the world around him. Attuned not only to the subtleties of the human mind, but to the infinite nuances in the natural world—mountains and rivers, birds, trees and flowers, wind, rain or the clean-swept air of a remote village, the kaleidoscope of changing seasons—Ou-yang Hsiu protrayed these in his prose and *shih*, and eventually in his *tz'u* as well[10].

One of his most quoted prose passages, written during a prolonged period of exile in Ch'uchow from 1048 on, aptly illustrates this dual attunement to nature and to the human heart:

> "However, Old Drunkard's heart is not set on wine, but lies somewhere betwixt the mountains and the rivers. The delight of mountains and rivers comes from the heart and is derived from wine."

[10]Themes other than love and the sorrows of the boudoir were not unprecedented in *tz'u* history. During the later T'ang when the genre was being developed, *tz'u* did not differ markedly either in theme or form from the *shih*, and *tz'u* about many subjects, including nature, are to be found as, for example, in the poems of Po Chü-i 白居易. The conventionalized world and poetic diction began later with the *Hua-chien* poets and persisted into the early Sung. Yet even within the *Hua-chien* school itself there is a discernible schism into two groups. The major one, led by Wen T'ing-yün, created poems whose most outstanding features were the voluptuousness, elegance and melancholy mentioned above. The other group, led by Wei Chuang 韋莊 (A.D. 836-910), wrote *tz'u* which were more restrained, less frivolous and somewhat more varied in theme. The tradition of Wei Ch'uang was extended about two generations later by Feng Yen-ssu 馮延巳 (A.D. 903-960) who wrote with great feeling both about love and sorrow, often against a backdrop of nature, and whose *tz'u* struck a responsive chord in Ou-yang Hsiu and greatly influenced his style.

"Shortly after, the sun sets over the mountains, the shadows of the revelers are scattered and the guests follow the Prefect as he returns home. A pall of darkness covers the trees, while the birds warble here and there as the guests leave. However, while the birds know the delights of mountains and trees, they do not know those of men; and while men know the delights of traveling with the Prefect, they do not know how the Prefect enjoys their pleasures. It is the Prefect who can share their pleasures while drunk and write about them while sober. Who is the Prefect? It is none other than Ou-yang Hsiu from Luling."[11]

Following the prolonged banishment at Ch'uchow, Ou-yang Hsiu spent a brief sojourn at Yangchow, the famous metropolis at the junction of the Grand Canal and the Yangtze; then requested a transfer to a smaller place where he might attract less attention. He was assigned to Yingchow, the beautiful lake country, where he settled his family permanently. Inspired by the charm of the area, he composed his series of thirteen lyrics about West Lake (in present day Anhwei, not the renowned West Lake of Hangchow), all written to the tune *Ts'ai-sang tzu*, describing that lake in all of its moods and variations:
Its bustle and gaiety:

Who does not delight in it—West Lake!	何人解賞西湖好
Its beauty knows no season.	佳景無時
Flying canopies chasing close on each other.	飛蓋相追
Oh to be among the flowers, drunk with jade goblet!	貪向花間醉玉卮
Painted pleasure boats, wine-laden—West Lake!	畫船載酒西湖好
Where gay are the sounds of pipes and strings	急管繁絃
And goblets of jade pass to and fro.	玉盞催傳
I drift on the placid waves, wine-lulled to sleep.	穩泛平波任醉眠

Its jewel-like serenity:

Clouds float by . . . beneath the boat.	行雲卻在行舟下
Sky and water are clear and limpid.	空水澄鮮
My gaze lingers now skyward, now below	俯仰留連
And I wonder—another world in the lake?	疑是湖中別有天
Cloud wisps, rosy in evening glow—lovely West Lake!	殘霞夕照西湖好
Flowers at its banks, duckweed floating by the shore.	花塢蘋汀
Endless stretch of tranquil waters.	十頃波平
	野岸無人舟自橫

[11] S.S. Liu. *Chinese Classical Prose*, pp. 187, 189.

At the deserted beach, boats gently right them-
*   selves.*

In the southwest, the moon is rising and floating   西南月上浮雲散
*   clouds disperse.*   軒檻涼生
At the railing it is cool and fresh.   蓮芰香清
How pure and fragrant the lotus!   水面風來酒面醒
A lake breeze revives my wine-flushed face.

And were it not for its pattern, set to the same tune, this final example from the
series seems far removed from the typical *tz'u*:

Sky and water—the loveliness of West Lake!   天容水色西湖好
Nature's face so fresh and new.   雲物俱鮮
Gulls and egrets relaxed in sleep.   鷗鷺閒眠
Following my wont, I listen to the pipes and   應慣尋常聽管絃
*   strings.*

Pure breeze, white moon . . . a perfect night.   風清月白偏宜夜
A lustrous field of jade.   一片瓊田
Who longs for treasured horse or fabled bird?   誰羨驂鸞
In my boat, I am an immortal!   人在舟中便是仙

The same sense of delight in the world around him is detailed in Ou-yang Hsiu's
prose writings and in his *shih* as, for example, in the following poem in the old
five-word style:

. . . . . .
I love the water below the pavilion.   但愛亭下水
Tumbling from the wild cliffs,   來從亂峯間
Singing as if falling from the skies,   聲如自空落
It runs out over the eaves   瀉向兩簷前
And down the rocky gorge,   流入巖下溪
Making hidden springs bubble and foam.   幽泉助涓涓

                                                          響不亂人語
Its voice does not disturb our talk,   其清非管絃
The pure tone so unlike that of pipe and strings.   豈不美絲竹
For lovely though they are,   絲竹不勝繁
Strings and flute are just too much.   所以屢攜酒

                                                          遠步就潺湲
So often, wine in hand,   野鳥窺我醉
I walk the distance to the falling waters.   溪雲留我眠
Wild birds espy my tipsiness,   山花徒能笑
Low clouds lull me to sleep.   不解與我言
The mountain flowers merely smile,   惟有巖風來

> *Not capable of conversing with me.*
> *Only the fresh cliff breeze comes*
> *To stir awake my wine-drowsed senses.* [12]
> . . . . . .

吹我還醒然

The water, clouds, birds, flowers and wind—all elements in his *tz'u*—appear in this poem as well. Only the mood is different. In the *tz'u*, these elements create a feeling of serenity and delicacy. In the *shih*, however, there is a robustness and vitality which result not only from the crispness and regularity of flow of the five-word metre, but from the transposition of the same elements to a more rugged setting. Here the serene waters of West Lake have been replaced by a tumbling mountain freshet, a lively spring and a wild music no less pleasing than the man-made sounds of pipe and string. Though the poet is still bemused by wine, as in his *tz'u*, here he too becomes more alive—no longer gazing in dreamy rapture at the beauty about him, but actively involved in his environment which, to reverse the picture, is now contemplating him! "The wild birds espy my tipsiness. Low clouds lull me to sleep." And although he explains that the flowers cannot walk with him, still he understands their laughter and joy in the same way as Chuang Tzu understood the fish. In the *tz'u* cited, the dynamic mood is muted and subdued, but the subjective and real involvement of the poet is apparent in both poems. Similarly, even in such a conventional poem on the sorrow of parting as the following:

To the Tune of *Yü-lou ch'un* 玉樓春

> *You've gone. I do not know how far.*　別後不知君遠近
> *All is cold and lonely. So much sadness!*　觸目凄涼多少悶
> *As you journey on, letters grow fewer.*　漸行漸遠漸無書
> *Across widening waters, no word.* [13] *Where can I*　水闊魚沈何處問
> *　ask?*
>
> *Deep in the night, bamboos beat an autumn dirge.*　夜深風竹敲秋韻
> *A million leaves cry out their grief.*　萬葉千聲皆是恨
> *On my lone pillow, I seek you in dreams.*　故欹單枕夢中尋
> *But no dreams come. The lamp flickers and dies.*　夢又不成燈又燼

The line, "deep in the night bamboos beat an autumn dirge," carries with it echoes of his *fu* on the "Sound of Autumn" (秋聲賦). Because of this association, the poem becomes more than a conventional expression of melancholy and conveys a sense of desolation and futility which are, to the poet, the very essence of autumn:

> . . . Oh, how sad! It is the sound of autumn. Can this be how it
> comes? Yes, this is the face of autumn: cruel and unfeeling; no trace

---

[12] *T'i Ch'uchow tsui-weng-t'ing chi* 題滁州醉翁亭記.

[13] Literally, "In the waters that separate us, the fish is lost," recalling the phrase 魚雁沈沈, in which the fish and geese are symbols for letters.

of mist or frost or cloud; bright and clear, with the sun brilliant in its high vaulted sky; its breath fierce and raw, penetrating our very bones. Its mood is chill and lonely. Mountains and streams are desolate and silent. And so the voice of autumn, bitter and icy, bursts forth in shrieks and wails.

Luxuriant plants and dense carpets of green vie in their lush beauty. Magnificent trees and rank vegetation delight the eye. Then autumn brushes the grass and the verdure fades; it comes upon the trees and the leaves are stripped. It wreaks havoc and destruction in a single breath of unexpended fury. For autumn is the agent of punishment and death.

Another such situation occurs in the following poem taken from the first of Ou-yang Hsiu's two cycles of *tz'u* to the tune of *Yü chia ao* 漁家傲, each of which describes the year, month by month, in twelve individual lyrics:

Eighth month—autumn's peak and the wind is fierce.　　　　　八月秋高風歷亂
Withered orchid. Shattered iris. Only red lotus at the shore.　　衰蘭敗芷紅蓮岸
The frost moon, full—　　　　　　　　　　　　　　　　　　　皓月十分光正滿
A cool radiance over the bank.　　　　　　　　　　　　　　清光畔
Year after year, how I miss the festive gatherings!　　　　　年年常願瓊筵看

Autumn sacrifices draw near. Grieving, I watch the homebound swallows.　　社近愁看歸去燕
Rivers and heavens, so vast . . . endless clouds.　　　　　　江天空闊雲容漫
Sung Yü in his time suffered deeply,　　　　　　　　　　　宋玉當時情不淺
Voicing melancholy grievances.　　　　　　　　　　　　　成幽怨
My home is a thousand li *away. I fear my heart must break!*　鄉關千里危腸斷

The time is once again autumn—lonely, chill. The intensity is at a somewhat greater level than in the previous *tz'u*. Again there is the implied description of another autumn, this time suggested by the reference to Sung Yü 宋玉 who wrote:

Alas for the breath of autumn!　　　　　　　　　　　　　悲哉秋之爲氣也
Wan and drear! flower and leaf fluttering fall and turn to decay.　　蕭瑟兮草木搖落而變衰
Sad and lorn! as when on journey far one climbs a hill and looks down on the water to speed a returning friend.　　憭慄兮若在遠行
登山臨水兮送將歸
Empty and vast! the skies are high and the air is cold.
Still and deep! the streams have drunk full and the

water are clear.[14]

Despite the machinations of political enemies and the spreading of malicious rumors, Ou-yang Hsiu's integrity as a man of Confucian ideals became increasingly apparent both through the writings which occupied him throughout his career, as well as through the performance of his duties in whatever capacity he chanced to find himself. By 1057, he was once again recalled to court and became Chief Imperial Examiner. He was further assigned the task of compiling the *New T'ang History*—a rare honor for an individual. On its completion in 1060, he was promoted to Assistant Military Commissioner and then, a year later, to Assistant Councillor in Charge of State Affairs. His friends were also given leading posts. For the first time he was solidly in power and succeeded in achieving stability in turbulent periods of reform. He served also as Secretary of the *Hanlin* Academy of eminent scholars and ultimately rose to the rank of Vice-Premier in which capacity he was able, because of his prominence, to carry as much weight as a full-fledged Prime Minister.

With all these official duties and responsibilities, Ou-yang Hsiu still found time for literary pursuits and the other pleasures abounding in Pien-ching where

> *New tunes and bewitching smiles*　　　　　新聲巧笑於柳陌花衢
> 　　*permeate willow paths and flower lanes;*[15]　按管調絃於茶坊酒肆
> *Sounds of pipes and strings*
> 　　*echo in teahouses and wineshops.*[16]

Moments of leisure were spent relaxing in these teahouses and wineshops, composing *shih* and adding to his already sizeable output of *tz'u*. Over the years, he had created some of the most romantic and endearing in the genre, often succeeding in endowing them with a greater depth of emotion and sense of reality than did many earlier *tz'u* poets. The scenes he describes with such empathy have been considered by some (in direct contrast to those who would deny he wrote love lyrics at all[17] to depict his own sorrows and frustrations in love during his earlier years. The following is one such example:

[14]Translated by David Hawkes in *Ch'u Tz'u, The Songs of the South*. (Beacon Paperback, Boston, 1962) p. 92.

[15]Willow and flower usually denote the gay quarters.

[16]Meng Yüan-lao 孟元老. Introduction to *Tung-ching meng-hua-lu* 東京夢華錄, written in 1147.

[17]Some went so far as to insist that the political enemies of Ou-yang Hsiu had themselves composed and circulated these "lascivious *tz'u*" in order to destroy his reputation, and thus some 73 of his lyrics were deliberately removed from later editions of his text, *Liu-i Tz'u* 六一詞 (The Tz'u of the Six Ones). (These censored poems, however, do appear in other collections of his work.) The *tz'u* were attributed to the well-known literary scholar, Liu Chi 劉幾 who, like many others, failed the doctoral examinations in 1057 as a result of the change in policy instituted by Ou-yang Hsiu who was then Imperial Examiner. A further anecdote relates how, a few years later, Liu Chi was able to imitate the ancient style favored by Ou-yang Hsiu so successfully that the latter, being extremely impressed by a paper by one Liu Hui 劉煇, awarded him first place in the examination. Not until afterward was he stunned to find out that Liu Chi and Liu Hui were one and the same person.

To the Tune of *T'a so hsing*　　　　　踏莎行

Through winding path of jade moss,　　　碧蘚回廊
Past deep courtyard of green willows.　　　綠楊深院
Stealing to our night tryst. The bamboo curtain　偷期夜入簾猶捲
　　is still rolled up.　　　　　　　　　照人無奈月華明
Spotlighting me, alas! the bright moonlight!　　潛身卻恨花深淺
I would hide, but flowers offer little cover.

　　　　　　　　　　　　　　　　　　密約如沈
Our rendezvous seems doomed;　　　　前歡未便
Last time did not go well.　　　　　　看看擲盡金壺箭
The marker in the water clock has reached its　闌干敲遍不應人
　　end.　　　　　　　　　　　　　分明簾下聞裁剪
I tap on the balustrade, but no one answers.
Clearly, from behind the curtain, the sound of
　　scissors cutting.

Much of the typical *tz'u* imagery is present in this poem—the jade moss, the willows, the silent courtyard, the flowers, moonlight and water, the bamboo curtain and the balustrade. But they appear in a context far from the usual. No one is leaning listlessly on the balustrade, the water clock does not echo emptily in the lonely night (glancing at its marker tallies, the lover realizes the lateness of the hour), behind the curtain is no languishing maiden, but a very real girl having the last word in a lovers' quarrel. There is a touching realism about the poem and, moreover, a feeling of identity with the lover—he could be tossing pebbles at a window today just as easily as tapping on a balustrade in Sung China nearly a thousand years ago. One can feel with him the terrible brightness of the moon, the inadequate shelter of the shrubs as he stands, illumined, within view of the uncovered window. As he waits he realizes there seems to be no hope of a meeting. Is it, he wonders, because last time they quarreled? Perhaps a gentle rap on the balustrade will bring her? But no soft voice answers—only the click of the scissors, startlingly loud and clear in the still night. This final touch imparts an eloquent climax to the poem. Had all been darkness and had the bamboo shades been drawn, he might have supposed that there was a mistake about the time or that the girl had unintentionally fallen asleep. But the rolled-up curtain, the girl herself tantalizingly out of sight, and the cold, metallic sound of snapping scissors at an hour when everyone should have been asleep, revealed very clearly that she had stayed up deliberately and knew he was there. No mournful drip of the water clock could have equalled the meaningful sound of the busy scissors.

Another lyric describes a happier rendezvous:

To the Tune of *Nan-hsiang tzu*　　　　南鄉子

This maiden so fair,　　　　　　　　好個人人
Deeply crimsoned her lips, faintly powdered her　深點脣兒淡抹腮
　　cheeks.　　　　　　　　　　　　花下相逢
We met by the flowers.　　　　　　　忙走怕人猜

> She hastened to go, lest anyone know. 遺下弓弓小繡鞋
> Leaving behind tiny crescents of embroidered
>   slippers. 剗襪重來
>
> 半嚲烏雲金鳳釵
> In stockinged feet she returns, 行笑行行連抱得
> Raven tresses and gold phoenix hairpins slipping. 相挨
> We walk, smiling. Walk, embracing. 一向嬌癡不下懷
> Tenderly close.
> Young and foolish, she lingers briefly in my arms.

As in the first poem, there is tension and conflict, as well as the passion of a stolen moment—elements which endow the poem with a reality for the most part lacking in the lyrics of the *Hua-chien chi*. It is reminiscent of Li Yü's description of a forbidden meeting with the young princess—his wife's sister—told from the viewpoint of the girl:

To the Tune of *P'u-sa man*　　菩薩蠻

> Bright flowers and moon clouded by light mist. 花明月暗籠輕霧
> A perfect time to go to my love. 今宵好向郎邊去
> Fearfully, I mount the fragrant steps, 剗襪步香苔
> Gold-embroidered slippers in my hand. 手提金縷鞋
>
> South of the painted hall we meet. 畫堂南畔見
> Briefly, I cling to him, trembling. 一向偎人顫
> "So hard it is for me to steal away, 好爲出來難
> Love me now with all your heart!" 教君恣意憐

Although the theme is almost identical, there is a difference in mood. In the lyric by Ou-yang Hsiu, the secret rendezvous has a light-hearted almost mischievous air about it. The first encounter is brief and suggests the conspiracy of the subsequent meeting when the girl returns quietly in stockinged feet, in charming *déshabillé*. The meeting is tender and lingering as they walk along, hand in hand, basking in each other's smiles and, briefly oblivious of all danger, embrace. But in the poem by Li Yü there is an undercurrent of something almost ominous. The moon is gloomy, the girl walks fearfully—one can almost sense her holding her breath—and when she reaches her lover, there is no basking in the warmth of mutual smiles. Instead, she leans against him, shivering, seeking not only his love, but refuge from the chill of the night and of her own apprehension.

In the following, Ou-yang Hsiu borrows another theme of Li Yü's—that of a charming coquette, adapting it to make it his own:

To the Tune of *Nan-ko tzu*　　南歌子

> Phoenix hairdo, gold-washed ribbon, dragons 鳳髻金泥帶
>   adorning her comb, 龍紋玉掌梳
> She approaches the window, exchanging smiles 走來窗下笑相扶

with him.
Charmingly, she asks if her brows are fashionably darkened.

愛道畫眉深淺
入時無

Toying with her brush, she snuggles close; begins her flower painting studies.
Idly dallying, she delays her embroidery work.
With winning smile she wonders, "How does one write 'mandarin ducks'?"

弄筆偎人久
描花試手初
等閒妨了繡功夫
笑問雙鴛鴦字
怎生書

The poem displays a perceptive insight into the charmingly transparent artifices of a young woman in love. What mirror could reflect her loveliness more than his admiring gaze as she bids him study her delicately drawn brows? What more subtle flattery of his male ego than to acknowledge his connoisseurship of feminine styles? What more innocent way to find herself so close to him? She lingers by his side, brush in hand, to create the illusion that it is he who is detaining her from more serious pursuits. After a token attempt at her embroidery and at tracing the outlines of flowers and characters to be embroidered, she again appeals to his wisdom—this time on a seemingly less frivolous plane—but she knows he will not fail to respond to the suggestion of mandarin ducks. In these small details and insights lies the charm of the poem and the special touches which give it life and a timeless universality.

Although Ou-yang Hsiu chose often to express his emotions frankly and directly in many of his love poems, he was also a master of the subtly disguised erotic lyric. He sang of the delights of love and of the passions of springtime, drawing over all a diaphonous veil of allusion which lent to his poems the charm of a landscape whose lushness and beauty are filtered through mists and hazes; the scenes have a soft radiance and muted loveliness, yet stir the imagination with what is hidden beyond view. The following poem seems to depict a tranquil spring day, but it is also replete with delicate imagery of a somewhat erotic nature:

To the Tune of *Yüan lang kuei*   阮郎歸

In Southern gardens, spring comes early—outing time!
Soft breezes carry the sound of horses whinnying.
Green plums are bean small; willow leaves curved like eyebrows.
Butterflies dance in the long day.

南園春早踏青時
風和聞馬嘶
青梅如豆柳如眉
日長蝴蝶飛

花露重
草煙低

Flowers are heavy with dew, mists low on the grass.
Everywhere lattice screens hang closed.
In the swing, I rest languorously with loosened garments.
In the painted eaves, a pair of swallows nest.

人家簾幕垂
鞦韆慵困解羅衣
畫梁雙燕棲

The mood is unmistakable. As nature awakens to spring, so do dormant human emotions. The undercurrent of stirring desires is delicately balanced by the almost overwhelming feeling of languor—the narrator, indolent, sways in the swing, and even the mists lie heavy on the flowers. There is a feeling of hypnotic passivity and of receptivity to the mood of nature.

In a *shih* counterpart, the identical theme and mood are repeated:

Green trees in full leaf, birds singing on the mountain.	綠樹交加山鳥啼
A fresh breeze ripples the waters and sets the petals flying.	晴風蕩漾落花飛
Birds sing, flowers dance, the prefect is drunk.	鳥歌花舞太守醉
Tomorrow, wine-glow gone, spring will have already vanished.[18]	明日酒醒春已歸

There is a mounting tension spreading from the burgeoning trees, the singing birds, the caress of the wind, the gay abandon of the flowers to the poet. Overcome by it all, he is drunk—more, perhaps, with spring and love than with wine.

With even greater boldness, the poet goes on to reveal his most intimate encounters in the green groves:

To the Tune of *I han yüeh*	憶漢月
Rosily voluptuous on branches slender and graceful,	紅豔幾枝輕裊
Newly blossoming in the East wind . . .	新被東風開了
Bending to the mist, they weep tears of dew. For whom so seductive?	倚煙啼露爲誰嬌
Provocative, they charm the butterflies, excite the bees.	故惹蝶憐蜂惱
Filled with thoughts of love, I wander in delight.	多情遊賞處
Longing, yearning . . . amid green groves, a thousand twists and turns.	留戀向
	綠叢千繞
But when the wine is drunk and pleasures done, it is hard to return.	酒闌歡罷不成歸
My heart is breaking with the waning moon— spring has grown old.	腸斷月斜春老

Enchanted by the seductive flowers, the poet abandons himself to the joys to be found among the thousand inviting paths in the green groves. But following the attainment of his desires, he concludes on a bittersweet note of sadness, a sudden welling up of melancholia. Again there is the reality of contrast in the mingling of pleasure and sorrow, recalling the meditative philosophy of Wang Hsi-chih 王羲之's *Lan T'ing Chi Hsü* 蘭亭集序 (Preface to the Orchid Pavilion Collection [of poems]):

[18]*Feng le t'ing yu ch'un* 豐樂亭遊春.

> Having attained one's desire, one grows surfeited and weary;
> the emotions change with shifting circumstances. How truly lamentable
> this is! That which had been so desired only a short while before, in the
> twinkling of an eye, has already become old and worn. Still one cannot
> but be moved by this. How much more then, must one be stirred by
> (an awareness of) the span of human life which must follow the laws of
> nature and, in the end, draw inevitably to its close!

The writings of Ou-yang Hsiu are like a tapestry through which is woven the unifying thread linking the unique sensibilities and inner world of this man with the external world in which he moved. Whether the latter was the world of politics and service to his country, of personal commitment to friendships and ideals; or of sensual pleasures, natural beauty and the way of the human heart, all of these found expression through his literary creativity. He revealed himself freely, both as the Confucian gentleman and scholar of whom Mencius spoke and as a compassionate human being who spoke with the eloquence of understanding to Emperor, common man and the feminine spirit. More than the style in which he chose to express himself, it was these qualities which have endowed both his prose and poetry with a timeless and universal appeal.

Coming from a man who was both his protégé and a great literary genius in his own right, these words of Su Tung-p'o 蘇東坡's, though they must be considered in the light of praise offered to a mentor, still convey a sense of the place occupied by Ou-yang Hsiu in Chinese history even to this day:

> He was like Han Yü in his discussion of the Great Way, like Lu
> Chih 陸贄 in that of human nature, like Ssu-ma Ch'ien 司馬遷 in record-
> ing historical events and like Li Po 李白 in writing poetry and *tz'u*.

鄭騫：柳永蘇軾與詞的發展

Liu Yung and Su Shih in the Evolution of *Tz'u* Poetry

By **Cheng Ch'ien**

Translated by **Ying-hsiung Chou**

LIU YUNG 柳永 (fl. 1034) and Su Shih 蘇軾 (1036-1101) did not seem to be on a par with each other. Su Shih was a grand master of his age, well versed in almost all genres and highly respected in the political world. Liu Yung, on the other hand, was known for his compositions in *tz'u* poetry alone—his achievement in *shih* poetry and prose was negligible. Basically he was a Bohemian scholar who "down on his luck, wandered through the country, with wine in the saddle." To put him alongside Su would thus seem inappropriate, for in terms of overall literary achievement, moral character and personal manner, needless to say, Liu lagged far behind Su. Nevertheless, Liu Yung's position in the history of *tz'u* was by no means interior to that of Su. In the evolution of this particular genre, the two masters were in fact of equal significance. Briefly speaking, Liu was instrumental in the development of its form while Su should be credited with the enrichment of its content.

In its earliest stage, *tz'u* was only a type of song, performed by singers to entertain guests at banquets and farewell parties. Its style, therefore, differed from that of *shih*. It had to correspond to the specific mood of the gathering. In addition, it had to be written with the singers' social positions as well as their verbal styles in mind. Since the singers of that time were mostly female, it would not be altogether fitting to have these teenage girls at sumptuous banquets sing—at the top of their voices—heroic laments to the beat of the red castanets in their hands. For that reason, the *tz'u* of the T'ang (618-907) and the Five Dynasties (907-960) dealt almost exclusively with silk quilts, geese in flight formations, remorse over separations and plaintiveness in spring. Its description did not generally go beyond that of gardens and pavilions, and its lyricism was characterized by ornate beauty.

In fact, the *tz'u* pieces of this period were restricted to these two aspects in both its intrinsic nature and its function. Admittedly by the Southern T'ang (923-936) Feng Yen-ssu 馮延巳 (903-960) with his stately elegance seemed to have become more diversified and more flexible than his predecessors in *Hua-chien chi*

The Chinese original was first published in Wen-hsüeh tsa-chih 文學雜誌 (Literary Review), *Vol. III, No. 1 (Sept. 1957), 25-31. The article was later collected in his* Ching-wu ts'ung-pien 景午叢編 *(Taipei: Chung-hua, 1972), Vol. I, pp. 119-27.*

花間集.[1] But even so, he surpassed them merely in sincerity, emotiveness, originality and subjectivism. Fundamentally he was still confined in theme to mournings over passage of time and concern for friends and relatives in distant places, nostalgia of the past and remembrances of old acquaintances. Of course, with Li Yü 李煜 (937-978) the scope of the aesthetic world and the depth of feelings far exceeded those of the T'ang and the Five Dynasties. Yet in *tz'u* Li Yü, like T'ao Ch'ien 陶潛 (365?-427) in *shih*, definitely transcended his age. Nonetheless despite the fact that they were both ahead of their time, their examples were not followed and no immediate change took place.

What was said above has to do with its content. As for its form, the Long Tunes (*Ch'ang tiao* 長調) had not yet come into being in the T'ang and the Five Dynasties. Instead, the Short Tunes (*Hsiao ling* 小令), which does not exceed sixty or seventy characters, were widely used in that period. They were just as restricted in form as in content. The restrictions in form had, moreover, its impact on content. Because of the limited length of the tunes, no matter how rich the feelings were or how complex the fluctuations might be, there simply was not sufficient room for undulations and amplifications. And precisely because of this restricted nature in both content and form, even by the T'ang and the Five Dynasties *tz'u* was still regarded as a minor craft and did not acquire the same prestige as poetry and prose. (As to whether the Long Tunes were existent but were not employed in literary compositions or whether the Long Tunes had not yet come into being in the first place, we shall have occasion to come back to this at a later point.)

The *tz'u* of the early Sung writers—such as Yen Shu 晏殊 (991-1055), Ou-yang Hsiu 歐陽修 (1007-1072) and Chang Hsien 張先 (990-1078)—did not really move beyond the realm of the T'ang and the Five Dynasties in content. Though stylistically some attempts had been made at writing the Long Tunes, the Short Tunes were still the predominant form. In the collections of Yen and Ou-yang, the Long Tunes account for no more than ten to twenty per cent. Chang Hsien was slightly more prolific in the Long Tunes which, however, took up but thirty to forty per cent of his complete works, not to mention the fact that technically this corpus left something to be desired. Chang, along with Yen and Ou-yang, could not exactly be called masters of the Long Tunes.[2] Liu Yung was a contemporary of Yen, Ou-yang and Chang, and was older than Su Shih by more than twenty years.[3] He was, however, the first *tz'u* poet conversant with the long form. Among the two hundred-odd *tz'u* pieces in the three *chüans* of *Yüeh-chang chi* 樂章集, together with the *Hsü-t'ien ch'ü-tzu* 續添曲子 (*Chiang-ts'un ts'ung-shu* ed. 彊村叢書本), approximately one

---

[1] An anthology of *tz'u* compiled by Chao Ts'ung-tso 趙崇祚 which includes five hundred pieces by the eighteen masters of the Five Dynasties (907-60). These works are generally limited in theme to the decadent life of the upper social class and are hence restricted in scope.

[2] Author's note: Chang Hsien has all along been a controversial poet in the history of *tz'u*. Chou Chi 周濟 was quite right in the introduction to his *Sung ssu-chia tz'u-hsüan* 宋四家詞選, where he said: "From

Chang's originality and strength one certainly derives great pleasure. Yet his cannot be called a well-rounded talent. Nor was he capable of great varieties."

[3] Author's note: Liu Yung passed the imperial *Chin-shih* 進士 examination in the first year of Yüan-yu 元祐 (1034) while Su Shih was born in the third year of the same reign (1036). Liu might have passed the examination very early in his career, but it was quite likely that he was older than Su by over twenty years.

hundred and thirty tune-titles were employed, of which some thirty pieces were written in the Short Tunes while eighty per cent were written in the Long Tunes. The number of the latter was unprecedented and his techniques were equally advanced (a point which we shall come back to later). Liu Yung's position in the history of *tz'u* was in fact built upon the quantity and quality of his works set to the Long Tunes.

The rise of the Long Tunes should not be lightly dismissed; it had a great deal to do with the development and perfection of *tz'u*. But when did the Long Tunes come into being in the first place? I earlier assumed that the Long Tunes were already present in as early as the T'ang and the Five Dynasties, but merely as musical tunes, often without lyrics having been written for them. The only exceptions were the works of some crude musicians and incompetent literati, in which case there were hardly any rhetorical or thematic merits to be mentioned; and hence their works were easily lost in transmission.[4] It thus follows that the *tz'u* handed down from the T'ang and the Five Dynasties were those set to the Short Tunes by literati scholars. The situation remained unchanged up to the early years of the Sung. Among the three hundred-odd tune-titles recorded in *Chiao-fang chi* 教坊記[5] compiled by Ts'ui Ling-ch'in 崔令欽 of the T'ang, many of these tunes along with their lyrics were lost. It is probable that some of them could have been in the Long Tunes. That was my earlier view but recently another view suggested itself to me. It is more likely that from the T'ang to the Five Dynasties and down to early Sung, not only did no one write in the Long Tunes; possibly the Long Tunes as a musical form had not yet come into being. If they had existed earlier, why had no one tried to set words to the Long Tunes during that long period of time when it was a popular practice to do so? The *tz'u* pieces set to the Long Tunes were mostly created in the Sung, just as the Long Tunes as a musical form were the creation of the Sung musicians.[6] Among the Long Tunes in which Liu Yung wrote, there were no more than twelve or thirteen tune-titles that could be found in *Chiao-fang chi*. They represented only one eighth of the total number, not to mention the fact that some of these titles might have been identical in name only. (Instances of different tunes with identical titles were plentiful in the T'ang and the Sung. For instance, *"Nü-kuan tzu"* (女冠子) and *"P'ao-chiu lo"* (拋球樂)—which were both in the Short Tunes in the T'ang and the Five Dynasties—were reset in the Long Tunes in Liu's *tz'u*.) There is, therefore, reason to believe that the Long Tunes came into being in the early Sung rather than in the Middle or the Late T'ang. Their appearance laid the cornerstone for *tz'u* in its evolvement into a full-fledged genre. If, on the contrary, *tz'u* writers had abided dutifully by the Short Tunes of the T'ang and the Five Dynasties, the days of *tz'u* would have been over in the Northern Sung. After all, how could the minor craft with its thematic and stylistic limitations constitute a genre of its own and lend itself to further development? Thanks mainly to the rise

[4]Author's note: There are in *Yün-yao chi tsa-ch'ü-tzu* 雲謠集雜曲子 (Chiang-ts'un ed.) a number of the Long Tunes which were sometimes considered to be *tz'u* pieces from T'ang. The claim, however, could not be substantiated.

[5]A personal account of the musicians' trade during the period of K'ai-Yüan 開元 (713-41). A significant document on the court music of T'ang.

[6]Author's note: Here the Long Tunes refer to what was adapted into *tz'u* after the Sung, having nothing to do with the tunes used in the *Ta Ch'ü* 大曲 dating back to the T'ang and the Sung.

of the Long Tunes, a major crisis of *tz'u* was averted. Moreover, the evolvement of *tz'u* into a literary phenomenon with all its spectacular dimensions did not occur until after the rise of the Long Tunes. And Liu Yung was precisely the first writer to be both prolific and skilled in the form in question. One can thus say that Liu Yung's position in the history of *tz'u* is built on the quantity and quality of his works in the Long Tunes. Let us here first review some traditional criticisms on Liu Yung for a clear picture of his contributions in this respect:

> Liu Yung's *Yüeh-chang chi* has been well liked over the years ... harmonized. Its narrative development is leisurely, with a beginning and an end. Ocassionally he could come up with nice turns of phrases. He is further capable of selecting the harmonious and sweet tunes to render his lyrics in. Nonetheless, he is inclined toward the plain and the vulgar, to the point of starting a style of his own. The uninitiated are especially fond of him.
>
> —Wang Cho 王灼,
> *Pi-chi man-chih* 碧雞漫志

> Though Liu's *tz'u* is of a vulgar style, his prosody is harmonious and his expressions to the point. A peaceful and prosperous world is fully depicted in his works. He is especially good at describing lives of stranded travelers and their journeys.
>
> —Ch'en Chen-sun 陳振孫,
> *Chih-tsa'i shu-lu chieh-t'i* 直齋書錄解題

> Liu Yung's descriptions are elaborate and detailed. His language is plain but rich in nuances. Inherent in it are *lush* beauty and restrained simplicity.
>
> —Chou Chi 周濟,
> *Chieh-ts'un-tsai lun tz'u tsa-chu* 介存齋論詞雜著

> Liu Yung's *tz'u* is refined, fluid, clear and intimate. He surpasses his predecessors in narration. Yet because his works are replete with descriptions of feminine charm, his style does not seem to be elevated.
>
> —Liu Hsi-tsai 劉熙載,
> *I kai* 藝概

> In his *tz'u* Liu Yung is capable of complementing the complicated with the straightforward, the dense with the sparse, and the swift with the becalmed. He is able to describe what is difficult to describe and express what is difficult to express and make everything appear natural. He is undoubtedly a giant of Northern Sung.
>
> —Fung Hsü 馮煦,
> *Hao-an lun tz'u* 蒿菴論詞

Though earlier criticisms on Liu Yung are quite voluminous, to save space we have cited here only two entries from the Sung and three from the Ch'ing, which are all quite to the point. To these critics, Liu's merits lay in narration and description which necessarily required the Long Tunes. Among Liu Yung's better-known pieces, *"Yü lin ling"* (雨霖鈴) and *"Pa-sheng Kan-chou"* (八聲甘州) have been widely acclaimed and need not be cited again. Let us quote a few other pieces instead:

To the Tune of *Yeh-pan yüeh*   夜半樂

Frigid clouds against the gloomy skies—
    In a blade of a boat,
I left the river shore on an impulse,
And passed the endless valleys and cliffs,
    Before coming to where the Yüeh river ran deep.
    The raging waves were gradually calming down,
    When in the sudden winds from across the woods
Came the calls of the traveling traders, each to each.
    Hoisting the sail high up the mast,
    In my Painted Fishhawk,
I skirted the southern shore, ever so swiftly.

Up came the glimmering banners over the taverns,
    Then a smoke-covered village in a huddle,
    And a few rows of frosted trees.
    In the fast-fading sunlight,
Home were the fishermen, sounding their clatters.
    Leaves from dying lotus were falling, one after another,
    While withering willows started to flicker.
At the shore, by twos and threes,
    Coy maidens tried to avoid
    This traveling stranger on the way
By talking and laughing among themselves.
A thought at this point of the journey:
"I have thoughtlessly fled her boudoir;
Now the drifting duckweeds will not stay."

For all her tender reminders, when is our next reunion?
    Saddened by separation, I felt my anguish
Over the belated return increasing at year's end.
    With eyes brimming with tears,
    I gazed down the road toward the capital,
Amidst a strayed goose's call, while the vast skies darkened.

凍雲黯淡天氣
扁舟一葉
乘興離江渚
渡萬壑千巖
越溪深處
怒濤漸息
樵風乍起
更聞商旅相呼
片帆高舉
泛畫鷁
翩翩過南浦

望中酒旆閃閃
一簇烟村
數行霜樹
殘日下
漁人鳴榔歸去
敗荷零落
衰楊掩映
岸邊兩兩三三
浣紗遊女
避行客
含羞笑相語

到此因念
繡閣輕拋
浪萍難駐
歎後約丁寧竟何據
慘離懷
空恨歲晚歸期阻
凝淚眼
杳杳神京路
斷鴻聲遠長天暮

To the Tune of *Chu ma tzu*   竹馬子

Up on a lone fortress, desolate in all directions,
    I looked about, from a towering pavilion,
        To find myself, face to face, with a bank of
        silent mist.
With raindrops hanging down from the elegant
    rainbow;
        And princely winds caressing the parapets,
        The summer heat within me seemed to be
        subsiding,
With a leaf, autumn took me by surprise,
        And late cicadas clamored in the dusk,
On the arrival of the autumn season.
All these bringing back pleasant memories of the
    past,
        I pointed a vague finger at the capital, lying
        Far, far away, neither amid the fog, nor in the
        mist.

With all these memories of the past revived,
        Fresh sorrows easily accumulated,
        While old friends could hardly be reunited.
High up from a lookout, I stood, all day long
        In exchange for speechless heartbreak.
All that I could see were bright clouds,
        Evening crows here and there,
        And the forlorn riverside city at dusk.
Meanwhile, the painted horn from the southern
    tower
Once again was bidding the sinking sun farewell.

登孤壘荒涼
危亭曠望
靜臨烟渚
對雌霓掛雨
雄風拂檻
微收煩暑
漸覺一葉驚秋
殘蟬噪晚
素商時序
覽景想前歡
指神京
非霧非烟深處

向此成追感
新愁易積
故人難聚
憑高盡日凝竚
贏得消魂無語
極目霽靄霏微
暝鴉零亂
蕭索江城暮
南樓畫角
又送殘陽去

To the Tune of *Feng kui yün*   鳳歸雲

        Late in autumn—
The western suburb cleansed with the crystal air
    after the rain.
        On the paths, night was about to run out
        And cold breeze was rising from my lapels
        and sleeves.
Above the horizon, the morning star continued to
    flicker,
        From above the branches.
Roosters' calls again were dying down
        While the first rays of the sun started to

向深秋
雨餘爽氣肅西郊
陌上夜闌
襟袖起涼飆
天末殘星流電未滅
閃閃隔林梢
又是曉雞聲斷
陽烏光動
漸分山路迢迢

驅驅行役

        emerge,
Unfolding as they did, the distant mountain paths.

    All that bustling on the way,
    While time and tide waits for no man.
    Meager profit and humble positions;
    Petty accomplishment and fickle fame—
All that to what avail?
    And why measure me against them?
    Forsaking my favorite sights,
    I have indulged myself in worldly pleasures,
    And let my aspirations transpire without
        second thoughts.
Fortunately Lake T'ai is still there, with all its
    mists and waves.
    With a sailful of wind and moonlight,
I must go back, and retire a fisherman, or a woods-
man.

苒苒光陰
蠅頭利祿
蝸角功名
畢竟成何事
漫相高
拋擲雲泉
狎玩塵土
壯節等閒消
幸有五湖烟浪
一船風月
會須歸去老漁樵

To the Tune of *An kung-tzu*

安公子

    At the distant shore, the rain gradually sub-
        sided.
With the rain subsided, the river sky seemed to
    turn dark at once.
Picking plants at the shoals, I was all alone
    Except for the company of gulls and egrets
        standing in pairs.
    A few specks of lights from fishing boats were
        visible,
    Dimly shining on the reed-infested shore.
        With painted oars at rest,
    Boat people exchanged greetings by twos and
        threes,
    And told of tonight's journeys,
By pointing at the mist-covered trees of the villages
    ahead.

My pursuit of official positions had turned into an
    over-extended journey
Leisurely I leaned against the oars and chanted.
My sense of distance being confused by a myriad
    of mountains and waters,
    I wondered where my hometown was.
    Since we parted last time,

遠岸收殘雨
雨殘稍覺江天暮
拾翠汀洲人寂靜
立雙雙鷗鷺
望幾點漁燈
掩映蒹葭浦
停畫橈
兩兩舟人語
道去程今夜
遙指前村烟樹

遊宦成羈旅
短檣吟倚閒凝竚
萬水千山迷遠近
想鄉關何處
自別後
風亭月榭孤歡聚
剛斷腸
惹得離情苦
聽杜宇聲聲
勸人不如歸去

> *I spent all festivals at lonely pavilions and halls.*
> *To add to that, the anguish reminded me*
> *Of the inflictions from the sorrows of separa-*
> *tions.*
> *Listening to the calls of the cuckoos,*
> *I was urged to go home, as early as I could.*[7]

These pieces along with such better-known works as *"Yü lin ling"* and *"Pa-sheng kan-chou,"* can all be described as: "harmonious in prosody," "refined and fluid," and "complementing the complicated with the straightforward, the dense with the sparse." Without employing the Long Tunes in the first place, how could all these good qualities manifest themselves? Wouldn't it have been a case of having the hands of a giant tied?

Thus it was only after the rise of the Long Tunes that the form of *tz'u* started to diversify. With the skilful use of this diversified form, never before employed in the T'ang and the Five Dynasties, Liu Yung was now able to transcend such conventional motifs as sorrows of love as well as remorse over separations, and to steer away from the domestic and the personal by giving voice to a deeper and more complex layer of meaning and a wider horizon of the spiritual world. The sense of desolation and the loftiness—as embodied in Liu Yung's descriptions of excursions in the mountains and on the waters, and in his treatment of thoughts provoked by watching distant places—could hardly be found earlier in the *tz'u* repertoire of the T'ang and the Five Dynasties. But ever since the appearance of Liu Yung, both the spirit and the outlook of *tz'u* underwent a radical change, so much so that the genre was consequently revitalized. It is for this reason that the rise of the Long Tunes must be seen as a major event in the history of *tz'u*, in which Liu Yung played the role of the innovator.

Be that as it may, Liu Yung's *tz'u* was qualitatively similar to that of his predecessors despite the fact that it could very well be less restricted in scope. Basically Liu still could not leave behind the descriptions of feminine charm and amorous feelings. For further development in content, one would have to wait for the appearance of Su Shih.

In the "*tz'u* talks" of the past, Su Shih was often mentioned alongside Liu Yung. But in most cases, Su was rated above Liu. Seldom had critics realized that the two were of equal significance in the history of *tz'u*. What follows are some typical examples:

> Though irregular meters (長短句) did not flourish until this dynasty, yet the vitality and sincerity which characterized our predecessors have deteriorated. Though Su Shih was not all that preoccupied with prosody, yet when he occasionally wrote in the song form, he was so totally enlightening as to open our eyes to new possibilities, with the result that practioners were greatly inspired. Nowadays young people erroneously criticized Su Shih for having changed prosodic rules in his crea-

---

[7]According to Li Shih-chen 李時珍's *Pen-ts'ao kang-mu* 本草綱目, the cuckoo reminds one of a sage ruler in Shu by the name of Tu Yü 杜宇. Its calls sound like *"pu ju kuei ch'ü"* (better go home).

tions of irregular meters, while at the same time a great majority of them either followed the path of Liu Yung or that of Ts'ao Tzu. Though the phenomenon was ludicrous, one need not laugh over it.

—Wang Cho,
Pi-chi man chih

Su Shih of Mei Shan cleansed once and for all the preoccupation with feminine charm and got rid of the overtly sentimental feelings. One is thus able to ascend high places for a distant view and troll with one's head lifted. One's unworldly aspirations and noble spirit can thus soar above the mundane world. *Hua-chien* poets are thus but attendants and Liu Yung but a footman.

—Hu Yin 胡寅,
Chiu pien tz'u hsü 酒邊詞序

The masters can be divided into two schools in the first place. Su Shih described himself by saying, "When inebriated, and writing in the cursive script, I could feel steams of wine issuing forth like breezes from my fingers." Huang T'ing-chien also said, "Su Shih's calligraphy carries with it the gale winds from the ocean." In reading Su Shih's *tz'u* one should likewise adopt a similar approach. Undoubtedly Su Shih would dismiss as fastidious any attempt to make narrow comparisons between himself and Liu Yung on minor points.

—Wang Shih-chen 王士禎,
Hua ts'ao meng-shih 花草蒙拾

Among the *tz'u* poets of the Northern Sung, only Su Shih with his outstanding achievement soars way above the worldly, making his work almost inimitable. The difference between him and his contemporaries is like that between heaven and earth. What is involved is not only artistic brilliancy. His temperament, his learning and his aspirations are simply not what the common run of artists could ever dream of.
—Wang P'eng-yün 王鵬運, as quoted by Lung Mu-hsün 龍沐勛,
T'ang Sung ming-chia tz'u-hsüan 唐宋名家詞選[8]

In the first three entries Su was placed above Liu, and the reason, as Wang P'eng-yün claimed, was due to the fact that Su's artistic brilliancy, temperament, learning and aspirations "are not what the common run of artists could ever dream of." Compared with Su, Liu was, of course, but one of "the common run of artists." Su soared in the sky like the Heavenly Horses. On the contrary, though Liu should not be compared to a harnessed horse, he was but "an ordinary pedestrian." In his *tz'u* Liu treated of the wanderings of vagrant souls and the thoughts of home on the part of stranded travelers. The unworldly aspirations and upright personality in Su, like winds in the sky and rain at sea, could nowhere be seen in Liu's *tz'u*. There is, in addition, a flaw in Liu: to tailor to the need of singing in the market place, he tended to yield at times to decadent feelings as well as low and humorous styles, to the point of being indiscriminate in his expression. That is why his works were

[8]Originally from Wang's *Pan-t'ang lao-jen i-kao* 半塘老人遺稿.

referred to by Wang Cho as "the plain and the vulgar," by Ch'en Chen-sun as "of a vulgar style"; and by Liu Hsi-tsai as stylistically not "elevated". Since *tz'u* is closely related to its author's character, Liu's style is a reflection of his temperament and his life style. His temperament was not exactly flippant, but his life style was totally decadent. In his despondency as a solitary vagabond, he spent practically all his time in enjoying the sights and sounds of dancing and singing and indulged himself in chanting poetry over sips of drinks, with the result that his unworldly aspirations and noble spirit, had he possessed any at all, had all but been dissipated. Su, by contrast, was respected all over the land, no matter whether he was in office or not. Without his knowing it, he had developed a sense of being different, of pride in addition with talent and learning, he belonged naturally to a different category from Liu Yung. These differences in life-style somehow surfaced in their works and accounted for the differences between Su's and Liu's works. Posterity accordingly rated the latter as inferior to the former. Such a rating was fully justified, for it was not until the appearance of Su's works that the horizon of *tz'u* was for the first time broadened and its status elevated. And it was not until then that *tz'u* was purged of its frivolous skills and enjoyed the same prestige as *shih* poetry and prose, and reached what Wang Cho referred to as "total enlightenment." Liu's contribution thus lay in expansions rather than enlightenment.

At the mention of Su's *tz'u*, one thinks invariably of "Recalling Antiquity at Red Cliff" (赤壁懷古), in which "the Great River flows to the east" (大江東去). Since it is a much recited classic, we need not quote it again in its entirety here, except to point out the fact that his "unworldly aspirations and noble spirit" fully surface in the lines. The piece is, moreover, characterized by the presence of the author through a process of the so-called "crystallization of personality and learning."[9] As a matter of fact, Su Shih's ability to broaden and elevate *tz'u* as a genre can be seen in a nutshell here. *Tz'u* pieces dealing with recollections of antiquity actually existed way back in the Five Dynasties, as in *"Chiang Ch'eng tzu"* (江城子) by Ou-yang Chiung 歐陽烔 (896-971):

Late in the afternoon, drooping reeds lined the Chin-ling shores.	晚日金陵岸草平
	落霞明
Under the bright twilight sky,	水無情
The waters flowed on with indifference,	六代豪華
Bringing all the prosperities of the Six Dynas-ties along	暗逐逝波聲
With the murmuring waves, into oblivion.	惟有姑蘇臺畔月
Only the moon above the Ku-su Terrace,	如西子鏡
Remained, like Hsi-shih's mirror,	照江城
And shone on the riverside city.	

In terms of literary techniques, it seems to be richer and more profound than Su's treatment of "The Great River Flows to the East." In comparison Su's work does

---

[9]Author's note: Quoted from the biographical sketch of Su Shih in Hu Shih's *Tz'u Hsüan* 詞選.

not read quite as smoothly. Yet Ou-yang's work can be likened to an immortal in the yonder sky. No matter how profound and rich and ingenious it may be, the work does not exactly relate to us directly. Su's work, on the contrary, confronts us with all its features, beard, brows and all. It is the creation of a man, not that of a god, and therefore it is more vivid and more down to earth. With Ou-yang's work —just as with the majority of works in *Hua-chien chi*—unless the reader is gifted and well-trained in letters, he will have some difficulties in understanding and appreciating it. Su's *tz'u*, on the other hand, moves the reader practically on a physical level because it is a total manifestation of self. Chou Yü 周瑜 (公瑾) (175-210)[10] then and Su Shih now seem to remotely echo and achieve a perfect communion with each other. The impact of his work is equivalent to "someone living inside the work, ready to step out," and thus is subjective and concrete, while that of the *Hua-chien* pieces is objective and imaginary, the latter being commendable more for their ingenious, rather than solid, aspects. Nelan Ch'eng-te 納蘭成德 in his *Lu-shui T'ing tsa-chih* 淥水亭雜志 had precisely this in mind when he said, "The *tz'u* from *Hua-chien chi* is like antique jade pieces, precious but not practical."

"The Great River Flows to the East" was often taken as the hallmark of Su's works. Yet *"Yung yü lo"* (永遇樂), though less known, seems to be even more characteristic of Su's art:

Bright moon like frost;	明月如霜
Fine breeze like water.	好風如水
The scene was clear and boundless.	清景無限
Fish were jumping in the winding creek,	曲港跳魚
And dewdrops rolling off the round lotus.	圓荷瀉露
All these went unappreciated, in solitude.	寂寞無人見
Boom—the midnight drum struck,	紞如三鼓
Clang—a leaf fell to the ground.	鏗然一葉
In the dark my amorous dream was interrupted,	黯黯夢雲驚斷
with a start.	夜茫茫
The night being so vast,	重尋無處
It was impossible to recapture the dream;	覺來小園行徧
I walked through every turn of the garden.	
A weary traveler at the end of the world,	天涯倦客
Gazing at the mountain path leading home,	山中歸路
Which lies hopelessly beyond the reach of my	望斷故園心眼
yearning eyes.	燕子樓空
Now that the Swallow Pavilion stands empty,	佳人何在
Where has the beautiful lady gone,	空鎖樓中燕
Leaving the swallows behind the locked door?	古今如夢
Past and present are like a dream	何曾夢覺
	但有舊歡新怨

---

[10]The commander-in-chief of Wu and the hero (赤壁懷古).
celebrated in Su's "Recalling Antiquity at Red Cliff"

From which one never really wakes up—   異時對
A dream filled with old joys and new sorrows.   黃樓夜景
Some day he who sees the Yellow Pavilion at night, 爲予浩歎
Will certainly heave a sigh for me.

Chang Yen 張炎 in his *Tz'u yüan* 詞源 described Su's work as endowed with "elegant charm and leisurely grace," while Chou Chi in his *Chieh-ts'un-chai lu tz'u tsa chu* claimed, "I value Su Shih for his blossoming beauty." What is described as "elegant charm and leisurely grace," as well as "blossoming beauty," constitute another facet in the beauty of Su's *tz'u*, aside from its characteristic virility which most of us are well aware of. The first stanza of "Yung yü lo" is a perfect demonstration of this often neglected side. Liu Yung could easily live up to the same verbal achievement. But the second stanza, beginning from "Past and present are like a dream" is by no means what Liu Yung could ever come up to. Liu simply lacked the kind of penetrative and outstanding imaginative power to produce such lines:

Past and present are like a dream
From which one never really wakes up—
A dream filled with old joys and new sorrows.

Nor does he possess the same noble and vigorous aspirations to produce such lines:

Some day he who sees the Yellow Pavilion at night,
Will certainly heave a sigh for me.

"Yung yü lo" was written in Hsü Chou 徐州 (P'eng Ch'eng 彭城), where he served as prefect.[11] It is subtitled: "Written after dreaming of P'an P'an 盼盼[12] while staying overnight at the Swallow Pavilion (燕子樓) in P'eng Ch'eng." The Yellow Pavilion referred to in the poem was also built by him while at Hsü Chou. Since he held the conviction that he could rival in immortality the heroes, Bohemian scholars and beauties of the past, he was thus confident that the future visitor "will heave a sigh for me!" Clearly the reference to himself is by no means the result of a random choice of words. With regard to the Yellow Pavilion, elsewhere in a *shih* poem ("A Response to Fan Ch'un-fu" 答范淳甫) he said:

Since the capital in our province produced Liu   吾州下邑生劉季
Pang   誰數區區張與李
Do ordinary Chang and Li need to be reckoned   重瞳遺跡已塵埃
with?   惟有黃樓臨泗水
The double-pupiled Hsiang Yü with his legend has   而今太守老且寒
since gone to dust,   俠氣不洗儒生酸

---

[11] In the year 1078.

[12] A beautiful singer and dancer who was the con-

cubine of Chang Chien-feng 張建封 (735-800). See James Liu, *Major Lyricists of the Northern Sung* (Princeton: Princeton University Press, 1974), p. 133.

> Leaving behind the Yellow Pavilion facing River
>   Ssu.
> Though I am but a poor old prefect, and my
>   pedantry
> Cannot be concealed with chivalrous spirit,
> I am still better off than Lü Pu, out of his wits at
>   Pai Men,
> Volunteering to serve Ts'ao Ts'ao on his saddled
>   horse.

猶勝白門窮呂布
欲將駿馬事曹瞞

He explained in his own annotations: "There used to be a hall in our prefecture for judiciary business, commonly known as the Hall of the Awe-inspiring Hsiang Yü 項羽 (232-202 B.C.). It was said to be no longer inhabitable; so I had it torn down and built the Yellow Pavilion (黃樓) in its place." Since he had the nerve to have Hsiang Yü's hall dismantled for reconstruction simply because it was haunted by its former owner's spirit, the ordinary run of Lü Pu 呂布, Chang Chien-feng and Li Kuang-pi 李光弼 (708-764) were definitely not his match. From this poem one can somehow visualize Su's virile quality and unrestrained nature, which could nowhere be found in Liu. Su's *tz'u*, however, was characterized by the omnipresence of self, just as the case of Liu's works. Both at the same time were more subjective and more down to earth than their predecessors in the T'ang and the Five Dynasties. And yet the self which surfaced in Su was elegant and candid while the self which was manifestated in Liu was pedestrian and self conscious. The differences in personality, learning, temperament and philosophy accounted for the divergences between the two masters. As far as content is concerned, Liu was inferior to Su.

Nevertheless, Su wrote very little in the Long Tunes—having employed no more than twenty-odd Long Tunes. Liu by contrast used over one hundred and ten Long Tunes. Su at the same time was not that concerned with prosody. Liu's language on the contrary was quite refined and fluid, not to mention its exultant qualities. In that sense Liu could be said to be playing "different tunes with the same excellence." As for his prosody, paradoxically from his apparent discordances are generated harmony and flexibility which are not to be found in Su's writings. Only in terms of aspirations and energy was Su a trail blazer of the school of Chang Hsiao-hsiang 張孝祥 (1132-1170), Lu Yu 陸游 (1125-1210) and Hsin Ch'i-chi 辛棄疾 (1140-1207). As far as techniques and artistries are concerned, Su did not open up the line of development of the school of Chou Pang-yen 周邦彥 (1056-1121), Chiang K'uei 姜夔 (ca. 1155-ca. 1221) and Wu Wen-ying 吳文英 (1200-1260). This is especially true with regard to prosody. Though *tz'u* no longer lends itself to singing, yet in our recitations we can easily feel how works from the school of Liu and Chou must have been song poetry with obvious melodious qualities. The writings from the school of Su and Hsin, by contrast, were invariably turned into *shih* poetry in irregular meters. Of course, *tz'u* does not necessarily have to differ from *shih* in content; yet somehow *tz'u* should ideally develop a style of its own. For this reason we cannot but subscribe to the interpretations of the earlier critics to the effect that Liu and Chou were, as it were, musical themes while Su and Hsin were variations. (Variations do not necessarily have to be inferior to themes and may actually be more accessible at times. The differentiations between themes and variations are but categories devised for the convenience of discussions. No value judgment is implied.) Su Shih created *tz'u* in the mode of *shih* and in so doing broadened the horizon and elevated the status of *tz'u*. Yet strictly speaking, *tz'u* did not owe its qualitative development to Su, an act which was to be consummated in the hands of Liu and Chou and their school. Though Su was a renowned master, he was not necessarily adept in the musical aspect of the art. Liu Yung, on the contrary, was an expert in the true sense of the word. Both in prosody and in form he did his best in employing new styles and new tunes as a means of laying the cornerstone for subsequent development in quality. That this "ordinary pedestrian" was able to stand on equal footing with the "soaring Heavenly Horses" was precisely due to this fact. Later Chou Pang-yen inherited the form from Liu Yung while at the same time surpassing the master in aspirations. In the same manner, Hsin Ch'i-chi took the content over from Su while at the same time putting a tighter rein on prosody than his master. The two late-comers were thus canonized as two saints in the genre. (Chou had previously been referred to as a *tz'u* saint, but Hsin's sainthood was unheard of before. One way or another, there can be more than one saint in the first instance.) It was not until the appearances of Chou and Hsin that *tz'u* flourished and reached its apex. The tasks of taking over from the past and of paving the way for the future fell on the shoulders of Liu and Su. Therefore I believe that the development of *tz'u* in form must be attributed to Liu while the growth of *tz'u* in content must be credited to Su.

顧隨：倦駝菴東坡詞說
Interpretation of Su Tung-p'o's *Tz'u*

By **Ku Sui**

Translated by **Huang Kuo-pin** and **Teresa Yee-wha Yü**

Introduction

SINCE I BEGAN TO study *tz'u*, I have never enjoyed reading the songs by Su Tung-p'o 蘇東坡 (1036-1101). The much celebrated "Eastward the River flows on" (大江東去) of *Nien-nu chiao* 念奴嬌 was lightly passed over by me, not to mention his other works. In the past, when I was teaching at the University at the Western City, I took up the discussion of Su's *tz'u* occasionally. One day, in the classroom, I selected his *Yung-yü le* 永遇樂: "Bright moon like frost" (明月如霜) for discussion with my students. I commented on it with elaboration and found my audience entranced. From then on, I gradually realized that Tung-p'o really possessed unequalled qualities and I must have done him injustice. After I finished interpreting the *tz'u* by Hsin Ch'i-chi in late summer this year, when autumn was about to begin, I was unoccupied and by chance had an annotated edition of the *Songs of Tung-p'o* by Lung Yü-sheng 龍楡生. Thus I went over his complete works and was able to tell the merits from the defects of his *tz'u* poems and I made a selection for comment. When I discussed the poetry of Hsin Ch'i-chi, I was only expressing in words the critical opinions I had locked up in my mind for years. What I am going to say about Su Tung-p'o now, on the other hand, is based on what I gathered from my brief encounter with his works over a few days. If my interpretation of Hsin can be said to have resulted from "gradual progress", that of Su, then, can be described as the product of "sudden enlightenment".

As for those who may have access to my interpretation and read it, I would advise them to read Su's *tz'u* first and read them all. When they study a piece, they should first read it quickly to get the gist, then read it carefully to understand its meaning, and finally close the book and meditate on it to grasp the spirit. There must be some that are superior and some that are inferior; some that are explicable and some that are beyond comprehension. But once the general conception of a poem is understood, those that are superior and explicable can be put aside, but those that are inferior should not be; nor should readers try to make far-fetched interpretations of those that are beyond their comprehension for the moment. Before taking up my interpretation they should read the original poems once more, then deliberate for a little while, asking themselves: "What is this chap Bitter Water going to say?" Then they should proceed to read my interpretation word by word and check it with the original poem. This is the proper way of learning. If they do not read it in this manner, but just glance over it as soon as they get hold of it, they would be doing injustice not only to Tung-p'o and Bitter Water, but also to themselves.

They should also bear in mind that true learning must not follow in the footsteps of other people, or have preconceived ideas. If my readers should say that my theory constitutes a cast-iron case, I would not be pleased at all, but would rather plead: "Not guilty!" If this be the case, how is Bitter Water going to face the students of poetry and how are the students of poetry going to face themselves? If on the other hand readers of my interpretation blame me for babbling, I wouldn't feel unduly vexed, but still I would feel that it was unfair. If this be the case, how are the students of poetry going to face Bitter Water and how is Bitter Water going to face himself?

Bitter Water lacking the ability of Ma Tzu 馬祖, whose shout at Po Chang 百丈 deafened his ears for three days, the reader will have to follow the example of Lin Chi 臨濟, who, returning to Huang Po 黃檗 after having received instruction from Ta Yü 大愚, smacked Huang Po on the face as soon as the latter opened his mouth;[1] otherwise, when will Bitter Water and the students of poetry be rid of their ignorance?

When I interpret *tz'u*, I seem to be discussing the theory of literature, but actually I am discussing the text. Students of poetry should try to grasp the spirit rather than understand the meaning of the *tz'u* under discussion. If they manage to understand many petty details without grasping the essence of the ancient classics, what is the point? If they can grasp the spirit, they need not ask whether Bitter Water agrees or not, because Bitter Water would be the first to ask whether they are attempting to grasp the spirit or not. Students of poetry should also try to learn by self-enlightenment and confirmation. If the interpretation by Bitter Water is worthless, why bother to read him at all? If it is worth reading, who is it that teaches him to interpret *tz'u* in this way? Aside from the interpretation of *tz'u*, if Bitter Water picks up a few questions in the Zen catechism and tries to discuss them with the readers, they should appreciate his earnest intention and not treat such discussions as trivial digressions. In any event, what I have said above is meant for students of poetry who wish to study under my guidance. As to those brilliant masters and severe critics, my interpretation is in black and white here, ready to be scrutinized, sifted and criticized. Even if they should go so far as to administer a thundering warning, I would still be glad to bear them.

---

[1] According to Zen Buddhism, neither reflection nor words are needed to restore a person to his original wisdom, that is, his innate understanding of Buddhist truth, which is generally obscured; the only way to enlighten the person is to shout at him or beat him with a club. Zen masters consider the use of reflection and words ineffective, for they cannot bring about one's enlightenment, whereas shouting and clubbing can.

To the Tune of *Yung-yü le*   永遇樂

Written After Spending the Night in Hsü Chou and   徐州夜夢覺登燕子樓作
Ascending the Swallow Tower After a Dream

明月如霜
好風如水
清景無限
曲港跳魚
圓荷瀉露
寂寞無人見
紞如三鼓
鏗然一葉
黯黯夢雲驚斷
夜茫茫
重尋無處
覺來小園行徧

Bright moon like frost;
Fine breeze like water.
The scene was clear and boundless.
Fish were jumping in the winding creek,
And dewdrops rolling off the round lotus.
All these went unappreciated, in solitude.
Boom—the midnight drum struck,
Clang—a leaf fell to the ground.
In the dark my amorous dream was interrupted,
with a start.
The night being so vast,
It was impossible to recapture the dream;
I walked through every turn of the garden.

天涯倦客
山中歸路
望斷故園心眼
燕子樓空
佳人何在
空鎖樓中燕
古今如夢
何曾夢覺
但有舊歡新怨
異時對黃樓夜景
爲余浩歎

A weary traveler at the end of the world,
Gazing at the mountain path leading home,
Which lies hopelessly beyond the reach of my
yearning eyes.
Now that the Swallow Pavilion stands empty,
Where has the beautiful lady gone,
Leaving the swallows behind the locked door?
Past and present are like a dream
From which one never really wakes up—
A dream filled with old joys and new sorrows.
Some day he who sees the Yellow Pavilion at night,
Will certainly heave a sigh for me.

tr. by Ying-hsiung Chou

Su Tung-p'o is certainly a master in depicting scenes, practically unequaled by his successors. Take this poem for example: lines 1-2 (Bright moon . . .), 4-5 (Winding stream . . .), and 7-9 (Boom . . .), are written apparently without effort. Indeed, they have accurately brought out both the feeling and the scene, happy in language as well as in content. However, when analysed in detail, they display various shades and levels, not haphazardly lumped together. Lines 1-2 give only a general description, but lines 4-5 subtly elaborate on it in detail. The fish in the winding creek will not jump except during quiet hours; the dew-drops on the round lotus leaves will not roll until deep in the night. These are actual scenes. Yet a person without keen perception would not be able to detect them, and a poet without supreme technique would not be able to describe them, let alone those who are dull of perception and superficial in observation. Lines 7-8 are unmistakably descriptions of the drum ("boom") and the leaf ("clang"), and clearly indicate the presence of sound. Yet they are dim and hazy, like light cloud and faint dew, like a few pointed peaks out of which a speck of colour can be clearly discerned. These two short lines cannot create such an atmosphere without the following line, which fittingly supplies the missing link. The words *"an-an"* 黯黯 (deep, deep), *"meng-yün"* 夢雲 (cloud-dream, amorous dream) and *"tuan"* 斷 (broken) more than complement and enhance the previous two lines; they fuse with them harmoniously as milk with water. The word *"ching"* 驚 (startle) is in the first level tone 陰平 and contains gentleness in its strength. Thus although it has a dynamic quality, it sets up tension and harmonizes with the preceding two lines. When we read them, listen to them, or even go so far as to feel them with our hands, we find no trace of angularity or ostentation. One cannot help chuckling over those who, conditioned by the view that Su's writings "oppress the reader like 'winds from the sky and rains from the sea' ",[2] regard him as a *tz'u* poet of the *hao-fang* 豪放 (powerful and free) school, and frequently pair him with Hsin Ch'i-chi. It is clear then that, as regards the aspects of Su's *tz'u* poetry just mentioned, these people are completely ignorant.

Let us drop this line of discussion for the time being and raise the hypothetical question: Has Bitter Water, interpreting Su's poem in the above manner, succeeded in grasping its gist? If the answer is "no", everything is done with, and you can pretend that Bitter Water has not said a word. The poem remains intact, and is none the worse for Bitter Water's remarks. If the answer is "yes", does it mean that, when Su composed this poem, he wrote it in accordance with the detailed considerations described by Bitter Water? No, certainly not. It was simply because his poetic world, long inherent in his genius, learning, temperament and spirit, came to the tip of his brush and gave rise to this wonderful poem, when his hand and heart, triggered by this fortuitous concourse, worked in unison. Otherwise, Su would only be a common sculptor who fashions mud into human figures. That is why Bitter Water often tells students of poetry that what he says of a certain poem takes time to say, while a poet like Su when he created poetry often did so in a split second. When he moved his brush, it was as swift as a falcon swooping down at the sight of a leaping hare. Consequently the finished poem bore no trace of the creative process. Those who are intelligent can grasp the spirit of the poem at a mere glance. Next come those who can grasp it by reading the poem aloud. Last come those who can do so only through listening to the intelligent reading it to them. Otherwise, even if Bitter Water tries to interpret the poem in all earnestness, like one cutting a melon and exposing all its seeds, even if the audience are all smiles when they are listening, and memorize thoroughly what Bitter Water says until they know his words backwards, the result will still be as disastrous as:

> *"You go your way, to the Hsiao and Hsiang Rivers,*   君向瀟湘我向秦
> *And I go my way, to the State of Ch'in."*[3]

---

[2]Translator's note: The phrase "winds from the sky and rains from the sea" is taken from Su's *tz'u Ch'üeh-ch'iao hsien* 鵲橋仙, by Chao I-tao 晁以道, one of Su's disciples, to describe the effect of singing Su's *Tz'u*. It was repeatedly used by later poets and critics and become almost a conditioned reflex when they characterized Su's style.

[3]Cheng Ku 鄭谷: Written after parting with his friend on the Huai River 淮上別友詩. The Hsiao and Hsiang Rivers are in the Southeast, while the State of Ch'in is in the Northwest.

Having digressed thus far, let us now go back to the poem. In lines 1 and 2, the word *"ju"* 如 (like) in the phrases *"ju-shuang"* 如霜 (like frost) and *"ju-shui"* 如水 (like water) is somewhat contrived. In lines 4-5, the characters *"t'iao"* 跳 in *"t'iao-yü"* 跳魚 (jumping fish) and *"hsieh"* 瀉 in *"hsieh-lu"* 瀉露 (rolling dew-drops) are somewhat laboured. Whatever merits these lines have, they are not as mellow and effortless as lines 7-9. As to line 3:

> *The scene was clear and boundless,*

and line 6:

> *All these went unappreciated, in solitude,*

Bitter Water used to suspect them to be the flaws in the whole poem, thinking that if the poet considered them to be the only way in which he could express his inspiration, he was incompetent, and that if the reader considered them to be the only way in which the poem could be made comprehensible, he was dull. In short, Bitter Water believed that these two lines served no purpose, either from the stand-point of the writer or from that of the reader. But now I have second thoughts. Why? Before I answer this question, let me explicate lines 10 and 11 first:

> *The night being so vast,*
> *It was impossible to recapture the dream.*

The word *"hsün"* 尋 (seek) refers to the phrase *"meng-yün"* 夢雲 (cloud-dream, amorous dream) in line 9. At this particular moment, the poet is not yet fully awake, probably still lying in bed, half asleep, trying to trace and recapture the broken dream. That is why only in the next line does he wake and walk through every turn of the garden.

Now, let us go back to the scenes depicted in the first 6 lines. Not only are they scenes the poet sees after he has awakened and walked through every turn of the garden, but they are also his realization, upon having awakened, walked through every turn of the garden, and seen the things around him, that during his sleep and dream, the frost-like moon, the water-like breeze, the jumping fish and the rolling dew-drops were there all the time. Alas! We may go to sleep and dream, but the moon itself is always like frost and the breeze like water while the fish go on jump-ing and the dew-drops go on rolling. We are born into this world, which is an endless sea of suffering, with endless karma-consciousness. We mistake illusion for reality and wickedness for goodness. Before our very eyes, there are so many beautiful things that have passed by without being noticed and enjoyed, not to mention those high above and far away beyond our reach. This is surely a great tragedy for men of ideas and integrity. Thus, line 3 "The scene was clear and boundless" and line 6 "All these went unappreciated, in solitude" are surely touching and yet restrained. How could one say then that these lines are flaws? Bitter Water must have been blind of one eye in those days; he must now offer his penitence to Su from the bottom of his heart.

As to the word *"meng"* 夢 in the phrase *meng yün* 夢雲 (amorous dream, literally cloud-dream), what does it refer to? Bitter Water thinks that it is a mere dream and does not necessarily refer to a particular dream. Perhaps one can let it refer to a particular dream if one wants, but it is certainly not a dream about Kuan P'an-p'an 關盼盼.[4] One of Wang Kuo-wei 王國維's poems has the following line:

> *How intolerable that dreams at night serve but to*   不堪宵夢續塵勞
> *continue mundane toils.*

According to Bitter Water, the dream in the night is nothing but toil of this mortal life. Su Tung-p'o here means exactly the same thing. That is why in copying the subtitle of this poem, Bitter Water intended to leave out "ascending the Swallow Tower", because in the poem we find nothing that hints at "ascending". It follows, then, that the phrase "written after awakening from a dream" alone would be adequate; why mention Hsü Chou at all? Bitter Water thinks that without the name Hsü Chou, "the Swallow Tower" in the poem would appear too abrupt, coming, so to speak, from nowhere. There is another text with the following subtitle: "Written after spending the night at the Swallow Tower and seeing Kuan P'an-p'an in my dream." On this subtitle, Chêng Weng-ch'o has passed the following strictures: "Su Tung-p'o would never use such fantastic nonsense as his subtitle." Chêng is correct, but then he quotes Wang Wên-kao's commentary and says that the poem was written after the poet had ascended the Swallow Tower in a dream and visited the place the next day. This, too, is pedantry, another case of "trying to recover the sword dropped into the river by cutting a mark on the side of the boat". At this point, students of poetry might ask what it is that entitles Bitter Water to speak with such finality, hardly realizing that rather than Bitter Water making a great deal of fuss over nothing, it is themselves who have failed to study the poem with care. Try to read the second stanza, which gradually unfolds the theme. It dwells only upon the tragic sense of life without a trace of romantic love. This is Su's true confession; Bitter Water need not go on with further interrogation to elicit evidence from him. Lines 13-15 lament the evanescence of life, which cannot even be compared to fallen leaves, for fallen leaves can still return to the roots. Lines 16-18 imply that whether people leave behind a good or bad name in history, everything in their lives will only serve as material for gossip in generations to come. Lines 19-21 ("Past and present are like a dream" 古今如夢) further suggest that for human beings, lost in the sea of suffering, karma-consciousness is intangible, affording hardly a firm basis for explanation. In the last three lines, the Swallow Tower reminds the poet of the Yellow Tower. A thousand years from now, posterity will think of Kuan P'an-p'an whenever they see the Swallow Tower. They will also think of Su whenever they see the Yellow Tower, which was built by Su himself. When will this lament, repeating itself from generation to generation, ever end? This is exactly what is meant by "succeeding generations are lamented by generations that succeed them." Thus, in the entire universe, from antiquity to the present, human beings, supposed to be

---

[4]Chang Chien-feng 張建封 (735-800)'s favorite concubine, who did not remarry after his death and locked herself up in the Swallow Tower built especially for her. •

superior creatures, are all in a great dream, with no hope of ever waking up. Consequently, man's predicament seems all the more tragic, because while he is dreaming, the moon is like frost, the breeze like water, the fish are jumping, and the dew-drops are rolling. This being the case, how can the poem have anything to do with the poet's ascending the Swallow Tower and dreaming of Kuan P'an-p'an? Let me ask you, discerning students of poetry, was Su awake when he was composing this poem or was he still dreaming? If he was still dreaming, then, Bitter Water is talking about a dream while dreaming himself! An ancient poet once wrote:

You cry in vain, until your tears become blood,	啼得血流無用處
You may as well keep silent for the rest of Spring.	不如緘口度殘春

Preface to the Appendix

AFTER I HAD DECIDED to discuss Su Tung-p'o's *tz'u* and made my selections, I went over them carefully. In so doing, I found that five anthology pieces, well known to the reading public, had been left out on the following grounds: since they had already been chosen by anthologists and were practically known to all, their merits must be quite obvious to discerning eyes and needed no further comment from me. On second thoughts, however, I felt that I had something to say about them after all. Hence my brief discussion of the five poems, now included in the book as an appendix.

Bitter Water
At the Temple of the Tired Camel

To the Tune of *Nien-nu chiao*	念奴嬌
Ancient Thoughts at the Red Cliff	赤壁懷古

Eastward the River rolls on,	大江東去
Washing away	浪淘盡
The traces of dashing men thousands of generations past.	千古風流人物
	故壘西邊
West of the old fortress, at the Red Cliff, it is said	人道是
Chou of the Three Kingdoms won his battle.	三國周郎赤壁
Now clouds crumbled over scattered rocks;	亂石崩雲
Furious waves, crashing upon the bank	驚濤裂岸
Hurl up a thousand heaps of snow.	捲起千堆雪
Vivid as a picture, the River and the hills—	江山如畫
What a host of heroes they once held!	一時多少豪傑
Imagine Chou Yü in those days,	遙想公瑾當年
When he had just married Younger Ch'iao:	小喬初嫁了

Ku Sui 顧隨, whose style is Hsien-chi 羨季, called himself Bitter Water (苦水, K'u Shui) because it was similar in sound to his name. He was born in 1897 in Hopei. Before obtaining his B.A. degree in English at National Peking University, he studied briefly at Pei-yang University in Tientsin. Upon graduation, he began his teaching career in several middle schools in Shantung and Tientsin, and finally settled in Peking, the cultural metropolis at that time. In 1928, he began to offer Chinese Literature courses at Yenching University and National Peking University, establishing himself as an all-round scholar of Chinese Literature and a *tz'u* 詞 specialist. During the Sino-Japanese war, he taught at Fu Jen University, where Professor Chia-ying Yeh Chao attended and began a lasting teacher-disciple relationship with him. Professor Ku continued to teach at Fu Jen University after 1949 until he was transferred to Tientsin Normal College in 1953. In 1960, he died of an illness at the age of 63.

Professor Chia-ying Yeh is herself an accomplished scholar of Chinese poetry and *tz'u*, having published several volumes of essays and many papers on her favorite topics and spent more than 25 years teaching at National Taiwan University, doing research at Harvard University, and serving as Professor of Chinese Literature at the University of British Columbia since 1969. A sense of profound gratitude to her former teacher has driven her to collect his writings through his colleagues, acquaintances and various other channels, with a view to having them reprinted in the future. It has taken her many years to assemble Professor Ku's publications, which include six volumes of regulated *shih* 詩 and *tz'u* (from 1928 to 1944, mostly limited editions and 2 titles are hand-copied), two volumes of *chü* 曲, and one volume of critical essays entitled *Interpretation of Su Tung-p'o's Tz'u*. She understands that Professor Ku has also written a book entitled *Interpretation of Hsin Ch'i-chi's Tz'u*, but so far she has not succeeded in tracing it.

Upon the request of the editor, Professor Chia-ying Yeh agreed to publish the lecture notes of her mentor's *Interpretation of Su Tung-p'o's Tz'u*, taken by her at China University (中國大學), Peking, as a part-time lecturer in 1943. These notes are by no means complete;

Full of youthful vigor,	雄姿英發
Wearing a silk turban and holding a feather fan.	羽扇綸巾
While he was chatting and laughing,	談笑間強虜灰飛煙滅
His powerful enemy scattered like flying ashes and smoke.	故國神遊
In this old country his spirit wanders—[5]	多情應笑我
Ah, the general would laugh at me,	早生華髮
For being sentimental and having grey hair at such an early age.	人間如夢
The world is like a dream.	一尊還酹江月
Let me but pour a libation to the River moon!	

The reputation of Su Shih as a *tz'u* poet was founded on this piece. It is on the strength of this piece, too, that critics have considered Su's style to be "powerful and free" (*Hao-fang* 豪放), and linked his name to that of Hsin. I seldom use the

---

[5]Lines 18-20 (故國神遊, 多情應笑我, 早生華髮 in the original) have generally been interpreted as: Su's mind has wandered back to his native land Szechwan, where, he imagines, he is laughed at by the spirit of his deceased wife for being sentimental. This explanation seems, however, to be out of place with the rest of the poem. Hence the interpretation in the translation.

nevertheless they represent the achievement of Ku Sui as an outstanding *tz'u* scholar and constitute part of his writings hitherto completely inaccessible to students of Chinese Literature. These notes were turned over in early 1979 to Professor Yeh's student, Miss Teresa Yu, who translated the five pieces in the Appendix and the Afterword. However, with admirable persistence, Professor Yeh finally succeeded in locating Bitter Water's *Interpretation of Su Tung-p'o's Tz'u* in its written form, which was serialized in the weekly literary supplement of a Tientsin vernacular newspaper from December 8, 1947 to April 1, 1949. A hand-copied version of the original manuscript was airmailed to and received by the editor in December 1979. After checking the original with the lecture notes, the editor found that the lecture notes were too brief and that some passages and sentences were missing. The first piece on *Yung-yü le* in the form of lecture notes, for example, was only about half the length of the original. While the editor was more than pleased with the discovery of the original, he felt compelled to reinstate the missing parts to the translations. Mr. K.B. Wong was thus called upon to translate the original Introduction, the first piece, and Short Preface to the Appendix in order to give the proper background of the entire collection of interpretative comments.

It must be pointed out that, while Bitter Water has a high regard for Su as a *tz'u* writer, as evidenced in his interpretation of the ten *tz'u* poems in the main section, he is somewhat reserved in his opinion of the five famous anthology pieces in the Appendix. Unfortunately, the main section runs much longer than the Appendix. As a result, only one piece of the former is given below in order to meet the demand of time. The interpretative comments presented may not give a balanced picture of or do justice to Bitter Water as a critic. However, it can be seen from the comments that Bitter Water is a very sensitive and discerning interpreter, who is not easily influenced by popular taste, but often detects the facile and superficial phrasing of well-known pieces. It is hoped that Bitter Water's *Interpretation* will be read as a sincere and perceptive reassessment of *tz'u* poets, not as a conscious and wilful attempt to reverse traditional and established opinions.

---

expression "powerful and free" in discussing *tz'u*, but this piece, I must say, belongs to that category indeed. The waning of heroes in the inexorable flow of time is a truly sad thought. Brought objectively to the surface in such a manner, the event is no longer pathetic and the poem becomes spirited and refreshing. The last five lines in stanza 2 well illustrate this point, not to mention lines 9-15.

"Powerful and free" as it is, this poem should not be hastily compared with Hsin's works. It lacks two essential qualities—strength and robustness—which mark Hsin's works, even though there is a touch of such qualities in lines 6-8. One would not be too wide of the mark even if one were to say that, in Su's complete works, only these three lines are comparable to Hsin Ch'i-chi's *tz'u* in terms of strength and robustness. The rest of this piece is full of leisurely grace and gentle contemplation, characteristic of his transcendent style. In this respect, stanza 1 is quite successful. By contrast, stanza 2 seems slightly superficial and facile, and is not truly in the style of grace and gentle contemplation. How is one to associate Chou Yü's youthful vigor with his marriage with Younger Ch'iao? Yet, this idea is not altogether unacceptable. But how is it possible that, while one was "chatting and laughing", a powerful enemy scattered like flying ashes and smoke?

In the past, when I came across "On Reading History" by Tso Ssu 左思 (250?-350?):

> *Glancing left, I conquered the Kingdom of Wu;* 左眄澄江湘
> *Looking right, I subjugated the Ch'iang and the* 右盼定羌胡
> *northern tribes.* 功成不受爵
> *I refused to accept any honor and title,* 長揖歸田廬
> *And returned to my farmstead after a deep bow.*

I thought it might not be too difficult to withdraw one's self from a spectacular success, but saying that he could conquer the Kingdom of Wu with a glance and subjugate the Ch'iang and the northern tribes with a look, Tso Szu must have been responsible for the habit of subsequent writers in talking big. I laughed at this and thought that either Tso was bluffing, or he was brazen. Although one cannot say that Tung-p'o is engaged in praising himself while overtly praising Chou Yü, it is difficult to deny that there is something akin in the essential spirit. Thus, though "this old country" of line 16 must be referring to the Three Kingdoms and "laugh at me" may refer to Chou Yü, while "having grey hair at such an early age" must be referring to the poet himself. These three lines, when linked together, do not make much sense. When Hsin Ch'i-chi wrote:

> *I do not regret missing the ancient sages;* 不恨古人吾不見
> *I only regret that they are unable to see how un-* 恨古人不見吾狂耳
> *disciplined I am!*

he was criticized for it. These lines by Su are even more superficial and deserve more reproach. In the first two lines after the break of the first stanza, in particular:

> *Imagine Chou Yü in those days*
> *When he had just married Younger Ch'iao.*

one can easily see how leisurely grace and gentle contemplation can degenerate into superficiality and frivolity. As for those who tried unsuccessfully to imitate Su's style and turned out clichés, they had only themselves to blame; Bitter Water cannot bring himself to lay this at Su's door.

To the Tune of *Shui-tiao Ko-t'ou*   水調歌頭

On Mid-autumn night of the year *ping-ch'en* I 丙辰中秋歡飲達旦大
drank till dawn to intoxication, after which, think- 醉作此篇兼懷子由
ing of Tzu-yu, I wrote this poem.

明月幾時有
> *Since when did the bright moon begin to shine?* 把酒問青天
> *With a cup of wine in hand I ask the deep blue sky.* 不知天上宮闕
> *I wonder what day it is* 今夕是何年
> *Tonight in Heaven.* 我欲乘風歸去
> *I long to ride back with the wind,* 惟恐瓊樓玉宇
> *But fear that the crystal halls and jade mansions* 高處不勝寒
> *Would be too cold on high.* 起舞弄清影

Rising to dance and frolic with my clear shadow—
How is it comparable with earthly joy?

何似在人間

Around the vermilion chamber,
Past the painted window,
The moon shines on the sleepless one.
The moon should have no ill feeling;
Why is it always full when men are separated?
Men have their joys and sorrows, their meetings
   and partings.
The moon has its bright and dim moments, its
   waxing and waning.
Since time began there has never been lasting per-
   fection.
I only wish that we could both be healthy and
   well,
To share the sight of this fair beauty thousands of
   miles apart.

轉朱閣
低綺戶
照無眠
不應有恨
何事長向別時圓
人有悲歡離合
月有陰晴圓缺
此事古難全
但願人長久
千里共嬋娟

Of all the *tz'u* poems by Su Shih, the one which has won most acclaim over the ages is *Nien-nu chiao*. In terms of poignancy, however, *Shui-tiao ko-t'ou* is surely the best. With its grand sweep, *Nien-nu chiao* may sound a little overpowering. This poem, by contrast, is mellow and serene in thought, and may be more appealing to most people. Personally, I believe the best part of the poem lies in the last four lines of the first stanza.

In the West poets and men of faith often glorify God, spurn reality, and try to seek eternal life in Heaven. On the other hand, those who are resentful and skeptical and believe in human instinct and reason would scorn the afterlife, feel quite contented with the mundane and the worldly and sing the praises of this earth. Personally, I think neither of these is relevant to the outlooks of the Chinese. The Chinese intellectuals, traditionally Confucian in their outlook, are concerned with the relationship between human nature and the universe. The Taoists, on the other hand, leave everything to nature and the Buddhists believe in negation and the void. The three streams of thought seem to diverge but end in fact in confluence. The writers derive their inspiration from *Li-sao* 離騷 and The *Book of Songs* while the recluses seek refuge in wild nature. They all try to forget themselves in wine and song or indulge in "the wind and the moon". As to those who express their feelings and discontent in the form of elegies or use poetry as a means of praise and eulogy, we need not discuss them. Thus, Chinese and Westerners display their sentiments through poetry in a very different manner. The Chinese who aim high are not necessarily religious fanatics; those who attach themselves to earthly pleasures are not necessarily realists. I used to think that the philosophy represented in the first stanza of this poem of Su's tallied happily with modern Western thought. On closer examination, I no longer think the same. Su does not seem to commit himself either to heaven or to earth. Because of his talent, he can afford to sound lofty and free, thus differing from the deliberately realistic approach of the West. In this respect, perhaps Chu Tun-ju 朱敦儒's famous couplet in *Che-ku t'ien* 鷓鴣天 bears a closer resemblance to Su's poem:

> *I am too lazy to return to jade halls and gold*　　玉樓金闕慵歸去
> *mansions,*
> *Let me get drunk in Loyang with plum blossoms*　　且插梅花醉洛陽
> *in my hair.*

The only difference is that Chu's lines are too plain in statement and makes too much of a pose, while Su's are more fluent and translucent, thus more appealing. They seem, nevertheless, to be in the same tradition. Han Yü expresses a similar feeling in his lines:

> *So long as I can put up with this world,*　　我能屈曲自世間
> *How could I follow you and live in the fairy*　　安能從汝巢神山
> *mountains?*

These lines sound bitter and blatant, when compared with Su's, which are marked by a gentle restraint.

The second stanza of Su's poem seems a little too mellow and sweet. This mellowness is one of Su's characteristics, shown often at the height of his lyricism. Those who try to imitate this closely, however, end up missing the true essence of his style, which often leads to undesirable effects. I disapprove of these works and would refrain from discussing them.

To the Tune of *Shui-lung-yin*　　水龍吟

To the Rhyme of Chang Chih-fu's *tz'u* "Willow　　次韻章質夫楊花詞
Catkins"

似花還似非花

> *It looks like a flower, but is not a flower.*　　也無人惜從敎墜
> *No one cares and lets it fall,*　　拋家傍路
> *Cast off to wander by the roadside,*　　思量卻是
> *So indifferent it seems*　　無情有思
> *Yet, as one ponders, so full of feeling.*　　縈損柔腸
> *Perturbed, on the point of opening, its sleepy eyes*　　困酣嬌眼
> *close,*　　欲開還閉
> *Dreaming, it follows the wind for thousands of*　　夢隨風萬里
> *miles*　　尋郎去處
> *In search of its lover.*　　又還被
> *Finally, it is wakened by the song of a warbler.*　　鶯呼起

> *I do not regret that the catkins have all fallen.*　　不恨此花飛盡
> *I only regret that*　　恨西園落紅難綴
> *All the fallen red petals in the Western Garden*　　曉來雨過
> *cannot be gathered anymore.*　　遺蹤何在

> *The rain ceases with the approach of dawn.*　　一池萍碎
> *Where have they left their traces?*　　　　　　春色三分
> *A pond full of broken duckweeds!*　　　　　　二分塵土
> *Ah, of all the colors of spring.*　　　　　　　一分流水
> *Two parts have gone to the dust,*　　　　　　細看來不是楊花點點
> *One to the flowing water—*　　　　　　　　　是離人淚
> *As I look closer,*
> *I see not catkins,*
> *But drops and drops of parted lovers' tears!*

I am an admirer of Wang Kuo-wei, my senior as a critic of *tz'u*. However, I cannot agree with him when he says that this is the best *tz'u* on external objects (*yung-wu tz'u* 詠物詞). Furthermore he goes on to say that although it is written in response to the *tz'u* by Chang Chieh 章楶 (?-1102) to the same tune, yet it sounds like an original. I do not consider sounding like an original sufficient reason for liking this poem. Is it because in the realm of poetry and *tz'u* I have no taste for "poems on objects"? In short, I cannot force myself to concur with Wang.

Tu Fu's poems may have heavy strokes, but no vulgar ones, but Li Po has occasional vulgar lapses. Hsin Ch'i-chi's *tz'u* may have crude expressions, but no vulgar ones, while Su Tung-po does have vulgar expressions. Is this because their learning could not measure up to their talent, so that in writing poetry and *tz'u*, even Li and Su, when careless in the least, would not be free from committing vulgarisms?

As to the *tz'u Shui-tiao ko-t'ou*, I do not have a high opinion of the second stanza, because, though not representing vulgarity, it borders on being vulgar. As to this poem, it is plain vulgarism. The first six lines of the first stanza is almost as vulgar and commonplace as some of the worst *san-chü* 散曲 written by minor Yüan and Ming writers. Lines such as "cast off to wander by the roadside", and "for thousands of miles in search of its lover" in particular, are obvious examples. The first two lines of the second stanza are fine, but the "fallen red petals" have nothing to do with willow catkins. The following lines:

> *The rain ceases with the approach of dawn.*
> *Where have they left their traces?*
> *A pond of broken duckweeds!*

are explicitly descriptive and lacks refinement, but nonetheless they are pleasing in their tender thoughts. It is a pity that the line

> *Where have they left their traces?*

sticks out in the middle, like a blemish on a piece of jade, spoiling the unity of the three lines as a whole. On the next three lines, beginning with:

> *Ah, of all the colors of spring*

Bitter Water would refrain from commenting. As to the final couplet which compares "catkins" to "parted lovers' tears", Bitter Water would exclaim: "No! No!" and more emphatically for the third time: "No!" Has anyone ever seen "tears of parted lovers" so light and frivolous? It is hard to understand why the poet wants to emphasize this by "looking closer". Now we know for sure that Su is not essentially a lyricist. For sentitive and subtle depiction of deep feelings, Su is clearly not equal to Hsin.

To the Tune of *Tieh lien hua*   蝶戀花

The flowers are shedding their faded red,	花褪殘紅青杏小
Under the tiny, green apricots.	燕子飛時
As swallows fly about,	綠水人家繞
Green waters encircle the houses.	枝上柳綿吹又少
Catkins on the willows are blown ever scarcer.	天涯何處無芳草
As far as the horizon, everywhere is a stretch of green.	牆裏鞦韆牆外道
	牆外行人
	牆裏佳人笑
Inside the wall a swing sways,	笑漸不聞聲漸悄
Outside lies the road.	多情卻被無情惱
Outside the wall is a traveller,	
Inside, a beauty's laughter.	
The laughter gradually softens, the sound gradually fades away.	
Ah, he who is full of feelings is troubled	
By one with none at all!	

One anecdote records that Chao-yün (朝雲 Morning Cloud), Su's concubine, was so overwhelmed with emotion every time she sang the fifth and sixth lines of this poem that she would not stop chanting those lines even when she was ill. After she died, Su stopped singing this *tz'u* for the rest of his life. I think this might be a true story. Yet Lu Chi (陸機) once wrote:

When the leaves are about to fall,	落葉俟微風以隕
The wind does not have to be strong;	而風之力蓋寡
When Meng Ch'ang wept on meeting the musician Yung Ch'iu,	孟嘗遭雍阿以泣
The melancholy music played only a small part.	而琴之感以末

Indeed, a leaf that is about to fall needs no help from the wind, and tears that are ready to be shed do not rely on sad music to hasten their flow. Perhaps this was why Chao-yün was moved to tears every time she came to those lines. Wang Yü-yang 王漁洋 writes of these two lines by Su:

Such delicacy of feelings may not even be rivaled by Liu
Yung. Who says that Su Shih knows only how to write lines such

as "Eastward the River rolls on . . . "? Su is extraordinary indeed! . . .

Perhaps Su is extraordinary, but I doubt his supremacy in depicting delicate feelings. Feelings and thoughts evolve when the heart meets with the external world. But in these two lines, Su's contemplations seem to override his emotions, so that he does not totally relate himself to reality. If the catkins are becoming scarcer as green grass grows all over the place, those who are easily moved would begin to mourn the passing away of spring. Yet on the other hand, the green grass is a sight to enjoy, and since it fills the horizon, one can seek a sense of joy wherever one goes. Isn't such a thought more contemplative than emotional, more objective than subjective? If we compare them with these lines from Hsin, we can immediately see the difference:

> *When finally he comes, spring will be gone.* 待得來時春盡也
> *The plums will be in clusters,* 梅結子
> *The bamboo shoots, too, will have grown into* 筍成竿
> *trunks.*

If I proceed with nitpicking, I may even say that "the green grass stretching to the horizon" contributes to the intellectual content of the poem at the expense of feeling, and the line "the catkins on the willow branches" is paying more attention to details than to essentials. Branch is a common noun and, therefore, embraces all trees while willow is a particular tree and has nothing to do with universal verdancy. However, I say this in order to warn students of poetry of the danger of excessive rhetoric, not to find fault with Su's *tz'u*. These two lines by Su have an open-minded candour and their carelessness may be overlooked. As to the second stanza, if it is not vulgar or cliché-ridden, it is at least trivial and superficial. As I have already discussed this point in detail in my interpretation of *Shui-tiao ko-t'ou*, I need not repeat myself here.

To the Tune of *Pu-suan tzu*   卜算子

Written During My Residence in Ting Hui Lodge,   黃州定慧院寓居作
Huang Chou

> *The crescent moon hangs on a spare* wu-t'ung *tree.*   缺月挂疏桐
> *The dripping of the waterclock has stopped;*   漏斷人初靜
> *Quiet has just fallen—*   誰見幽人獨往來
> *Who sees the recluse go his solitary way?*   縹緲孤鴻影
> *Dim and distant, the shadow of a lone wild goose.*
>
> *Roused, he turns his head*   驚起卻回頭
> *In quiet sorrow which no one knows.*   有恨無人省
> *From cold branch to cold branch, searching in vain*   揀盡寒枝不肯棲
> *for a place to roost,*   寂寞沙洲冷
> *He finally lands on a bleak, lonely shoal.*

Of the five poems included in this appendix, I like this one best. In such a short poem Su has used the character *jen* (人, "man", "person") three times.[6] That is open-minded and free indeed and one should not be niggardly enough to find fault! Lines 1 and 2 of the poem give a quiet, lonely feeling, and when Su mentions "the recluse", he is referring to himself. The shadow of the solitary wild goose, dimly discernible, is a description of the bird as well as a self-portrait of the poet himself. Who is startled? It is the poet, startled by the bird. Who turns his head? The poet again. Like the bird, he, too, is "in quiet sorrow". The phrase "no one knows" indicates that only Tung-p'o is stirred, and no one else. The last two lines of the second stanza tell us that the wild goose travels from one cold branch to another in search of a place to roost, and rests on a lonely shoal. There are no trees to shelter him but only frosts to invade him. That accounts for the sorrow. Consequently, the poet and the wild goose become one and cannot be separated.

This being the case, it seems to follow that I approve of this poem without any reservation. Why, then, have I excluded it from my selection of Tung-p'o's *tz'u* and put it in the appendix? It is difficult to justify myself but there is a reason. As far as literary expression is concerned, this piece is quite adequate. But "the world" created is by no means unique: it can be found in traditional Chinese poetry through the ages. A writer need not be deliberately quaint and different so as to depart from the usual practice and common sense. Nor need he fall into ready patterns so that he looks like the pale shadow of past masters. This *tz'u* by Su hardly fits in the latter category. Its style, however, is imitative and its taste lacks individuality. Moreover, it is not poetry of the highest order and would not make a good model for later poets, as it tends to encourage crude imitations. It may be pointed out that Bitter Water is making a mountain out of a mole hill by repeating himself endlessly. A story goes that a person was very much in love with his young wife. One day he saw his mother-in-law, who turned out to be an ugly old hag. When he returned home, he divorced his mate. His friends and relatives were all puzzled by what he did and wanted to find out the underlying reason. "My wife will doubtless look like her mother in future." Bitter Water seems to be in the same quandary. When a scholar sets out to achieve great things, he must take former sages and saints as his models. When a Buddhist disciple makes a vow, he must aim to become a Buddha or a holy man, for one intending to reach the top often ends up in the middle. In order to prevent degeneration and deterioration, there is no harm in aiming high. This is my personal view and does not relate to Su's *tz'u*. However, deep in my heart, there is a sense of dissatisfaction. It occurs to me that every time I read this poem, I sense a ghostly spirit which, though not fierce and ferocious, is nevertheless intangible and nebulous. I would not normally be pleased with the sight of an immortal who disdains man's food, not to mention a phantom having nothing to do with the human world. Some say, "Ch'ü Yüan 屈原 wrote about strange spirits too. Are you going to apply the same criteria to his works?" The answer is that the ghost in Ch'ü

---

[6]The character occurs in line 2 in the original as 人初靜 (literally "*men* first silent", rendered as "quiet has just fallen"); in line 3 as 幽人 ("obscure *person*", rendered as "recluse"), and lastly in line 6 as 有恨無人省 ("has sorrow no *person* understands/knows", which I take to be "quiet sorrow"). I have taken the liberty to translate these lines freely, as it would be impossible to retain the identity of the character "人" in each case without making the translation unreadable.

Yüan's *Chu-tz'u* 楚辭 is figurative and that the poet shows a deep and genuine concern for man's sufferings and vicissitudes. In Su's poem, however, "the recluse" is actually a spirit and his "quiet sorrow" is that of a spirit, too. People may not sympathize with my view, but I am speaking with all sincerity and in all fairness. By this standard, I evaluate not only Su's works, but also the works of all ancient poets. Even in my personal writings, I have always abided by this principle, creative as well as critical.

Afterword

WHEN I FINISHED MY interpretation of Hsin's poems, the chill of autumn deepened, followed by spells of continuous heavy rain. When at times it grew sunny, the wind came in gusts, so that I relapsed again into my chronic cold. In idleness, I tried to write something about Su's *tz'u* to while away my time. As I was under no pressure, the work went on smoothly and was completed only in twelve days. On reviewing what I had written, I felt compelled to include an afterword.

In discussing literature, Ts'ao P'i 曹丕 states in his *Tien-lun lun-wen* 典論論文 that the essence of a piece of writing is its *ch'i* 氣 (spirit, literally "breath", "air"). He says that *ch'i*, whether clear or murky, is a quality that cannot be cultivated. From this statement, it is clear that, by *ch'i*, Ts'ao P'i means "innate spirit", which is inborn. I have not come across any comments on *ch'i* in *The Analects*. As for Mencius, he says, "I nurture a magnanimous *ch'i* (one which fills up all between heaven and earth)". Wang Ch'ung 王充 states in *Lun-heng* 論衡: "I nourish *ch'i* to guard myself with". I know nothing about Mencius' magnanimous *ch'i*, but if Wang's *ch'i* stresses the idea of nurturing one's health and life, it is different from that of Mencius'. Liu Hsieh 劉勰 writes about the cultivation of *ch'i* (*yang-ch'i* 養氣, which is a combination of Mencius' *yang* and Ts'ao P'i's *ch'i*) in *Wen-hsin tiao-lung* 文心 彫龍: "When one's spirit is overcome by darkness, the more it is spurred on, the duller it becomes. In literary and artistic creation, therefore, it is important to maintain temperance and a readiness of expression, to rest one's mind in tranquillity and soothe one's *ch'i*. When one feels vexed, one should at once stop pursuing." What Liu means by *ch'i* is the flow of inspiration in the process of literary creation. He believes that, if one works too hard, one becomes "weary in spirit and sapped in vitality." His concept of *ch'i* is different from Ts'ao's.

Since Su Ch'e 蘇轍 mentioned that *ch'i* can be cultivated, that idea of *ch'i* has become established in the minds of critics. While Ts'ao believes that *ch'i* is inborn, Han Yü speaks of a vigorous *ch'i* and Su Ch'e the cultivation of *ch'i*. And in order to attain a vigorous *ch'i*, one has to foster it. However, contrary to Ts'ao's notion that *ch'i* is inborn, this seems to be acquired through inculcation and study in later life. As for those who followed Han and Su's interpretation, they tried to manufacture *ch'i* by forcing a kind of faked vitality, and called it powerful and free spirit. When applied to creative writing, this faked vitality will never make a work immortal. When cherished by a person, it manifests little of his true self. This is why I have no sympathy with the *hao-fang* style in discussing *tz'u* poetry. Su and Hsin have been considered "powerful and free" poets of the highest esteem. Yet they have little in common. Su displays a gentle expressiveness in his depiction of scenes whereas Hsin can win the reader's unreserved admiration in his description of feelings. Hsin's poems do have depiction of scenes too but they lack the gentle expressiveness of Su. Similarly, Su's works also describe feelings but they are no comparison to Hsin's in depth and subtlety. As for poems with an intellectual and philosophical content, they opened up fresh territory: Hsin is more involved with the human and the earthly while Su tends to escape to Taoism and Buddhism. Their difference can aptly be described by the two terms: *ch'u* 出 (transcendent) and *ju* 入 (secular).

After the Han and Wei periods, Taoist philosophy became doctrines for magicians and alchemists, which, when pushed to an extreme, developed into a belief in immortality and sublimation of the soul. As for Buddhism, it evolved and gave rise to the Zen school, whose ultimate expression was the practice of meditation and sudden enlightenment. The aftermath of this surge of belief flooded the country for many years.

Those who enjoyed abstract philosophizing found a direction for their endless discussions. Those who believed in metaphysical speculations pursued it as a path to further knowledge of one's own inner nature. Poets too were not able to put themselves outside this trend. They either imparted momentum to it or fell into its pitfalls. Li Po's poetry, for example, has affinities with Taoism. Wang Wei, on the other hand, adopted a Buddhist outlook. In the Six Dynasties, the only person who could stand aloof and stay out of all this was T'ao Ch'ien 陶潛, T'ao's poetry is sober, simple, unadorned, written in the true Confucian vein, and mellow to the highest degree, unequalled by poets who followed in his steps. However, there are poets who, though not comparable to T'ao, have also mastered the craft of poetry, and distinguished themselves with a style of their own. Tu Fu and Hsin Ch'i-chi are two such poets in *shih* and *tz'u* respectively. Though they have not attained a penetrating vision of life, yet with their strength, fortitude and sense of mission, they have indeed striven to do their best generations after their predecessors, and to stem the raging tide of the day.

Su likes to use Buddhist expressions in his poems, but he is not a true Buddhist. Lines such as:

> *The running brook is Buddha's tongue,*　　　　溪聲便是廣長舌
> *Isn't the mountain view one's pure self!*　　　　山色豈非清淨身

and,

> *With two hands I try to cover all the water in the*　　兩手欲遮瓶裏水
> 　　*bottle,*

have nothing to do with Zen Buddhism and deserve nothing better than a blow from the master. They may suggest a twinkling of understanding but they are not true Zen enlightenment. Su's imitative Zen phrases are all too superficial. Lines found in the *tz'u Nan-ko tzu* 南歌子 (which runs: whose music are you singing? . . .) and *Ju meng ling* 如夢令 (written beneath Yung-hsi's Pagoda in Ssu Chou) may not be clichés but are nevertheless imitative. My younger brother Liu-chi 六吉 thinks that these lines from the poet's own *shih* "On visiting the Gold Mountain Monastery", gave the most vivid picture of Su in this respect:

> *It was neither a ghost nor a human.*   恨然歸臥心莫識
> *In grief I lay on my way home,*   非鬼非人定何物
> *Puzzling over its true identity.*

Indeed, Su's poetry is neither ghostly nor human. There is a touch of the immortal spirit in many of his descriptive phrases. Lines such as: "Competing to hold on to the cold branch, they (the birds) gaze at the jade pistils . . ." (*Nan-hsiang tzu* 南鄉子) and "Coming down from high above . . ." (*Mu-lan-hua* 木蘭花) all seem to be free from the dust of the world and abstain from man's food. Many other lines depicting scenery are filled with a celestial spirit, far removed from Zen. I used to be fond of the following lines, thinking that they suggest a touch of sudden enlightenment:

> *In gentle despair I rise from bed,*   推枕惘然不見
> *In front of me the river in vast expanse,*   但空江月明千里
> *And a moon that shines over a thousand miles.*   憂喜相尋
>   風雨過
> *Joy and despair come in turn;*   一江春綠
> *After the storm,*
> *A stretch of spring green.*

Now I think that only the first example is close to Zen; the second is merely good, clever *tz'u*, having nothing to do with Zen. Su is after all closer to the Taoist than to the Buddhist. His works are always ethereal, with a lingering grace that exerts a salutary influence on the reader. What, you may ask, is the difference between the two, since they both renounce the world? The main difference is: in Zen, one transcends through living and stoic acceptance of life; in Taoism, one simply runs away from life and sufferings. The Taoist wants a long life; the Buddhist, non-existence. One is motivated by greed, the other, reconciled through self-denial.

Su Shih is critical of Liu Yung 柳永 as a poet, but he says that, in terms of loftiness, Liu's *Pa-sheng kan-chou* 八聲甘州, can rival the works of T'ang poets. From this judgment, one can deduce what Su himself is striving after. In *Pa-sheng kan-chou*, Liu rises above all feelings of sadness and joy through his lofty contemplation in much the same way as Su does in many of his *tz'u*. Lines such as "After the frost, the vastness of the long Huai River is lost" (*Mu-lan-hua*) and "Without wind the flowers fall on their own" *(Tieh lien hua)* are good examples. The first stanza of *Yung-yü le* is, on the other hand, a change from the sober and vigorous to the gentle and delicate, from the rugged to the smooth and harmonious. Hsin Ch'i-chi has these few lines in his *tz'u Ch'ing-yü-an* 青玉案

> *A hundred, a thousand times I search for the sight*   衆裏尋他千百度
>   *of her among the crowd.*

> *Suddenly, as I turn my head,*   驀然回首
> *There she is,*   那人卻在
> *Under the dim and fading light!*   燈火闌珊處

They have an intensity arising from the mingling of joy and sadness. They are, therefore, lines written by one who has come to grips with the world. Su, on the other hand, tends to rise above joy and sadness. Consequently, he is inclined to renounce the world. That being the main difference between the two poets, how can the term *hao-ch'i* 豪氣 (heroic spirit) be justified?

周邦彥詞

Nine Tz'u *by Chou Pang-yen*

Translated by Julie Landau

To the Tune of *Tieh lien hua*

Leaving Early

A moon so bright the crows are restless
Night's end drips through the clepsydra
Someone already draws water from the well—
The call to rise: two bright eyes
Shed tears that blossom on the pillow, cold and
    red

Hands touch, a frosty wind blows the shadow of
    her hair,
How can he think of going?
Words of parting pain the ear.
Above the stairs, the handle of the Dipper passes
    the rail,
Out in cold dew, far away, cocks call, and call

蝶戀花
秋思

月皎驚烏栖不定
更漏將殘
轆轤牽金井
喚起兩眸清炯炯
淚花落枕紅棉冷

執手霜風吹鬢影
去意徊徨
別語愁難聽
樓上闌干橫斗柄
露寒人遠雞相應

177

To the Tune of *Su Mu Che*

Burning gharu wood
Dispels the summer dampness,
Birds and sparrows greet the day
Chattering and peeping about the eaves at dawn.
Early sun dries last nights rain from leaves
Floating in clear rounds on the water.
The lotus, one by one, nod in the wind

I don't belong here,
When can I go
Home to Wu Men?
I have stayed on in the capital so long,
Would May fishermen even remember me
If a small oar and a light boat
Took me in dreams, back to the lotus pond?

蘇幕遮

燎沈香
消溽暑
鳥雀呼晴
侵曉窺簷語
葉上初陽乾宿雨
水面清圓
一一風荷舉

故鄉遙
何日去
家住吳門
久作長安旅
五月漁郎相憶否
小楫輕舟
夢入芙蓉浦

蘇幕遮
燎沈香
消溽暑
鳥雀呼晴
侵曉窺簷語
葉上初陽乾宿雨
水面清圓
一一風荷舉
故鄉遙
何日去
家住吳門
久作長安旅
五月漁郎相憶否
小楫輕舟
夢入芙蓉浦

To the Tune of *Yeh yu kung*

Falling leaves, the sunset on the river
Rippling for a thousand miles.
On the bridge, harsh winds pierce my eyes
I linger,
The day fades,
Lamps are lit along the streets

In the cold under my window in the old house
I hear each leaf that falls from the Wu Tung by the
    well.
My quilt won't hold me, alone, I can't stay still—
Who would know
That for her
I write this?

夜遊宮

葉下斜陽照水
捲輕浪
沈沈千里
橋上酸風射眸子
立多時
看黃昏
燈火市

古屋寒窗底
聽幾片
井桐飛墜
不戀單衾再三起
有誰知
爲蕭娘
書一紙

満庭芳

夏景

To the Tune of *Man-t'ing fang*

Written on a Summer Day on
No-thought Hill in Li Shui

Wind has matured the infant oriole
Rain fattened plums
At noon the shade of trees is true and round
On low ground near the hills
Damp clothes need incense smoke to dry
Quietly, I watch birds frolic,
Beyond the little bridge, new green splashes
I linger against the rail,
Yellow reeds, Bitter Bamboo—[1]
Would I could drift in the boat at Chiu-chiang

風老鶯雛
雨肥梅子
午陰嘉樹清圓
地卑山近
衣潤費鑪煙
人靜烏鳶自樂
小橋外
新綠濺濺
凭欄久
黃蘆苦竹
擬泛九江船

[1] This line quotes from Po Chü-i's *P'i P'a* Song, and the following line alludes to the same poem.

容我醉時眠
先安簟枕
歌筵畔
急管繁絃
不堪聽
顯頹江南倦客
長近尊前
且莫思身外
來寄修椽
飄流瀚海
年：如社燕

Year in year out, like the punctual swallow
I go back and forth over the vast desert
Lodging on long rafters—
Why look beyond the moment?
I'll keep close to the wine.
Wretched, spent, a stranger from the south,
I hate the sound of the fast pipes and jumbled
    strings,
Wide of both feast and song
I'll spread my mat and pillow
Then I can sleep, when drunk

年年
如社燕
飄流瀚海
來寄修椽
且莫思身外
長近尊前
顦頓江南倦客
不堪聽
急管繁絃
歌筵畔
先安簟枕
容我醉時眠

滿庭芳 夏景

風老鶯雛
雨肥梅子
午陰嘉對清圓
地卑山近
衣潤費爐煙
人靜烏鳶自樂
小橋外
新綠濺濺
憑欄久
黃蘆苦竹
擬泛九江船

To the Tune of *Chieh yü hua*

Lantern Festival

Candles flare and melt in the wind
Staining the paper lotus with red dew,
Market lanterns dazzle one another
Moonlight cascades over tiled roofs
Light clouds scatter
The bright moon goddess longs to join
Lovely girls in light dresses
Their waists slender as those of Ch'u.
Flutes and drums clamor for attention—
Peoples' shadows blend in disarray—
The scent of musk drifts, lingers, everywhere

解語花

元宵

風銷焰蠟
露浥烘爐
花市光相射
桂華流瓦
纖雲散
耿耿素娥欲下
衣裳淡雅
看楚女
纖腰一把
簫鼓喧
人影參差
滿路飄香麝

因念都城放夜
望千門如畫
嬉笑游冶
鈿車羅帕
相逢處
自有暗塵隨馬
年光是也
唯只見
舊情衰謝
清漏移
飛蓋歸來
從舞休歌罷

It brings back nights at the capital, when, curfew
    waived,
Lights on a thousand gates turned night to day,
Changed streets into a pleasure ground—
The wave of a silk handkerchief from a gilded
    carriage
And where we met
Horses kicked up dark dust—
This year's festival is as bright,
Only love has faded.
Time moves on,
Coaches, calash flying, come again,
Let them pass, let the dance end, for me the songs
    are over

因念都城放夜
望千門如畫
嬉笑游冶
鈿車羅帕
相逢處
自有暗塵隨馬
年光是也
唯只見
舊情衰謝
清漏移
飛蓋歸來
從舞休歌罷

解語花 元宵
風銷焰蠟
露浥烘爐
花市光相射
桂華流瓦
纖雲散
耿耿素娥欲下
衣裳淡雅
看楚女
纖腰一把
簫鼓喧
人影參差
滿路飄香麝

To the Tune of *Yü mei-jen*

Fences of small farms are scattered along the wind-
    ing path
Trees emerge from mist—day dawns.
In the cold, mountain peaks float as if on nothing
At the first bell from the wilderness, a lone skiff
    sets sail

I bundle up, urge the horse on to find a post
    station
Only wine will ease my sorrow
Ducks asleep in the rushes of a pond by the slope,
Startled by my passing, fly up, only to find each-
    other again

虞美人

疏籬曲徑田家小
雲樹開清曉
天寒山色有無中
野外一聲鐘起
送孤蓬

添衣策馬尋亭堠
愁抱惟宜酒
菰蒲睡鴨占陂塘
縱被行人驚散
又成雙

To the Tune of *P'u-sa man*

Plum Blossoms in the Snow

The silver river has three thousand bends
Wild ducks bathe in it; cranes fly above the pure
    green waves
But where is the boat bringing him back,
Now the evening glow is on the tower by the river?

Heaven, jealous of the rioting plum blossoms,
Heaps the branches with snow.
Deep within the yard, she rolls up the shade,
Overcome with pity for one freezing on the river

菩薩蠻
梅雪

銀河宛轉三千曲
浴鳧飛鷺澄波綠
何處是歸舟
夕陽江上樓

天憎梅浪發
故下封枝雪
深院捲簾看
應憐江上寒

應憐江上寒
深院捲簾看
故下封枝雪
天憎梅浪發
夕陽江上樓
何處是歸舟
浴鳧飛鷺澄波綠
銀河宛轉三千曲
菩薩蠻
梅雪

To the Tune of *Lan-ling wang*

Willows

Rows of willows neatly shade the bank
Strand by strand they green the mist
Along the Sui Dykes—I know them all already,
Branches trailing to the water, catkins blowing—
    hue and cast of partings
When I come, I climb the hills to gaze toward
    home—
Who knows what it is to be a weary stranger in the
    capital,
On the road of post stations
Year in, year out?
The willow strands I've broken measure out a
    thousand feet

蘭陵王
柳

柳陰直
煙裏絲絲弄碧
隋堤上
曾見幾番
拂水飄綿送行色
登臨望故國
誰識
京華倦客
長亭路
年去歲來
應折柔條過千尺

梨花榆火催寒食
愁一箭風快
半篙波暖
回頭迢遞便數驛
望人在天北

悽惻
恨堆積
漸別浦縈回
津堠岑寂
斜陽冉冉春無極
念月榭攜手
露橋聞笛
沈思前事
似夢裏
淚暗滴

Had I time I'd search for traces of the past
But once again, wine and sad music speed me on
Lanterns light the farewell dinner
Pear blossoms and elm fires press toward the Day
    of Cold Hearths—
I hate the wind that carries me faster
As the boat poles the warm waves
Several stations have raced by before I turn
And see you at the far edge of heaven

Chill misery
Grief piled on grief
Gradually, the churning of the water where we
    parted
At the pier grows quiet,
Reluctantly, the sun sets on a boundless spring
I remember how we held hands by the moonlit
    pavilion
And listened to a flute at a dew covered bridge.
Lost in the past
Now like a dream
My tears fall stealthily.

閒尋舊蹤跡
又酒趁哀絃
燈照離席
梨花楡火催寒食
愁一箭風快
半篙波暖
回頭迢遞便數驛
望人在天北

悽惻
恨堆積
漸別浦縈回
津堠岑寂
斜陽冉冉春無極
念月榭攜手
露橋聞笛
沈思前事
似夢裏
淚暗滴

蘭陵王　柳

柳陰直
煙裏絲絲弄碧
隋堤上
曾見幾番
拂水飄綿送行色
登臨望故國
誰識
京華倦客
長亭路
年來歲去
應折柔條過千尺

閒尋舊蹤跡
又酒趁哀絃
燈照離席

To the Tune of *Liu-ch'ou*

Written After the Roses Faded

Time to wear light clothes again, taste wine
How I regret the days and nights I've thrown away!
If only spring had stayed a little
And not brushed past
Now suddenly there's nothing left
Ask where the flowers are:
Last night brought wind and rain . . .
Those whose beauty toppled kings are buried with
    Ch'u Palace
But where each filigree hairpin fell there is a
    fragrant remnant—
Disheveling the peach path,
Fluttering along a lane of willows . . .
Who will pity one who pines for them?
Only matchmaking bees and butterfly messengers
That knock from time to time at my window.

六醜
落花

正單衣試酒
恨客裏
光陰虛擲
願春暫留
春歸如過翼
一去無跡
爲問花何在
夜來風雨
葬楚宮傾國
釵鈿墮處遺香澤
亂點桃蹊
輕翻柳陌
多情爲誰追惜
但蜂媒蝶使
時叩窗隔

東園岑寂
漸蒙籠暗碧
靜遶珍叢底
成歎息
長條故惹行客
似牽衣待話
別情無極
殘英小
強簪巾幘
終不似一朵
釵頭顫裊
向人敧側
漂流處
莫趁潮汐
恐斷紅尚有相思字
何由見得

The east garden is quiet
Gradually thick with green
That stealthily coiled beneath the sprays
I sigh for
A long shoot catches as I pass
Pulls at my clothes as if about to speak
The sorrow of parting never ends
The faded flower is nothing
Better pin it to my turban
Where it will no longer seem
A blossom trembling in your hair
As it leans toward me
Petals drift everywhere—oh, do not drift away
    with the tides—
Your broken red may still have words of love
For me to see!

東園岑寂
漸蒙籠暗碧
靜遶珍叢底
成歎息
長條故惹行客
似牽衣待話
別情無極
殘英小
強簪巾幘
終不似一朶
釵頭顫裊
向人欹側
漂流處
莫趁潮汐
恐斷紅
尚有相思字
何由見得

六醜 落花

正單衣試酒
恨客裏光陰虛擲
願春暫留
春歸如過翼
一去無跡
為問花何在
夜來風雨
葬楚宮傾國
釵鈿墮處遺香澤
亂點桃蹊
輕翻柳陌
多情更誰追惜
但蜂媒蝶使
時叩窗隔

Appreciations of Tz'u

By **Yü P'ing-po**

Translated by **Ying-hsiung Chou** and **Winnie Lai-fong Leung**

From *Tu-tz'u ou-te* 讀詞偶得 (Random Notes on Reading *Tz'u*)

To the Tune of *P'u-sa man*

菩薩蠻

Hillock upon hillock
Golden sunlight flickering,
Her cloud-hair about to drift over
Her fragrant snow-white cheeks.
Reluctantly, she paints her moth-eyebrows,
Slowly, she dallies with her make-up;

小山重疊金明滅
鬢雲欲度香腮雪
嬾起畫蛾眉
弄妝梳洗遲

With mirrors front and back
She studies the flowers.
Images of her face and flowers
Set off each other in the mirrors,
On her freshly-ironed silk vest
Golden partridges in pairs.

照花前後鏡
花面交相映
新貼繡羅襦
雙雙金鷓鴣

Wen T'ing-yün 溫庭筠 (813?-879)

Exegesis

The phrase *"hsiao-shan"* 小山 (hillock) refers to the golden screen. This interpretation is supported by the line *"chen-shang p'ing-shan yen"* 枕上屏山掩 (above the pillows is the enfolding screen) from another of his poems. The three words *"chin-ming-mieh"* 金明滅 (golden sunlight flickering) depict the morning sunlight reflected on the painted screen. The combined descriptions of sunlight and a beautiful woman had appeared in such ancient poems as *"Tung-fang-chih-jih"* 東方之日 (The Sun of the East) of *Shih-ching* 詩經 (The Book of Songs) and *"Shen-nü fu"* 神女賦 (The Rhymeprose on the Immortal Lady) of *Ch'u-tz'u* 楚辭 (The Songs of Ch'u) as well as in numerous other later literary works. This line starts with the description of a scene and is saturated with bright colors.

190

Line 2 describes the heroine's appearance before she has risen. In ancient times, the screen was placed beside the bed. The phrase *"pin-yün"* 鬢雲 which refers to her disheveled hair generates the descriptions of the various stages in doing her make-up. Although the phrase *"yü-tu"* 欲度 (about to drift over) appears difficult to explain, it is extraordinary in effect. If this line was changed to *"pin-yün yü-yen"* 鬢雲欲掩 (cloud-hair about to cover) its meaning would be more straightforward and clear, but the poetic effect would be greatly weakened. This line depicts not just a beautiful lady on a fair day but in a gentle breeze on a fair day. The essence of this line lies in the two words *"yü-tu"*. Though a bit obscure, they are not unintelligible.

The central idea of the poem is in lines 3 and 4. The words *"lan"* 嬾 (lazy) and *"ch'ih"* 遲 late are the key words. In describing love, the poet begins with what is intangible, and attains the effect of great clarity and elegance. Here, the theme of love is implied through the heroine's reluctance to rise and begin her make-up. The word *"nung"* 弄 (to dally with) in the phrase *"nung-chuang"* 弄妝 (to dally with make-up) is striking because it hints at the twists and turns in her mood and hence heighten the refined and gentle qualities of the poem.

The word *"chuang"* 妝 in line 4 leads into the second stanza. I have used a semicolon to indicate the stanzaic division instead of a full stop. This poem follows a single linear structure. The focus of the description shifts from the scene to the woman. The actions of the heroine are presented in succession: from lying in bed to getting up, from washing to combing her hair, from putting flowers on her hair to looking into the mirror and finally to changing her clothes. These seem to be random descriptions but in fact they are tightly interwoven.

Wen, by focusing on the descriptions of the heroine's make-up process, actually succeeds in his real aim of describing love. This shows his superb poetic technique. In order to avoid belabouring the process of making herself up and hence losing the sense of proportion, he ends the poem with the line *"shuang-shuang chin-che-ku"* 雙雙金鷓鴣 (golden partridges in pairs). This line hints at love but on the surface it is still about her appearance. I think this arrangement is similar to the one used in the first half of the first act in the drama *"Huan-hun-chi"* 還魂記 (The Record of the Returning Soul).

To the Tune of *P'u-sa man*   菩薩蠻

Porcelain pillow inside the crystal curtain,   水精簾裏頗黎枕
Warm and fragrant mandarin-duck brocade   暖香惹夢鴛鴦錦
*   provokes dreams.*   江上柳如煙
Misty willows line the riverside,   雁飛殘月天
Wild geese flying across the fading-moon sky.

Lotus thread tinted with light autumn hues,   藕絲秋色淺
Colorful streamers curvedly trimmed,   人勝參差翦
                                                                 雙鬢隔香紅
                                                                 玉釵頭上風

> *Fragrant flowers separate the locks on her*
> *temples,*
> *Jade pins wavering in the breeze.*

Wen T'ing-yün

Exegesis

This poem begins with the greatest crystalline clarity that one could possibly imagine. The scene described in Li Shang-yin 李商隱 (813-858)'s line *"shui-ching t'an shang hu-p'o chen"* 水精簟上琥珀枕 (On the crystal mattress lies the amber pillow) bears some resemblances. One should, however, not take them too literally. Semantically, the phrase *"yüan-yang-chin"* 鴛鴦錦 (mandarin-duck brocade) apparently refers to the bed covers and the like. In poetry, as a rule however, it is not necessary to mention the object explicitly. The warmth and fragrance cause the heroine to dream, and the verb used here *"je"* 惹 (to provoke) is extraordinary. The third and fourth lines which abruptly unveil a grand vista are much quoted lines. Initially, I was inclined toward following the interpretation formerly proposed which saw "What follows the line *'chiang-shang . . . '* as a brief description of the dream". But thanks to a friend's suggestion, I realised that such an interpretation left room for dissent. After careful consideration I am now convinced that it is a mistake. Wen T'ing-yün's *tz'u* are characterized by the juxtaposition of congruous images which automatically become assimilated, and the reader is left to provide his own interpretation, without having to search for the relationships between images for these already exist by the mere fact of juxtaposition. . . .

Without doubt, these two lines are marvellous. If cast in the *shih* form they completely conform to the *shih* prosody in term of tonal pattern and syntax. Nonetheless, they would suffer from languorousness, and this example appropriately demonstrates the basic difference in nature between *shih* and *tz'u*. . . .

The second stanza presents a scene of the heroine after she has got dressed. That the phrase *"ou-ssu"* 藕絲 (lotus threads) refers to her garment is borne out by the lines in Wen's poem to the tune *Kuei-kuo yao* 歸國謠 (Song of Returning to the Homeland) which runs,

> *Dancing skirt hangs limply as breeze ceases,*   舞衣無力風斂
> *Lotus threads tinted with autumn hues.*   藕絲秋色染

The phrase *"jen-sheng"* 人勝 refers to her hair ornament. The custom of trimming multi-coloured silk and attaching it to a hairpin on the seventh day of the Chinese new year was recorded in *Ching-Ch'u sui-shih chi* 荊楚歲時記 (The Record of Yearly Observances of the Ching-Ch'u Area). The fact that this image also appears in the lines

> Her jade pin wavering in the breeze,   玉釵風不定
> Her lonely steps moving back and forth.   香步獨裴回

in the poem *Yung ch'un fan* 詠春幡 (On the Spring Streamers) in the third section of his poetry collection shows that it is one of his favorite images. *"Fan"* and *"sheng"* 幡勝 refer to the same type of ornament. The line, "Fragrant flowers separate the locks on her temples" is a continuation of the previous line. The word *"ke"* 隔 (to separate) effectively describes the picturesque beauty of the flowers pinned on her hair. *"Hsiang-hung"* 香紅 (fragrant red) refers to the flowers. The final line is especially skilful because the word *"feng"* 風 (breeze) vividly brings out the entire scene. Not only is the flower fragrance drifting around her hair, but also the hairpins and colorful streamers are charmingly wavering in the gentle breeze. . . .

The second stanza ostensibly appears somewhat unconnected to the first, but a close examination shows that they are related: *"hsiang-hung"* 香紅 (fragrant red) echoes *"nuan-hsiang"* 暖香 (warm and fragrant) and *"feng"* (breeze) corresponds to lines 3 and 4. But, these are merely formal connections with which we need not concern ourselves. What is significant is that this rhythmic flow conveys a sense of the passage of time which arouses deeper feelings with its indescribable sorrow. . . . *"Jen-sheng"* is definitely not a space-filler but matches perfectly the line *"yen-fei ts'an-yüeh-t'ien"* 雁飛殘月天 (Wild geese flying across the fading-moon sky). The scene portrayed in this line is similar to the one in Hsüeh Tao-heng 薛道衡 (540-609)'s *Jen-jih shih* 人日詩 (Poem on the Seventh day of the New Year) which runs

> He left for home after the departure of the   人歸落雁後
>   wild geese,   思發在花前
> My thought of him welled up before the
>   blossoming of the flowers.

Wen's poem not only portrays a sense of the swift passing of youth, but also effortlessly evokes the lament of a woman in her secluded chamber over a distant lover. Like a luxuriant embroidery or a finely orchestrated score, this poem was rich in sensual appeal. This implicit way of describing sorrow is typical of the *tz'u* of the T'ang and the Five Dynasties. After the Southern T'ang, even as *tz'u* became more popular, its old spirit gradually disappeared and the elevated style of Wen T'ing-yün and Wei Chuang 韋莊 (836-910) was not to be seen again.

From Ch'ing-chen tz'u shih 清眞詞釋 (Notes on Ch'ing-chen Tz'u)

> To the Tune of *Tieh lien hua*   **蝶戀花**
>
> *The moon so bright the alarmed crows*   月皎驚烏栖不定
>   *became restless,*   更漏將殘

While the night was running out through the
*   water clock,*
A pulley working up and down the golden
*   well.*
Wakened by the sound, she opened a pair of
*   glittering eyes,*
Whose dewy tears had soaked the pillow, wet
*   and cold.*

轆轤牽金井
喚起兩眸清炯炯
淚花落枕紅綿泠

執手霜風吹鬢影
去意徊徨
別語愁難聽
樓上闌干橫斗柄
露寒人遠雞相應

Hands locked; frosty winds against shadowy
*   sideburns.*
How reluctant to leave!
How sad the parting words!
But upstairs the Dipper's handle had since
*   crossed the rail.*
A man out in cold dew, and cocks' calls back
*   and forth.*

Chou Pang-yen, styled name
Ch'ing-chen (1056-1121)

The first three lines in stanza 1 describe what the woman in bed heard, who is about to be separated from her beloved, and through this depict the break of dawn. One must attribute the success of the section to the exclusively auditory nature of the experience. (The bright moon is merely the cause of the crows becoming restless; the emphasis is on the birds' calls, not the moon-light.) What the woman hears in bed also paves the way for the fourth line about "the glittering eyes." The crows' calls, the almost dripped dry water clock and the pulley are all sounds which interrupt the woman's dream. Lines 4 and 5 in fact deal with the sorrows of separation felt by the woman in bed. While line 4 visualizes to the last detail her sadness and apprehension before her man's departure—a line which fully exemplifies Chou Pang-yen's fine artistry in delineating the sorrows of separation. In terms of physical actions, the line describes the woman being unexpectedly awakened by the noises. Theoretically her eyes should be sleepy, but here they are described as glittering which shows how observant the poet is of details. It is a natural physiological phenomenon to wake up with sleepy eyes—if one is unexpectedly awakened after a good night's sleep, that is. But, of course, it would have been a minor flaw on the part of the poet if he had described a woman about to be separated from her lover in the same way. Chou's *Tsao mei fang* 早梅芳 may shed some light on this particular line:

As I was being disturbed in my dream,
Dawn was already here at the door.

正魂驚夢怯
門外已知曉

By dealing with the immediate what lies beyond the immediate is also conveyed. Through his concrete description of the woman lying in bed in the early morning, the poet actually captures all shades of sadness throughout the night. In one single line, the sorrow of the woman seems to be on the verge of surfacing with full force. The next line about the dewy tears deals with the separation on a different level and does not deal with the same thing as the previous line. The reader's doubt about this can be expelled by the use of the word "cold". The pillow here actually refers to the cotton stuffing inside. Normally warm tears, however profuse they may be, can at most moisten the pillow case, without saturating the cotton stuffing inside, let alone turning the entire pillow cold. Now that it is said to be cold, the extent of the copious tears and the heart-breaking sorrow at the moment of separation can be imagined. Line 4 therefore describes the scene when the woman abruptly wakes up, while line 5 follows it up by delineating her action before rising. Two distinct phases of narrative progression are implied. The two lines, moreover, are impregnated with all shades of feelings aroused by the forthcoming separation. Anyone treating the two lines as an undifferentiated unit disqualifies himself as a competent reader. At this point the woman and her lover are forced to leave the bed, no matter how reluctant they may be, for the man has to be on his way soon. It is a moment which lends itself to further treatment in stanza 2. Lines 6, 7 and 8 deal with what happens after they have risen by moving the locale from the room to the yard. The last two lines of the stanza deals on the other hand, with what happens after leave-taking, and the locale shifts from the steps to the road outside. Line 9 is in a rather leisurely manner, while line 10 is an extremely swift movement. So the impression we get in the first three lines of the second stanza is the reluctance before the departure, while the last two lines have to do with the hastiness of the separation. The tone and feeling are intertwined, while its content and form are both taken care of. As for the last two lines, one describes the deserted boudoir, the other the vast wilderness. In one sweeping treatment the two worlds are conjoined. There is ingrained in it the longing of the one left behind in the empty room for her beloved abroad, which cannot be fully expressed through language. Wen T'ing-yün's *Keng-lou tzu* 更漏子 concludes with "one cock's call from the village." Here the number of the fowl is multiplied, which shows how skilful Chou Pang-yen can be in applying magic touches to his predecessor's marvellous compositions, and in bringing to the surface the flavour beyond the ordinary flavour. All those discussions on the distinctions between creativity and imitation only serve to reflect the ignorance of the critics.

To the Tune of *So ch'uang han*   瑣窗寒

Crows caw amidst the willows in the dark.   暗柳啼鴉
In a light gown I linger.   單衣竚立
The little curtain at the vermillion door   小簾朱戶

Together with purple t'ung *flowers quietly*
         lock   桐花半畝
The doleful rain in the courtyard.   靜鎖一庭愁雨
It splashes on empty stairs incessantly   灑空階夜闌未休
Throughout the night.   故人剪燭西窗語
Chatting with my friend by the west window   似楚江暝宿
And trimming the candlewick,   風燈零亂
I recall my sojourn on the River Ch'u   少年羈旅
In the evening amidst flickering lights
During my youthful travels.   遲暮
                                                         嬉游處
Now I am old,   正店舍無煙
In the Forbidden City,   禁城百五
Where I have my pleasure trip,   旗亭喚酒
No smoke rises from chimneys of inns,   付與高陽儔侶
For it is Cold-food Festival.   想東園桃李自春
In the taverns I order wine,   小脣秀靨今在否
Offering it to my drinking companions.   到歸時定有殘英
Peaches and plums must be blooming in the   待客攜樽俎
         East Garden.
But, is the fair one
With her dainty lips and beautiful dimples
         still there?
By the time I return home
There will certainly be withered petals
Waiting for the visitor who comes with a
         bottle of wine.

Old Exegesis

Chou Chih-an 周止庵 (Chou Chi 周濟, 1781-1839) praises lines 8, 9 and 10 (The line numbers refer to the original Chinese text) for being "outstanding and extraordinary". Hsia Jun-an 夏閏庵 (Hsia Sun-t'ung 夏孫桐) comments that "emotion being interfused with scenery, these lines are not superficial" (These two comments are correct, though Chou's comment seems to be too brief. Hsia's comment is especially to the point. If we compare this poem to the one set to the tune *Jui-lung yin* 瑞龍吟 (Auspicious Dragon Sings) we will see that in the former the emotion is revealed through scene whereas in the latter, the scene is revealed through emotion.)

Exegesis

Line 1 sets the background for the approaching rain in late spring. Lines 2 and 3 introduce the human setting. Lines 4 and 5 depict the scene when the rain starts. The following lines go from the night rain to future talk about the rain and then the reminiscence of the poet's sad feelings of his over-extended journeys in Ch'u. Every line unveils an imaginary scene and yet unfolds a deeper level of meaning. Up to line 6, the scene described is still a concrete one but it becomes illusory in line 7 with the allusion to Li Shang-yin's lines,

> *When shall we be able to trim the candle*   何當共剪西窗燭
>   *together beside the west window,*   卻話巴山夜雨時
> *While talking about this rainy night on the*
>   *Pa Mountain?*

Ch'en Yüan-lung 陳元龍 (1652-1736) had completely missed Chou's point when he quoted from Wen T'ing-yün's lines

> *She turns her head, smiles and talks to the*   回鸞笑話西窗客
>   *guest by the west window.*

The scene revealed in Li's poem is a mixture of the illusory and the naturalistic. If we render this line in prose, it becomes, "How I wish I could have my old friend here to trim the candle and talk with me by the west window?" which is not a description of an actual scene. Lines 8, 9 and 10 depict an illusion within an illusion. Is this why Chou Chi praises them for being "outstanding and extraordinary"? At that time the poet was leading a solitary life in his late years; how could it be possible for him to be talking about the past with his love by the west window? As his longing to stay with his love is already an illusion, his thoughts suddenly shift from his love to his earlier over-extended journeys. To elucidate this situation, Ch'en quoted from Tu Fu's lines

> *As the wind begins to blow, the spring lamp-*   風起春燈亂
>   *lights flicker;*   江鳴夜雨懸
> *As the rain starts falling, the river roars.*

Both deal with over-extended journeys, and yet the differences between that undertaken during one's youth and that made in one's old age are obvious. The first stanza, despite its seemingly unrelated lines, smoothly flows into the second. On the surface, the structure appears loose, but, in fact, it is tight and inevitable. Such a divine technique surely deserves appreciative savouring on the part of the reader.

The second stanza is quite straightforward. The parallelism between the phrases *"ch'ih-mu"* 遲暮 (late years) here and *"shao-nien"* 少年 (youth) exemplifies Chou's masterful way of opening and ending a stanza. While the poem goes this way and that in the first half, with the appearance of the phrase "ch'ih-mu" the theme of the poem comes to the foreground. The following lines bring up the Han-shih 寒食 (Cold-food) Festival in a natural manner. The unobstructed flow from line 17 to the end of the poem exemplifies Chou's typical style. These lines which constitute the core of the poem comment on something to the effect that during his late years there may be withered flowers to keep him company while drinking, but where is she, the one with dainty lips and beautiful dimples? The two words *"fou"* 否 (no) and *"ting"* 定 (will be) are half intentionally and half unintentionally used in two consecutive lines. The word "ting" has the connotations of "perhaps" or "ought to". It is, however, stronger in implication and lies halfway between the abstract and the concrete. One example can be seen in Tu Fu's lines,

> *I have heard that you are staying in a monas-* 聞汝依山寺
>   *tery by a hill,*   杭州定越州
> *Is it in Hang-chou or Yüeh-chou?*

In commenting on the poem *Jui-lung yin* Chou Chi says, "It is merely a variation on the poem 'Beach Blossom and Human Face' ". This song is a similar case in that Chou Pang-yen borrows from lines used before for re-creations. Those who attack him as "lacking in creativity" simply don't understand him.

  The rain scene vividly described in the first stanza is not mentioned again in the second. What follows line 13 focuses on the poet's low spirit and his lack of interest in the approaching festival, thus having nothing to do with descriptions. A further reference to the rain is therefore not called for. The Chi-ku-ke 汲古閣 edition gives the title *"Han-shih"* (Cold-food Festival). What is described in the first stanza must be an actual scene of rain. According to the *Ching-ch'u sui-shih-chi* (The Records of Yearly Observances of the Ching Ch'u Area) "One hundred and five days after the winter solstice there will be fierce winds and heavy rain. That day is what is called the Cold-food Festival." Hence, the meaning of the tune title still is appropriately rendered in the descriptive passage.

陸游詞

Ten Tz'u by Lu Yu

Translated by James P. Rice

訴衷情

當年萬里覓封侯

匹馬戍梁州

關河夢斷何處

塵暗舊貂裘

胡未滅

鬢先秋

淚空流

此生誰料

心在天山

身老滄洲

To the Tune of Su chung-ch'ing

In the past, I travelled
Ten thousand miles in search of glory,
I was stationed at the Liang-chou border.

Where are my broken dreams of
Wilderness passes and rivers?
Dust has darkened my old sable coat.

The Tartars not yet defeated,
My temple hair has turned grey
And tears flowed in vain.

This life,
Who would have predicted?
My heart at Tien Shan frontier
My body in a riverside lodge.

訴衷情

當年萬里覓封侯
匹馬戍梁州
關河夢斷何處
塵暗舊貂裘

胡未滅
鬢先秋
淚空流
此生誰料
心在天山
身老滄洲

夜遊宮　記夢寄師伯渾

雪曉清笳亂起
夢遊處
不知何地
鐵騎無聲望似水
想關河
雁門西
青海際
睡覺寒燈裏
漏聲斷
月斜窗紙
自許封侯在萬里
有誰知
鬢雖殘
心未死

To the Tune of *Yeh yu kung*

Presented to Shih Pai-hun After Recalling a Dream

A snowy dawn—
As the Tartar pipe blares
Starting up here and there,
In my dream I travel to
An unknown place
Where armed cavalry
Without a sound
Move like rivulets of water.

I am reminded of a frontier river—
West of Goose Gate
Or perhaps the border of Ch'inghai.

I awake in the cold light
Of the lamp,
The water clock has stopped,
Moonlight slants through
The paper window.

It is my ambition
To achieve fame ten thousand miles away.

Understand me:
Even though my temples have faded,
My heart still yearns for glory!

夜遊宮
記夢寄師伯渾

雪曉清笳亂起
夢遊處
不知何地
鐵騎無聲望似水
想關河
雁門西
青海際

睡覺寒燈裏
漏聲斷
月斜窗紙
自許封侯在萬里
有誰知
鬢雖殘
心未死

漁家傲 寄仲高

東望山陰何處是
往來一萬三千里
寫得家書空滿紙
流清淚
書回已是明年事

寄語紅橋橋下水
扁舟何日尋兄弟
行徧天涯眞老矣
愁無寐
鬢絲幾縷茶煙裏

To the Tune of *Yü chia ao*

Presented to Cousin Chung Kao

Gazing eastward
Where is my homeland?

Going and coming—
Thirteen thousand miles.

Writing home—
I fill the pages in vain,
Sad tears flow,
A letter in return:
The New Year already past.

I sent the message through the water
Below the Red Bridge:
On a flat boat—
When can I sail to seek you?

Travelling to the edge of the earth
I have become truly old.

Sadness—
No sleep,
Strands of my temple hair
Hanging in the tea's mist.

漁家傲
寄仲高

東望山陰何處是
往來一萬三千里
寫得家書空滿紙
流清淚
書回已是明年事

寄語紅橋橋下水
扁舟何日尋兄弟
行徧天涯眞老矣
愁無寐
鬢絲幾縷茶煙裏

鵲橋仙

華燈縱博
雕鞍馳射
誰記當年豪舉
酒徒一一取封侯
獨去作
江邊漁父

輕舟八尺
低篷三扇
占斷蘋洲煙雨
鏡湖元自屬閒人
又何必
官家賜與

To the Tune of *Ch'ueh-ch'iao hsien*

鵲橋仙

Colored Lanterns—
Indulging in games of chance,
Engraved saddles gallop by
Shooting targets,
Who remembers that year's heroic deeds?

華燈縱博
雕鞍馳射
誰記當年豪舉
酒徒一一取封侯
獨去作
江邊漁父

Those fond of the cup
One by one become office-holders,
Alone, I leave for the riverside
To become a fisherman.

My light boat is eight feet long with
Three lowered awnings,
I relish the duckweed island
All by myself in the misty rain.

輕舟八尺
低篷三扇
占斷蘋洲煙雨
鏡湖元自屬閒人
又何必
官家賜與

Mirror Lake: always
The place for people at leisure,
No need for Imperial favor!

莫莫莫
錦書難託
山盟雖在
閑池閣
桃花落
淚痕紅浥鮫綃透
人空瘦
春如舊

錯錯錯
幾年離索
一懷愁緒
歡情薄
東風惡
滿城春色宮牆柳
黃縢酒
紅酥手

釵頭鳳

To the Tune of *Ch'ai-t'ou-feng*　　釵頭鳳

Pink, moist hands,　　　　　　　　　　紅酥手
Choice yellow wine,　　　　　　　　　　黃縢酒
City full of spring colors—　　　　　　滿城春色宮牆柳
Willows behind the palace wall.

East Wind—malicious,　　　　　　　　東風惡
Chance for love is scarce,　　　　　　　歡情薄
My heart—filled with sadness,　　　　　一懷愁緒
Several years of separation.　　　　　　幾年離索

Wrong, wrong, wrong!　　　　　　　　錯錯錯

Spring the same as before—　　　　　　春如舊
She has grown thin in vain,　　　　　　人空瘦
Tears leave red traces　　　　　　　　淚痕紅浥鮫綃透
On her silk scarf.

Peach blossoms fall,　　　　　　　　　桃花落
Deserted pond and pavilion.　　　　　　閑池閣
Our mountain vow still stands,　　　　山盟雖在
But gilded letters cannot be sent.　　　錦書難託

Never, Never, Never.　　　　　　　　莫莫莫

鵲橋仙 夜聞杜鵑

茅簷人靜
蓬窗燈暗
春晚連江風雨
林鶯巢燕總無聲
但月夜
常啼杜宇

催成清淚
驚殘孤夢
又揀深枝飛去
故山猶自不堪聽
況半世
飄然羈旅

To the Tune of *Ch'ueh-ch'iao hsien*

At Night Hearing the Cuckoo's Cry

Beneath thatched roofs
    Everything is quiet—
Lanterns in rough windows
    Are dimmed,
The wind and rain of late spring
    Spread over the river.

Forest orioles and nesting swallows
    Are silent—
There is constantly the cry
    Of the cuckoo
On this moonlit night.

Quickening the flow of sad tears,
    Cutting short my lonely dream,
It selects a branch
    Deep among the trees
And flies away.

Even at home
    I could not bear to hear it—
Let alone,
    After half a lifetime of drifting!

鵲橋仙

夜聞杜鵑

茅簷人靜
蓬牕燈暗
春晚連江風雨
林鶯巢燕總無聲
但月夜
常啼杜宇

催成清淚
驚殘孤夢
又揀深枝飛去
故山猶自不堪聽
況半世
飄然羈旅

鷓鴣天

家住蒼煙落照間
絲毫塵事不相關
斟殘玉瀣行穿竹
卷罷黃庭臥看山

貪嘯傲
任衰殘
不妨隨處一開顏
元知造物心腸別
老卻英雄似等閒

To the Tune of *Che-ku t'ien*

Retired—
A green mist at sundown,
Not a trace of
Worldly affairs affects me.

Having poured the last of the jade wine,
I thread through the bamboo grove—
Being done with my "Huang Ting",[1]
I lie down and look off at the mountains.

I want to go about whistling, carefree—
Letting myself grow old and feeble,
Nothing to prevent me from offering
A smiling face everywhere I go.

I should have known earlier
The Creator had other intentions—
An old warrior,
I am leaving my past glories behind.

[1] A Taoist text.

鷓鴣天

家住蒼煙落照間
絲毫塵事不相關
斟殘玉瀣行穿竹
卷罷黃庭臥看山

貪嘯傲
任衰殘
不妨隨處一開顏
元知造物心腸別
老卻英雄似等閒

何時又作南來
看重易藥市
元夕燈山
花時萬人樂處
鼓帽垂鞭
閒歌感舊
尚時？
流涕尊前
君記取
封族事在
功名不信由天

To the Tune of *Han kung ch'un*

*Starting from Nan-Cheng coming to Ch'eng-tu
on Official Business*

Feathered arrows, carved bows—
I remember calling my falcon
Atop the ancient rampart,
And killing a tiger on the vast plain.

A Tartar pipe is blowing, evening,
Returning to my tent,
Snow weighed down the green coverlet.

Unrestrained in my drunken writings,
Dragons and snakes
Fly and settle on my colored notepaper.

I was unduly praised for
My poetic feelings and military planning,
For a time, my talents were considered tran-
scendent.

漢宮春

初自南鄭來成都作

羽箭雕弓
憶呼鷹古壘
截虎平川
吹笳暮歸野帳
雪壓青氈
淋漓醉墨
看龍蛇
飛落蠻箋
人誤許
詩情將略
一時才氣超然

漢宮春

羽箭雕弓
憶呼鷹古壘
截虎平川
吹笛暮歸野帳
雪壓青氈
淋漓醉墨
看龍蛇
飛落蠻箋
人誤許
詩情將略
一時才氣超然

Now I am ordered to come south,　　　　　　　何事又作南來
I watch the Double Ninth Herb Fair,　　　　　看重陽藥市
The first full moon, mountains of lanterns.　　元夕燈山

Blossom time—crowds of people, making merry,　花時萬人樂處
Men with caps slant, whips hanging down.　　　攲帽垂鞭

At the sound of a song, I think of the past,　　聞歌感舊
Still from time to time,　　　　　　　　　　　尚時時
My tears flow when I have the bottle beside me.　流涕尊前

Sir, remember:　　　　　　　　　　　　　　　君記取
A scholar could very well become a General,　　封侯事在
I do not believe fame and merit depend on heaven.　功名不信由天

盡道錦里繁華
歎宮閣畫永
柴荊添睡
清愁自醉
念此際
付與何人心事
縱有楚柁吳檣
知何時東逝
空悵望
鱠美菰香
秋風又起

To the Tune of *Shuang t'ou lien*

Presented to Fan Chih-neng, Advisor

White temple hair—
Like scattered stars,
I wake up to my unfulfilled dreams,
Merely a lodger in this world.

Sad and lonely like a sick horse,
Silent and unnoticed,
My heroic fervor of those years—
Completely gone.

I am haunted by dreams of the hills
And streams of home,
Separated by layer upon layer
Of mist and water.

I have travelled ten thousand miles,
Old friends have all dispersed,
Who remembers visits to Green Gate?

雙頭蓮
呈范致能待制

華鬢星星
驚壯志成虛
此身如寄
蕭條病驥
向暗裏
消盡當年豪氣
夢斷故國山川
隔重重煙水
身萬里
舊社凋零
青門俊遊誰記

雙頭蓮　呈范致能待制

華鬢星星，
驚壯志成虛，
此身如寄。
蕭條病驥，
向暗裏、
消盡當年豪氣。
夢斷故國山川，
隔重重、煙水。
身萬里，
舊社凋零，
青門俊遊誰記。

Everyone says Ch'eng-tu is beautiful, but—
In my office full of leisure,
I sigh at how the days seem to last forever,
Spending more time
Sleeping in my hut.

In pure sadness I get drunk,
Thinking of this time—
To whom can I
Tell the feelings of my heart?

Even if my rudder were from Ch'u
And my mast from Wu,
Who knows when I could sail East?

Longing in vain
For fishcakes and the fragrance of Zizania,
Now that the autumn wind is again rising.

盡道錦里繁華
歡官閒畫永
柴荊添睡
清愁自醉
念此際
付與何人心事
縱有楚柁吳檣
知何時東逝
空悵望
鱠美菰香
秋風又起

卜算子詠梅

驛外斷橋邊
寂寞開無主
已是黃昏獨自愁
更著風和雨

無意苦爭春
一任羣芳妒
零落成泥碾作塵
只有香如故

To the Tune of *Pu-suan tzu*

Song of the Plum

卜算子

詠梅

Outside a courier post
    By a broken bridge
        Quiet and lonely,
            It blossoms without a lord:

Already dusk
    Alone and grieving,
        In the wind and rain.

Having no wish to vie with spring
    It allows all flowers
        Their jealousy.

When its blossoms are
    Ground into mud and dust,
        Only the fragrance will be as before.

驛外斷橋邊
寂寞開無主
已是黃昏獨自愁
更著風和雨

無意苦爭春
一任羣芳妒
零落成泥碾作塵
只有香如故

The *Tz'u* Music of Chiang K'uei:
Its Style and Compositional Strategy

By **Liang Ming-yüeh**

Introduction

CHIANG K'UEI 姜夔 (PAI-SHIH), known as one of the *tz'u* masters of all times, stands as the single most studied poet-musician in Chinese history. The majority of the studies on Chiang's *tz'u* songs, the only extant collection of *tz'u-yüeh* (*tz'u* music), concentrated mainly in the areas of notational interpretations, including translation of notational symbols and performance practice, and speech-musical tonal correlations. In spite of their contributions, they are not without discrepancies. This article is an attempt toward making an indepth, analytical study of Chiang K'uei's seventeen *tz'u* songs, including (1) clarification of interpretational differences by major researchers, (2) stylistic understanding of the compositional process (strategy), and (3) application of the theoretical, structural criteria to a creative situation, i.e., musical composition in Chiang K'uei's style. Thus, the primary emphasis of this investigation is addressed to music rather than to poetry, as a first step toward making some concrete and substantial revelations about Chiang's *tz'u* songs.

Chiang K'uei, Poet and Musician (1155-1221)

CHIANG K'UEI—ALSO KNOWN by his courtesy name, Yao Chang 堯章, or more familiarly by his style, Pai-shih tao-ren 白石道人 (Whitestone Taoist)—was born in Poyang 鄱陽 in present-day Kiangsi Province. His father, Chiang O 姜噩, was a district magistrate of Hanyang County, Hupei Province, who died early, leaving Chiang partially to the support of his married sister. As a youth, Chiang had already exhibited a love for and distinguished himself in calligraphy, music, and poetry to the extent that he enjoyed fame as a prodigy among the literati in the Hanyang area where he lived for almost twenty years. Chiang's literary career was later influenced by the poet Hsiao Te-tsao 蕭德藻, who was so impressed with Chiang's literary talents that he later offered his niece in marriage, and brought Chiang to Wushing in Chekiang Province in 1186. Ten years later Chiang moved to Hangchou and lived in the urban cultural centers of the lower Yangtze region for the rest of his life.[1]

[1] For further biographical information see Lin 1978: 48-61.

In spite of his eminence as a man of letters, Chiang never held an official position, partly by circumstance and partly by choice. He led instead the life of a wandering bard, and supported himself by selling his calligraphy and by remaining under the patronage of his gentry friends, such as Chang Chien 張鑑 and Fan Ch'eng-ta 范成大, the latter an established poet in his own right. It was Fan Ch'eng-ta's tune that Chiang set to lyric in Song Four, *Yü-mei-ling* 玉梅令 (Jade Plum Ling). It was also for Fan that Chiang composed a eulogy in Song Nine, *Shih-hu hsien* 石湖仙 (Stone-Lake Immortal). (See Example 3 for the list of songs and their series number.) In between composing poems, selling his calligraphy, and playing the *hsiao* 簫 and *ch'in* 琴 (vertical flute and seven-stringed zither, respectively), Chiang spent his most memorable times as a traveller and guest at the estates of Fan and Chang. Chiang's *tz'u* compositions were undoubtedly performed and appreciated among his patrons' audience, for troops of singing-girls and musicians were readily available at the two estates. According to his own writings, Whitestone Taoist evidently lived a leisurely life—in spite of his somewhat eccentric nature and his negative attitude toward the prevailing socio-political practices. Understandably, Chiang, like other patriots and traditionalists, found contemporary 12th- and 13th-century China to be extremely turbulent. The Northern Sung capital (present-day Kaifeng) was taken over first by the barbarian invaders from Central Asia (1126) and then by the Juchen dynasty which carried out its campaign Southwards until it conquered the entire area north of the Yangtze River. From then on, war posed a constant threat—in fact, Hangchou itself fell in 1276, after Chiang's death. But the Hangchou of Chiang's time was the relocated imperial capital, a huge urban center set amidst the most scenic terrains and was to become the largest and most prosperous city within a few decades. Swarms of people and their noise filled the streets— beggars struggling for daily survival, vendors outshouting each other and selling everything from hot water to toys, foreign traders negotiating in the teahouses while singing girls entertained their guests upstairs, and, of course, the numerous court families each employing wasteful retinues of domestics, entertainers, and other dependents. Such was the situation with which Chiang K'uei had to deal, one which we find reflected in his works. His poetry (both *tz'u* and *shih*) is a constant description of outside sensations and inner feelings: nostalgia for the singing girls, nationalistic sentiments for the occupied northern homeland, guilt of a jobless life, and escape from reality, which was frequently transformed into reminiscences of glory of the past. Through speech and tonal (musical) expressions, these perceptual experiences were further transformed into introspective ones. Although he died in obscurity, Chiang's poetry and songs have captivated generations of poet-musicians and lovers of poetry who empathize in his heart-felt convictions. Readers throughout the ages will undoubtedly continue to find themselves sharing the restrained passion in lines such as the following two from *Shih-hu hsien* (Song Nine):

> *Wealth and fame, like floating clouds—Where*
> *are they now?*
> *I only delight in the green fragrance and red*
> *dancing of the lotus.*

Editions and Studies

CHIANG K'UEI'S POETIC WORKS, consisting of approximately 80 remaining *tz'u* poems, are certainly among the most published in Chinese literature. Some 45 editions, (in manuscript and printed form) have been published, mostly from 1679 till 1909 during the Ch'ing dynasty (Ch'iu 1959: 12-24); but the majority are purely poetic editions, containing no music notations. The earliest extant editions bearing music are three 18th-century works, which fortunately have preserved the seventeen songs, which will be the subject of our discussion. The 1737 manuscript edition is attributed to Chiang Ping-yen 江炳炎 (but first printed in 1913 by Chu Hsiao-tsang 朱孝臧, hence referred to as Chu edition), the 1743 printed edition was by Lu Chung-hui 陸鍾輝 (known as Lu edition), and the 1749 printed edition was by Chang I-shu 張奕樞 (known as Chang edition). All three editions were said to have been derived from a 1350 manuscript in the hands of the Yüan scholar Tao Tsung-i 陶宗儀, although discrepancies exist among them. Supposedly, neither Lu, Chiang, nor Chang worked directly with the Yüan manuscript but, rather, each relied on inter-mediary copies which were declared to have been copied from the Yüan manuscript. At this point in time, we can only speculate whether the differences were the result of inadvertent copying-printing errors or of difficulties in deciphering the notation. After all, the style of notation, *chih-tzu p'u* 指字譜, used in these *tz'u* songs had already been a lost art by the time of the 18th century, editions and scholars from then on have been proffering their interpretations.

Between the late 18th-century to 1967, some sixteen studies on various aspects of Chiang K'uei's *tz'u* music have been advanced. Of these, the most significant examinations dealing with the musical interpretations of the songs were those which appeared after mid-1950's. They include: *Studies of the Composed Songs by Chiang Pai-shih of the Sung Dynasty* 宋姜白石創作歌曲研究 (1957) by Yang Yin-liu and Yin Fa-lu 楊蔭瀏, 陰法魯, *A Comprehensive Examination of the Songs by Whitestone Taoist* 白石道人歌曲通考 (1959) by Ch'iu Ch'iung-sun 丘瓊蓀, "Secular Chinese Songs of the Twelfth Century" (1966) by Laurence Picken, and *Song, Dynasty Musical Sources and Their Interpretation* (1967) by Rulan Chao Pian. The extensive Yang and Yin study is a performance-oriented edition containing transcriptions of the seventeen *tz'u* songs, ten ritual songs and a *ch'in* song. Emphases are also placed on a biographical study of Chiang, a comparative and critical study of the interpretation of side notation 傍譜, transcription into staff notation, and translation of the original text into vernacular Chinese. The transcriptions are made on a largely evaluative and personal basis and historical findings are correlated with contemporary 20th-century understanding. Hence, in my opinion, it is an excellent source for the modern song performer. On the other hand, Ch'iu's work which was formulated about the same time as was the above-mentioned study, concentrates solely on the seventeen *tz'u* songs, and certainly ranks as one of the most thorough studies on the subject to date. It is simultaneously a musicological as well as a literary investigation, which incorporates a historical and systematic approach to the study on editions, notational symbols, and speech and musical tonal correlations, including intonational patterns of the major Chinese dialects. Ch'iu furthers this speech/tonal comparison in Chiang's seventeen songs by presenting it in graphic contours of melodizations which are not only informative but also innovative as compared to other contemporaneous studies. The transcriptions are the result of a critical comparison of the three editions (Lu, Chang, and Chu), with reference to the historiographical material at hand.

The two important English sources, one by Laurence Picken and the other by Rulan Chao Pian have contributed to making Chiang K'uei's songs more accessible to Western scholars and musicians. The "Secular Chinese Songs of the Twelfth Century" by Picken presents a combined Eastern and Western view of the seventeen songs, including English translations of song texts, plus analogies and comparisons drawn broadly from Western, Eastern, and Asian music practices. Picken also cites earlier Chinese *tz'u* studies particularly those of Yang and Yin (1957) and Ch'iu Ch'iung-sun (1959). In his transcriptions, Picken applies the nominal mode theory as found in the Ch'iu study rather than the introduced (outside mode) pitch hypothesis of the Yang and Yin study. However, the emphasis of the Picken study is clearly a rhythmic interpretation, and what he proposes is a reconstruction of songs into a rhythmically balanced and "squared", equal eight-unit framework. As related to Chiang's *tz'u* songs, the book *Song Dynasty Musical Sources and Their Interpretation* by Rulan Chao Pian contains information mostly of a historical and literary nature, and is a useful source for its copious notes and references. Pian's transcriptions are not meant to be practiced as they are; although pitches are given in staff notational format, rhythm is missing, and so are the musical interpretations for the various ornamental signs. (More detailed comments on the above-named studies will be included later as they relate to specific points, and particularly in our musical analysis.)

Notation of the Seventeen *Tz'u* Songs

THE SEVENTEEN *TZ'U* SONGS of Chiang K'uei are notated in an early Sung style called *chih-tzu p'u* "character tablature notation", also familiarly known as *pang p'u* "side notation", or *su-tzu p'u* 俗字譜 "popular character notation" in the later Sung dynasty. Three types of symbols are used as the basis for the seventeen *tz'u* notation: pitch symbols, rhythmic symbols, and symbols for embellishment. Beginning with the pitch symbols, there are eleven noted (See Example 1).

Example 1

These symbols were evident in the earlier, Sung dynasty style of notation called *chih-tzu p'u* or "character tablature notation" for wind instruments—*hsiao*, *ti* 笛, *kuan* 管, etc. A few words on the characteristics of this early form of *chih-tzu p'u* is prerequisite to understanding its relationship to the pitch notation and key/mode designation of the songs.

Little is known of the Chiang style of *chih-tzu* notation since it has become archaic even before the earliest-existing editions of the late 18th century. However, in all probability, the notational symbols were originally derived from the finger position symbols for playing the *hsiao*, an end-blown vertical flute with five frontal fingerholes and one in the back. Chiang's song are musically and poetically associated with the *hsiao* (Yang and Yin, 1957: 68-69). In the quatrain "Kuo ch'ui hung" 過垂虹 (Passing "Drooping-Rainbow" Bridge) Chiang writes, "Hsiao Hung sang quietly while I played the *hsiao*" (小紅低唱我吹簫). Functioning as tablature symbols, the ten pitch names, *ho* through *wu*,[2] (refer back to Example 1) have the following definitions: (1) *ho* "ㅿ", 合 (close) means to close all six fingerholes of the *hsiao*; (2) *ssu* "マ", 四 (four) means to close four frontal fingerholes; (3) *i* "一", 乙 (secondary) means to close a subordinate fingerhole thereby producing a neutral pitch (more discussion later on the *i* note); (4) *shang* "ㄥ", 上 (ascending) a homonym of *san* 三 (three), means to open three frontal fingerholes; (5) *kou* "ㄥ", 勾 (hook) means to curve or crook the finger when covering a portion of the fingerhole; (6) *ch'ê* "人", 尺 (foot) means to close the fingerhole which is one foot away from the blowing hole; (7) *kung* "ㄱ", 工 (labor), a homonym of *k'ung* 空 (empty) means to keep all frontal fingerholes empty, i.e., open; (8) *fan* "リ", 凡 (all) means to open all fingerholes including the one in the back; (9) *liu* "久", 六 (six) means to cover all six holes (overblown octave of pitch *ho* is produced); (10) *wu* "ㄋ", 五 (five) means to close five fingerholes (four frontal and one back fingerholes; hence, overblown octave of pitch *ssu* is produced).[3] With a knowledge of the tablature

[2] The eleventh symbol *i-wu* ㄋ is not a tablature-derived symbol, although it appears to have a pitch meaning. The symbol can be interpreted as *i*—on *wu* ㄋ which would result in another neutral interval, a heightened $\overset{+}{F}$, between F♮ and F#. If indeed Chiang K'uei used the *i-wu* in his seventeen songs, scholarly opinions differ on this point; it could indicate that even during Chiang's time, the transformation from tablature to pitch notation had already begun.

[3] The tablature phenomenon of Chiang's seventeen *tz'u* notation has often been overlooked, perhaps obscured by the tendency to regard Chiang's notation as an early form of *kung-ch'ê* 工尺 pitch notation, *together* with the other known Sung dynasty notations mentioned in the *"Ch'in-lü shou"* by Chu Hsi and in the *Tz'u Yüan* by Chang Yen. Although these three notational examples have similar notational symbols, that of Chiang is tablature-based while those of Chu and Chang are pitch-based. Furthermore, the functional aspect of the pitch notations cited in the Chu and Chang works is questionable since, for example, it would not be possible to apply the "chro-

matic" scale characteristic of the notation mentioned by Chu and Chang to a fixed-pitch Chinese aerophone instrument. Thus, if Chiang's notation is recognized as a *chih-tzu* tablature notation (idiomatic to the flute), we can probably draw two conclusions regarding Sung notational system. First, Chiang's *chih-tzu* notation is the earliest type of *kung-ch'ê* notation, and that the symbols of the Sung *su-tzu* popular character notational system were originally derived from tablature notation, based on the *hsiao* flute fingering position. Second, both the notations cited in Chu's and Chang's writings are meant to be a general type of notation for pitch reference in theoretical discussions, not for use in applied music. The reader may recall that idiomatic notations existed for the *ch'in* and *sê* zithers during the Sung dynasty. Hence it is most likely that the *kung-ch'ê* notational system (referring to all notations using the *ho, ssu, i, shang*, etc. concept) originated as a tablature notation, idiomatic for the *hsiao* instrument. I thank Prof. Ts'ao Cheng of the Central College of Music in Peking for his verification of the tablature meanings in correlation with a flute type of instrument.

foundation of the pitch symbols that appear in the notation of the seventeen songs, we can now discuss their intervallic relationship. As has been pointed out by Yang the *hsiao* of today is similar to that played by Chiang K'uei in the Southern Sung period and which he used for notational reference (1957: 69). Bearing in mind the organological similarity together with the practical meaning of *chih-tzu p'u*, we can propose the following intervallic relationships of the seven pitches within the first octave:

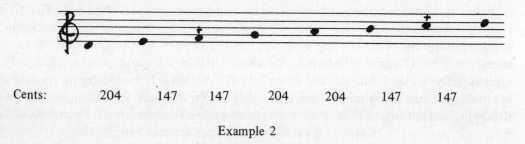

Cents: 204   147   147   204   204   147   147

Example 2

Aside from the major second interval of 204 cents and the pure fifth interval of 702 cents, the unusual intervals are those between pitches E to F, F to G, and B to C, C to D each of which is theoretically equal to 147 cents. The neutral intervals surrounding the neutral F and C pitches, mentioned previously, are slightly larger than tempered half-step intervals. In descriptive terms, it means that the indicated pitch $\overset{+}{F}$ is higher than a tempered F♮ by approximately 47 cents and lower than a tempered F♯ by approximately 53 cents, similarly with the neutral $\overset{+}{C}$ pitch. (Please note that I am not referring to the Chinese music tonal system; rather, I am illustrating the probable intervallic relationships produced by the open fingering of the *hsiao*.) In other words, the resulting series will form a T (tone), NT (neutral tone), NT, T, T, NT, NT hierarchy. Now perhaps the reader wonders why so much attention is given to the *hsiao* tuning. The answer is that without knowing this fundamental tuning characteristic, one could not begin to understand: (1) what the music of Chiang K'uei actually sounded like, and (2) how eleven pitches can accommodate six keys without having recourse to any additional accidental pitches. To elaborate on the latter statement, let us examine the key designations in relationship to the notated pitch symbols.

The total seventeen songs utilize six different key signatures (cf. Yang and Yin 1957, Ch'iu 1959, and Pian 1967). For the key signature designations I shall refer to the Yang and Yin transcriptions: (1) key in C (Songs no. 2, 3, 6, 7, and 17); (2) key in D (Song no. 8); (3) key in E (Song no. 4—notice that D♯ is not used in this song and notationally only 3 sharps, key in A, are required)[4]; (4) key in F (Songs no. 1, 5, 10, 11, and 16); (5) key in G (Songs no. 9, 12, and 15); and (6) key in A (Songs no. 13 and 14). In view of the above keys, one would immediately inquire into the possibilities for the necessary sharps and flats since only G♯ is included among the eleven pitch symbols. Let us begin our explanation with the sharp key signatures,

---

[4]Since the pitch D♯ does not occur in Song Four, three sharps (F♯, C♯, and G♯) would be practically sufficient, but one must still recognize that "do" is on E.

i.e., keys in G, D, and A (disregarding key in E for the practical reason mentioned above). The additional sharp pitch symbols required would be $F^{\#}$ for key in G, $F^{\#}$ and $C^{\#}$ for the key in D, and again only $F^{\#}$ and $C^{\#}$ for the key in A since $G^{\#}$ is already present, essentially requiring only two additional sharpened pitches—$F^{\#}$ and $C^{\#}$. Recalling the neutral pitches $\overset{+}{F}$ and $\overset{+}{C}$ and their adjacent intervals E to $\overset{+}{F}$, $\overset{+}{F}$ to G and B to $\overset{+}{C}$, $\overset{+}{C}$ to D, we can immediately understand why Chiang did not bother to notate the $F^{\#}$ and $C^{\#}$ pitch symbols ... because of the double functions of the neutral pitches which I shall call "equivocal pitches". The pitch $\overset{+}{F}$ can be considered $F^{\natural}$ (although sharper than the tempered F) or as $F^{\#}$ (although lower than the tempered $F^{\#}$) depending upon the given key and in view of the fact that the *hsiao* is not a tempered instrument. In the actual performance of these equivocal or neutral pitches, psychoacoustic factors and physical manipulation can inititate a "tonization" process or adjustment toward the recognized tonic "do". For example, the *hsiao* performer could blow slightly harder or softer, as in the undulation technique, in order to achieve a slightly higher- or lower-pitched tendency, respectively on the equivocal pitches. For Western audiences, unused to hearing Chinese music, the neutral pitches may indeed sound strange, but they provide the "in-between" tonality characteristic of traditional Chinese music even to the present day.

List of Seventeen Songs by Chiang K'uei

1. Ke-hsi-mei ling 羈溪梅令 — Plum on the Far Side of the Stream Ling
2. Hsing-hua-t'ien ying 杏花天影 — Apricot Blossom Sky Shadow
3. Tzui-yin-shang hsiao-p'in 醉吟商小品 — Little Drunken Song in Shang
4. Yü-mei ling 玉梅令 — Jade Plum Ling
5. Ni-shang chung-hsü ti-i 霓裳中序第一 — Middle Prelude of Rainbow Skirt, no. 1
6. Yangchou man 揚州慢 — Yangchou Man
7. Ch'ang-t'ing-yüan man 長亭怨慢 — Long Pavilion Lament Man
8. Tan-huang-liu 淡黄柳 — Golden Willows
9. Shih-hu-hsien 石湖仙 — Stone-Lake Immortal
10. An-hsiang 暗香 — Hidden Fragrance
11. Shu-ying 疏影 — Dappled Shadows
12. Hsi hung-i 惜紅衣 — Compassion for Red Dress
13. Chiao-shao 角招 — Harmonious Chiao
14. Chih-shao 徵招 — Harmonious Chih
15. Ch'iu-hsiao yin 秋宵吟 — Autumn Night
16. Ch'i-liang fan 凄涼犯 — Desolate Fan
17. Ts'ui-lou yin 翠樓吟 — Green Tower

Example 3

Having discussed the pitch possibilities with the sharp keys, let us turn to the key in F, the last of the six key categories unaccounted for. The key in F is somewhat problematic here, since the required B♭ cannot be produced on the *hsiao* through open fingering, calling for, instead, a forked finger technique. The practice of this latter technique in Chiang's time is not totally inconceivable. For in 1340, the *Shih-lin kuang-chi* 事林廣記 by Chen Yüan-ching 陳元靚 compiled a table of forked fingerings, but this publication dated about 140 years after Chiang's time (Yang and Yin 1957: 14-16). In the light of the evidence from the three earliest extant editions, we can conclude that: (1) the symbol for B♭ was either ambiguous or inconspicuous and therefore had been overlooked by copyists; or (2) the key in F, that is, "do" tonic on F, may not necessarily involve a B♭ pitch, as in the theory proposed by Lü Pu-wei 呂不韋 of the 3rd century B.C. in *Lü-shih ch'un-ch'iu* 呂氏春秋. Accordingly, the F tonic scale could be structured F-G-A-B-C-D-E-F, using a sharp fourth degree from pitch F, which is realized through the cycle of the fifth method. No conclusions can be drawn at this time, however. In my analysis, I have considered the B♭ to be a part of the original notation for predominantly musical reasons. It is a coincidence that two of the most beautiful songs in the collection, Songs Ten and Eleven, are in key F, and that the alteration from B♭ to B is musically inconceivable in both pieces.

Thus far, I have correlated the eleven pitch symbols and resulting intervallic aspects to the key designations which, except for Song Two, were made by Chiang himself. In summary, the pitch symbols used by Chiang K'uei for the seventeen *tz'u* songs have the following indications:

(1)   The 11 pitch symbols are sufficient for the songs included, with the possible exception of a B♭ pitch.

(2)   The compositional pitch language is seven-tone scaled (without semitones, unlike the tempered diatonic scale).

(3)   The range of pitches for all seventeen songs is confined to an octave plus a minor third.

(4)   The tuning system of the songs is based on the *hsiao* tuning which includes the two neutral, equivocal pitches and related neutral second intervals.

(5)   Other known Chinese theoretical systems of tuning such as the cycle of fifths cannot be applied to these songs. Therefore, it is clear that theoretical and practical applications do not necessarily coincide. This, to me, is the most significant evidence illuminated by Chiang's *tz'u* music, as far as pitch is concerned.

(6)   During Chiang's time twelve-pitched notation was known to have existed, (speaking more in terms of date of publication rather than applicational theory). For example, the *Ch'in-lü-shuo* 琴律說 (published ca. 1190) by Chu Hsi 朱熹 mentioned sixteen pitch symbols (twelve semi-pitches plus four semi-pitches), and the *Tz'u-yüan* 詞源 (published ca. 1280) by Chang Yen 張炎 mentioned nineteen pitch symbols (twelve plus seven). Nevertheless, Chiang did not know of their existence or did not use these pitch symbols for a good reason; that is, his style of *tz'u* music *did not* consist of semi-tone intervallic relationships outside the diatonic scale. This im-

plication is important for our understanding of his modal language. Otherwise, there seems to be no other reason for Chiang not to use, for example, the twelve plus four pitch symbols in his *tz'u* notation.

Rhythmic Symbols

To arrive at some understanding of the real meaning, i.e., a performance realization, of the rhythmic symbols used in notating the seventeen *tz'u* songs (written some 700 years ago) is a most difficult task. Even within a given genre, the notational system in Chinese music was not unified. Discrepancies occurred from person to person, school to school, and varied with geographical locations. Therefore, Chiang's notational system would have to be considered as a personal style of notation, constituting the only one of its kind from late twelfth-century China. Moreover, Chiang's *tz'u* music had not been handed down by word of mouth and is known to us only through the written notations. In fact, the compositional and performance tradition of *tz'u* music had been lost in subsequent dynasties soon after Chiang's time. Therefore, the interpretation of the rhythmic symbols as discussed here is tentative, and my conclusion is mainly the result based primarily on a comparison of the important *tz'u* scholarships by Yang and Yin (1957) and Ch'iu (1959). No attempt will be made to pursue in detail the various arguments concerning the interpretation of rhythmic symbols drawn from other studies.

There are two basic types of rhythmic symbols used in the seventeen songs: *chu* 住 (literally meaning big pause) and *ta* 打 "フ" (literally meaning strike). They are all prolongation symbols which are located under the pitch symbols. Within the *chu* category there are symbols respectively for the *ta-chu* 大住 "タ" (big "pause") and *hsiao-chu* 小住 "リ" (small "pause"). The *ta-chu* symbol apparently has a number of varieties, e.g., 夯, 少, 力, allegedly resulting from copying errors or from subsequent ideographical stylizations in which the full character had been transformed first into an abbreviated form and then perhaps to a more ambiguous grass style of writing. The *hsiao-chu*, when notated under the pitch symbol, is meant to add a syllabic "beat" to the designated text word, thereby totalling two "beats". The *ta-chu* symbol, when written under the pitch symbol, is meant to add two syllabic "beats" to the designated word, thereby totalling three "beats". (See Shen Kua 沈括, esp. 538.) The *ta* symbol, according to Ch'iu (1959: 101) and Yang (1957: 27), is similar in meaning to the *hsiao-chu* in that it is also a two "beat" character. For this reason Yang feels that the symbols of *hsiao-chu* and *ta* should be considered as one type, however, without further questioning their application. Here, Ch'iu's statistical analysis as to the frequency of each symbol is helpful. He informs us that the majority of *ta-chu* prolongation signs occur in the *man-tz'u* 慢詞 (long tune), i.e., mostly from Song Six onwards. Conversely, most of the *hsiao-chu* symbols are applied before Song Six in the *ling* 令, short songs (except for Song Five which is a long tune). *Ta* is applied in both the *ling* and *man-tz'u* songs.

In considering the functional relationship between the prolongation symbols and the poetic-textual structure, it is obvious that the majority of prolongation symbols coincide with rhyming lexigraphs at the ends of lines (133 examples). The next frequent occurrences happen at the caesuras within lines (49 examples). This is followed by 40 examples of prolongation symbols variously placed, other than at ends of lines and caesuras. The least frequent use of these symbols are at the ends of non-rhyming lines (29 examples). (Cf. Yang 1957: 29, also Pian 1967: 68-69.) In comparing the individual functional application of these three prolongation symbols, we find that *ta-chu* are most frequently associated with rhyming lexigraphs, whereas *ta* is applied to the other text-structure periodizations (caesuras, non-rhyming syllables, etc.). It should be noted that these statistics should be considered only in relative terms, in view of discrepancies among editions and among scholarly studies. They provide, however, broader conceptualized understandings, rather than absolute formulas.

The Ch'iu study theorizes further on the performance realization of the prolongation symbols. It proposes that the *chu* symbols, both large and small, designate that the wooden block (*pan* 板) be struck at the end of each prolongation, and the *ta* symbol designates that the drum (*ku* 鼓) be sounded on the downbeat of a syllable so marked. These percussive sound additions are based on the practice of the classical *K'un-ch'ü* 崑曲 of the Ming dynasty, and while interesting, the hypothesis is questionable. Ch'iu's study, on the one hand, suggests the use of the percussive instrumental punctuation which is in fact a northern *pei-ch'ü* 北曲 practice called *ch'ang ch'uan* 唱賺 (Cheung 1975: 348-356), and, on the other hand, he restricts the rhythmic interpretation of Chiang's *tz'u* music to a 4/4 duple framework. The effect seems to be somewhat contradictory and adds a rhythmic confusion to the songs. Furthermore, whether a synchronized rhythmic scheme was indeed practiced in *tz'u* music in 12th-century China has yet to be studied. As for the function of the prolongation symbols in Chiang's *tz'u* music, we can only propose that, first, the criteria for musical-rhythmic units are in general determined by the textual-sectional devices, resulting in a logo-rhythmic contour rather than melo-rhythmic contour. Secondly, the rhythmic reference density is one word (syllable) per beat. Therefore, Shen Kua's comment on the *chu*, mentioned previously, becomes clearer; that is, the prolongations are based on the addition of one or two rhythmic reference points (beats) to the one word (or note, or syllable) per beat format.

In this light, the efforts of the studies by Ch'iu, Yang and Picken, on synchronized rhythmic compartmentalization appear rather ambitious. Caution must be exercised in imposing a twentieth-century "chrono-rational" habit (whether Oriental or Occidental) upon a *tz'u*-song tradition practiced some 700 years ago and for which we have no "chrono-musical" taste. As for the poetic-metrical system of the *tz'u* songs, this level of understanding will be selectively discussed in the analysis portion of this article.

Finally, if the prolongational symbols for *chu* (pause) and *ta* (strike) have the lexical implication of some kind of break, we can extend this understanding to its musical meaning. My observation is that when the *ta* symbol occurs at a caesura and at the end of a line (textual pausation), the prolonged beat must be followed by a break before proceeding to the next syllable. In addition, a brief crescendo dynamic emphasis is to be given on that pitch which can be notated as ♩♪. .[5] Based on this

---

[5] Note that this assumption is also influenced by   traditions.
the performance of *K'un-ch'ü* and Amoy singing

crescendo interpretation, the "striking" implication of *ta* can be comprehended as an internal "attack", and thus on this hypothesis we can no longer associate *ta* with *hsiao-chu* function as a single type of prolongational symbol. Furthermore, the *ta* symbol in its prolonged and dynamic function is applied to both the *ling* poem as well as to the *man tz'u* poem. As for the two types of *chu*, the small *chu* is applied mostly to the *ling* poems and the big *chu* to most of the *man tz'u* poems. The distinction between *chu* and *ta* is clear. Since the *chu* means a "pause", therefore, a pause is required at the end of a prolongation, hence, a breathing requirement. Obviously, the dynamic interpretation is not conclusive and further research by other scholars is necessary. The dynamic treatment in *tz'u* music is definitely an important aspect since *tz'u* is very much a pathogenic type of verbal/speech expression, and one would likewise expect that the possibilities for patho-rhythmic implication would be substantial.

Embellishment Symbols

IN THE NOTATION OF THE seventeen songs, three embellishment symbols occur: *chê* 折 "ㄅ" (deflection), *fan* 反 "ﾉ" (unsettled), and *chih* 掣 "ﾉ" (diminution). The interpretation of these embellishments in studies of recent decades have been most controversial. Recalling that the *tz'u* practice survived only as a poetic form, subsequent *tz'u* researchers have collated information from various sources in an effort to decipher Chiang's *tz'u* notation. Music sources proximate to Chiang's time, such as those by Chu Hsi, Shen Kua, and Chang Yen, have yielded important insights, but shortcomings exist in that most of these sources were written by scholars who were not proficient practicing musicians (as opposed to theorists), nor were they specifically knowledgeable in the *tz'u* performing tradition. The investigation on *tz'u* practices led to comparisons with other vocal traditions of historical or contemporaneous time. For example, the 1625 and 1862 publications by Wang Chi-tê 王驥德 and Chang Wen-hu 張文虎, respectively, provide comparisons with vocal genres more than 400 years after Chiang's time. Analogies have also been drawn from the vocal style of K'un-ch'ü classical opera, an ancient but still viable art form with a predominant oral tradition.

First, let us compare the discrepancies in the Ch'iu and Yang studies concerning the *fan* and *chih* embellishment symbols. Ch'iu believes that *fan* and *chih* are separate symbols, the *fan* being placed on the right side of the pitch symbol in the notation, and the *chih* being placed below the pitch symbol. Whereas, Yang refers to *fan* and *chih* as one and the same symbol called *i* 洩, although their positions in the notation are different.[6] Both Ch'iu and Yang offer convincing arguments for the use of their terminology. The views presented by other studies will be included in later discussion where appropriate. Before examining the functional application of the three symbols in terms of embellished (additional) pitch(es) and duration, we shall discuss their comparative occurrences and positions within the song notations.

---

[6] Although the Ch'iu, and Yang and Yin studies did not initiate the use of the embellishment nomenclature, their works are cited here as the most prominent studies on the subject to date.

The *chê* symbol occurs on the first or the first two syllables preceding a rhyming word. It also occurs at a beginning or middle syllable of a non-rhyming line, seldom on the syllable preceding the end of it, and never on the syllable preceding the end of a stanza. It appears to me that musically, *chê* occurs on modally or melodically significant notes, i.e., the tone at the end of a song (final) and on the absolute rhyming pitch(es).[7] (In most cases the rhyming pitch(es) is related a fifth interval above or fourth below the final as in a dominant-tonic relationship, and in some cases, a third interval above or below the final.) When a *chê* is applied in the middle of a line, the added pitch appears to be generally ornamental in nature, sometimes with prolongational emphasis, rather than a pitch oriented embellishment. (See Ch'iu 1959: 50-57.)

The *fan* symbol (based on Ch'iu's statistical study) is applied only to the *man tz'u* songs, where it is usually preceded by a one syllable beat, i.e., without a prolongation sign. The placement of *fan* generally has the following criteria. (1) on a syllable preceding a rhyming syllable that is marked, as previously mentioned under the discussion of prolongation symbols, by either a *chu* or *ta* symbol; (2) on a note, mostly on pitches *liu* (D) and *chê* (A), preceding (hence preparing) a third or fourth interval that leads to a resolution note; and less often (3) on a syllable at the end of a textual line (though not the end of a musical line) that is followed by a large disjunct interval, i.e., a fourth or fifth.

The *chih* symbol, like the *fan* symbol, only occurs in the *man-tz'u* songs. It is unlike the other secondary symbols (including those of rhythm and embellishment) in that *chih* also has a diminution meaning in addition to its embellishing function, which results in a diminishing of the duration of the pitch to which the symbol is affixed. In musical terms, the effect of *chih* can be described as: the down beat occurring on the designated pitch and the up beat on the added pitch(es)—neighboring tone or passing tone, etc. Statistically, the *chih* connected pitch generally follows a prolongated pitch. Its occurrence is most frequently on the syllable(s) preceding the end syllable of a rhyming or non-rhyming line, the end pitch of which is often marked by a *ta* type of prolongation. *Chih* in this position may appear on a single preceding syllable, two, or even three consecutive, preceding syllables. The embellishment of two or even three consecutively placed syllables significantly differentiates the *chih* from the *fan* symbols. (Thus, my interpretation is contrary to Yang's treatment of *chih* and *fan* as one symbol called *i*.)

After the statistical study on the occurrence and placement of the embellishment symbols, one is faced with the problem of what pitches or other ornamentational and durational criteria are involved. The solutions are all hypothetical depending on what stylistic or theoretical method one wishes to comply with and what one's scholarly attitude is, i.e., based on Ming, Ch'ing, or present-day interpretations.

---

[7]In this study, the term rhyming pitch is used in two senses. In a specific sense, a rhyming pitch refers to that pitch which coincides with a textual rhyme syllable and is designated as an "absolute" rhyming pitch. In a general sense, a rhyming pitch (by name rather than function) frequently occurs in a non-rhyming position and has the significance of a home tone or reciting tone—the most frequently occurring pitch(es). In this latter usage, it is called a "nominal" rhyming pitch.

On the matter of the *chê* symbol, one of the most well-known statements comes from the ca. 1086 publication, *Pu pi-t'an* 補筆談, *Meng-hsi pi-t'an* 夢溪筆談 by Shen Kua:

> The sound of *chê* 折 [is] not applied to *ho* 合 pitch, [it means] to deflect one *fen* 分 [a Chinese measurement roughly equivalent to one/tenth of an inch], two *fen*, even to seven-eight *fen*. The manner of fingering [to produce *chê* sound] requires full or partial fingerhole covering, the manner of blowing [on a flute instrument] requires light and heavy [soft and strong]. For the *sheng* [mouth-organ] and the *hsiao* [end-blown vertical flute] all matters [depend] on the breath [in blowing]. For the stringed instruments it involves sliding and stopping.
>
> (*Pu pi-t'an*, esp. 538)

Shen's comments offer a variety of interpretational possibilities. For example, Yang understood the matter on *fen* to be related to duration and dynamics rather than to pitch deviation (1957: 23), whereas Ch'iu considers *fen* to mean a pitch variant which when applied to the flute finger technique has the meaning of covering certain portions (*fen*) of the finger-hole (1959: 51). Picken also interprets *fen* as a pitch variant, but specifies that the "change in pitch might be as little as a comma or as much as a tone" (1966: 139).

It seems to me that the comments on *chê* by Shen have a broader musical meaning rather than its strict performance applications. The *fen* analogy in reference to the *ch'in* (seven-stringed zither) practice indicates the degree of the pitch embellishment: (1) one *fen* (using the seventh stud as a given pitch) indicates a minor second, (2) two *fen* indicates a major second, and (3) between 7 and 8 *fen* indicates a minor third interval. That is to say, when a given pitch has a sign of *chê*, one could embellish the given pitch (according to *ch'in* practice) by applying a minor second, a major second, or even a minor third interval.[8] Shen's comments on the full and partial finger technique can refer to a sliding tone technique (for flute instrument), which is still practiced in present folk flute musical style, and also to an added pitch embellishment. Shen's comment on the light and heavy blowing technique for flute can refer to (1) a musical, dynamic interpretation, i.e., the attack and release approach to timbre definition, and (2) an undulation (vibrato) effect. In concluding the above quoted discussion of *chê*, Shen Kua simply but most significantly says that the "how to" was the professional knowledge of the trained musician (probably referring to the oral tradition) and not for outsiders.

In the *tz'u* interpretational studies by recent scholars, all agree that a pitch marked by the *chê* symbol should be followed by an added neighboring tone leading to the following designated pitch. Ch'iu specified an upper neighboring tone, Yang theorized either an upper or lower neighboring tone according to the conduct of the melodic movement of the given phrase. This interpretation is adopted from

---

[8] In *ch'in* practice, there is generally no distinction made between the seven and eight *fen* within the same tuning; rather an inbetween point is usually referred to as "seven to eight *fen*." In certain situations, however, separate reference may be made to either the seven or the eight *fen* alone, in different tunings.

the *hua* 豁 and *lo* 落 interpretational conventions found in *K'un-ch'ü* opera. Ch'iu on the other hand, gives an interpolated dimension to the *tz'u* songs. In addition to the *chê* practice included above, he calls for a "hidden" (unnotated) deflection called *an chê* 暗折, which would fill in or bridge a large intervallic gap at the end of a line and where no *chê* has been notated. In this case, either a lower or upper neighboring tone could be applied (Ch'iu 1959: 53). If Shen Kua's comments on *chê* has any relevance to Chiang K'uei's *tz'u* songs, it would seem to be that the timbre (sliding tone), durational, and dynamic conventions of *chê* ought to be considered in addition to its pitch embellishing aspect.

The combined *fan* and *chih* symbol called *i* in the Yang and Yin study was interpreted as: (1) a bridging-passing figure consisting of one or two added bridging pitches (according to the anhemi-pentatonic scale rather than non-harmonic sense), and (2) a neighboring figure consisting of an added upper or lower neighboring tone plus a repeated primary pitch. *I* can also be interpreted as a single upper or lower neighboring pitch when inserted between two conjunct pitches (1957: 27). According to Ch'iu, *fan* is a neighboring figure treated as a tri-tone consisting of the added neighboring pitch and repeated primary, given pitch. *Chih* is a separate symbol and is described by Ch'iu as a bridging-passing tone of shorter duration to be inserted between designated pitches (1959: 107-108).

In concluding this section on the notation of Chiang K'uei's *tz'u* music, one would have to consider, at least before a conclusive study can be made, that the notation implemented along the side of the text is an instrumental notation for a flute type of instrument. There is no evidence as yet to support it as vocal notation since the interpretation of the pitch, rhythm, and embellishment symbols pertains to idiomatic terms for instruments. As mentioned earlier, the interpretation of the secondary symbols are most problematic. Only through the accidental retrieval of additional 12th-century poetic songs (notation), and through related musicological studies, such as on the *t'an tz'u* 彈詞 of the present-day southern narrative song tradition, would it be possible to shed new light on the interpretation of *tz'u* songs.

The incompleteness or skeletal characteristic of the *tz'u* notation is obvious and to understand why, we must consider the implication of Shen Kua's comment about "know how" being in the hands of trained musicians. Although contributory, it is not possible here to pursue an examination of the theoretical and historical foundation of Chinese notational practice in relation to the more established and prevalent practice of oral transmission, but a few words are necessary.

Within the orally transmitted, regional instrumental traditions of the early twentieth century, such as the percussion ensemble of Ch'ao-chou 潮州 and the Honan *cheng* 箏 (zither) music, the recitation of notation (*tu p'u* 讀譜) was a popular practice. This oral convention consisted of reciting pitches by their names and secondary symbols, such as for prolongation and embellishment, by their respective symbolic terminology rather than by actual notes or processes. To illustrate, let us apply this method to line 11 of Song Eight which begins: *"Yen-yen fei-lai . . ."* The recited notation would be as follows, (brackets are my clarification): Fen [C^5], Liu [D^5], Wu [E^5], Fan [embellishment], Liu [D^5], Chih [embellishment]. Notice that rhythm is inherent in the reciting process itself. If one were to apply this recited notation convention to Western music (single line), one would recite the solfège syllables and call out appoggiatura, cambiata, etc., without any further description. I believe that this type of oral reciting convention was anciently practiced, being handed down from one generation to another among professional musicians, most of whom were not well-educated and could not explain or document their practice in writing. Moreover, when literati wanted to adopt and assimilate certain folk music genres, the orally communicated conventions of performance practice were not readily transmittable to a written medium. Therefore, if it is possible to reconstruct the performance tradition of the *tz'u* songs, one would have to re-interpret the written tradition with the help of existing "old-school" master musicians.

The Music of Chiang K'uei's Seventeen *Tz'u* Songs

TZ'U POETRY AT ITS inimitable best has always been an ingenious blending of poetry and music. Before *tz'u* was adopted by the literati sometime in the 9th century, it had been known as a folk tradition called *ch'ü-tzu tz'u* 曲子詞, song *tz'u* poetry. The music of *ch'ü-tzu tz'u* was primarily of the *yen-yüeh* 燕樂 tradition, that is, the popular music of non-indigenous origins (as opposed to the indigenous *ch'ing-shang yüeh* 清商樂 style), mainly from Sino-Central Asiatic hybridized styles, and which appeared in banquet and entertainment music. With the introduction of *tz'u* as a literary poetic expression, a new type of song was launched into being, quickly gaining prominence among succeeding generations of poets. The music composed for this *tz'u* song incorporated folk song elements into the existing literary styles, which were then set to a new poetic *tz'u* structure. While the poet-musicians Liu Yung 柳永 and Chou Pang-yen 周邦彦 are among the earlier eminent figures in *tz'u* musical and poetic compositions, Chiang K'uei is considered the last giant; in fact, his *tz'u* music is peerless, being the only corpus with notation surviving.

In general, Chiang's *tz'u* music, like his poem, can be characterized as being in the literati style. By his time, the previous popular, folk musical influence was waning and *tz'u* was on its way toward becoming a musicless poetic expression. As noted by Hsia Ch'eng-t'ao 夏承燾, Chiang's poetic style was a synthesis between the regional Kiangsi poetic style and that of the late T'ang dynasty (10th century), particularly as manifested by Lu Kuei-meng 陸龜蒙, a poet whom Chiang admired (1963: 6). In many respects, Chiang's music also seems to be a synthesis of regional elements and the remote 10th-century style of music.[9] Chiang's fondness for music of previous periods, particularly of the T'ang, is undisguised; Chiang definitely attributes the melodies of both Songs Three and Five to music long before his time (presumably T'ang dynasty). The eccentric manner of his musical behavior should not come as a surprise to us since: (1) to absorb an older tradition is a source of inspiration and material in the compositional process, such as was practiced even in the West among the great 19th-century composers; (2) to be well-informed of

---

[9] As an example, the identical SL structure (refer to page 999 of this study) that occurs in Chiang's Song Ten *"An-hsiang"* (Hidden Fragrance) also occurs in No. Seventeen (*Yu chi-ch'ü-tzê* 又急曲子) of the 9th century *p'i-p'a* notation from Tunhuang (see Hayashi 1957: 70). Since this subject is not the focal point of this essay, further discussion will have to appear in a later publication.

history was not only educationally required [in the education of the elite literati];
one of the idiosyncracies of the scholar-gentry was to live and think in the manner
of centuries ago; and (3) to follow in the steps of an existing older tradition had
always been considered a stepping stone to the higher level of a personalized and
creative approach.

The language of Chiang K'uei's *tz'u* music is diatonic and modal. The tonal
range of these seventeen songs are limited to an octave plus a minor 3rd interval,
i.e., from pitches D^4 to F^5. The range could be considered to be vocally suitable,
but it is more a result of the notation's tablature origin, i.e., defined by the idioma-
tic limitations of the end-blown vertical flute (and other types of flute instruments).
Chiang's music is lyrical in style although motivic rather than melodically oriented,
in conjunct motion with interruptions of dramatic intervallic leaps, and generally
follows a descending contour, being appropriate to the overwhelmingly melancholy
textual meanings. The *tz'u* poetry and music incorporate a mixture of programmatic
impressions and romantic expressiveness, very personal and introspective in nature.

Of the seventeen songs: (1) thirteen are known to be composed by Chiang
(Songs One, and Six through Seventeen); (2) two are borrowed melodies (Song
Three, a recovered *p'i-p'a* melody, and Song Five, a section from *Ta-ch'ü* 大曲
Grand Song and Dance Suite with instrumental accompaniment, presumably from
the T'ang dynasty); (3) one by his poet-musician friend, Fan Ch'eng-ta (Song Four);
and (4) one from an unknown source (Song Two). The majority of the songs were
set to music during the period from 1176 to 1196 when Chiang was between the
ages of 21 and 41. These songs thus represent the middle period of his career.

The seventeen songs can be divided into two types according to their poetic
forms: there are four *ling* (short song), and thirteen *man-tz'u* (long tune).

The ensuing analysis of examples of Chiang's own songs (composed by himself
rather than using borrowed music material) will delineate the different levels of
musical structure in order to arrive at some idea of Chiang's musical style and his
creative procedure. Because of limited space, a selective sampling is necessary;
therefore, one *ling* (Song One) and two paired *man-tz'u* (Songs Six and Seven)
will be analyzed, and only One and Six will be transcribed. (For transcriptions of
the other songs, the reader can consult the Ch'iu publication (pp. 104-114) or the
English version of the Picken study (pp. 95-114) for primary pitch references.)

The Methodology of the Analysis

In the analysis of Examples 4 and 5, and transcriptions, two types of signs
will be used to indicate poetic structure. The dotted bar line indicates the end of
a non-rhyming verse line and the solid bar line indicates the end of a rhyming verse
line. The comma on top of the staff indicates the occurrence of a caesura as in
measure 1 of Song One transcription. Thus the measures in the analysis are based
on the stanzaic structure.

In the examination of the musical structure of the songs, three levels are
delineated. The first level is established by the isolation of three-tone motivic units
(MU) through which construction of mosaic fragmentation of a song becomes
evident. This level is labelled the surface level, abbreviated SL, and is graphically

notated as groups of three filled note-heads with upward facing stems ♩♩♩. The second level is established by isolating the notes that are modally significant, which in most cases are the absolute rhyming (meaning the pitch correlated with a rhyming syllable) and final pitches. These modally important notes constitute the skeletal aspect for the thematic idea and shall be called hidden level (HL). In Examples 4 and 5, HL pitches are distinguished from SL pitches by their downward facing stems. HL pitches with hollow note-heads ⌐ indicate that they are more important, i.e., occurring more frequently, than the HL pitches with darkened note-heads ⌐. Where an SL pitch coincides with an HL pitch, both upward and downward facing stems will be evident. The filled, stemless note-heads indicate the third structural level, modificational level (abbreviated ML) and contain the pitches which function as prefixes, infixes, and suffixes to the above notes, mostly modifying the MU. Hopefully, this three-level isolation method of structural analysis will provide some understanding of Chiang's music compositional process as related to the musical-thematic criteria (manifested in SL) and the linguistic criteria (manifested in HL). In other words, the surface level structure is significant in delineating the synchronic stylistic features of Chiang's songs (meaning the style of a given time), whereas the skeletal presentation of the hidden level would be more indicative of the poetic rhyming rules. Finally, the position and function of the ML "fix" pitches in conjunction with textual-inflectional rules provide some indication of Chiang K'uei's personal musical stylization. For instance, in Example 7, the ML pitches (indicated in parentheses) provide a kind of stylistic coloring or personality which helps to distinguish the otherwise similar melodic materials of the paired Songs Six and Seven.

The primary reference for my staff transcription of Songs One and Six is the Chang edition, though the Lu and Chu editions are also used for comparisons. When a discrepancy occurs, the majority opinion is followed. If three alternatives are given, the Chang interpretation is followed—though with an evaluation of the surrounding melodic conduct and a cross-comparison of the parallel structure in another stanza (of the same song).

The prolongational symbols, *hsiao-chu* and *ta-chu*, extend the basic beat by two more, thus totalling three beats; but at the end of the third beat, a brief pause (notated as an eighth rest) is indicated: ♩ ♪⁷. As mentioned previously in the discussion of rhythmic symbols, *hsiao-chu* is mainly applied in the *ling*, and *ta-chu* mainly in the *man-tz'u*, thus both symbols rarely occur in the same song. The exception does present itself, however, in Song Six: parallel measures 5 and 15. *Hsiao-chu* (small *chu*) functions here as a breath pause ♩ ♪⁷ marking the first cadential pitch in the ongoing long phrase. The phrase ends two pitches later with a *ta-chu* which is notated ♩ ♪⁷. The prolongation *ta* symbol may occur within a line at the caesura, and/or at the end of a line; in both cases the symbol prolongs the pitch (to which it is affixed) and includes a brief rest, such as notated: ♩ ♪．⁷. (An accent may also be interpreted on a pitch where *ta* is indicated, but more appropriately at the end of a line.)

The embellishment symbols are treated here in a tentative manner. The *chê* symbol is interpreted as an embellishment consisting of a simple neighboring tone. The determination of upper or lower neighboring tone correlates with the speech tone: the level tone *ping sheng* 平聲 (shown as — in transcriptions) is ornamented with a lower neighboring pitch, and the oblique tone *chê-sheng* 仄聲 (shown as ＼) is ornamented with an upper neighboring pitch.

The interpretation of *fan* and *chih* embellishment symbols is variable, depending upon the surrounding melodic contour and modal emphasis. These symbols may each be interpreted as one, two, or sometimes even three added pitches (but always within a single beat, rhythmic density reference) and function either as bridging (passing) tones (based on a 7-tone scale rather than a 5-tone scale) or neighboring tones. In the transcription of Song Six (Song One being a *ling*, thus having no *fan* and *chih*), I have interpreted the *fan* embellishment as a compound neighboring motion, represented by four sixteenth-notes including the principal pitch (see measure 17, beat 6), and the *chih* embellishment as a bridging-passing motion (see measure 11, beat 1). Thus, comparatively speaking, *fan* appears more important as a melodic-pitch figure, whereas *chih* is more prominent as a mechanical bridge and rhythmic device. The musical application of *fan* and *chih*, as well as interpretation of other more or less arbitrary symbols, is a result of my musical instinct and experience with the performance and literature of 14th-century Northern *ling* songs, Japanese *Gagaku* music, and *ch'in* (seven-stringed zither) music before the 12th century. With the recovery of additional Sung dynasty song notation and after many more analytical comparisons of existing song repertoires, it will be possible to be more certain about the *tz'u* song practice.

A cipher analytical method is included in portions of the analysis where numbers are thought to be visually clearer than staff pitches and where a moveable "do" system is expedient. The cipher number presentation in conjunction with the moveable "do" system is: 1 as "do", 2 as "rei", 3 as "mi", etc., with "do" always representing the tonic of a key, e.g., in the of F, "do" is on F.

In addition to the correlation between the embellishment symbol *chê* and the speech tones, the Yang and Yin, and Ch'iu studies indicate a general correlation (although inconsistencies have been noted) in Chiang K'uei's *tz'u* songs between musical contour and two types of speech tones: *p'ing* 平 level (symbolized —), and *chê* 仄 oblique (symbolized ＼). However, the historical discrepancy is that the literature during Chiang's time, at least theoretically, referred to four speech tonal levels as: *p'ing*, *shang* 上, *ch'ü* 去 and *ju* 入. Yang proposes that perhaps in Chiang's songs, the *shang*, *ch'ü*, and *ju* speech tones were considered as one type, *chê* (oblique). The application of speech tonal rules to musical contour will be further discussed within the Song One analysis.

Analysis of Song One: "Ke-hsi-mei ling" *(Plum on the Far Side of the Stream Ling)*

This *ling* composed in 1196 is presumably one of the last compositions within the seventeen *tz'u* song collection. The poetic text is in two stanzas, each consisting of two lines, with the stanzaic structure: 7, 3, 9, 5. The absolute and nominal rhyming pitches are D (cipher 6 or "la") and G (cipher 2 or "rei"); the final pitch is on cipher 2, and the mode (2, 3, 4, 5, 6, 7, 1̇, 2̇) is a 2 ("rei" mode) or in Sung nomenclature, *yü-tiao* 羽調. (An underlined cipher number indicates an absolute rhyming pitch but in actual usage, these pitches also appear in non-rhyming capa-

Song One

city.) It is apparent that the modality of Song One is engineered by skeletal pitches D and G; resolutions of musical phrases are on the modal "tonic" and "dominant" (see Example 4).

Example 4

The HL structure in similar measures 1 and 3 show repeated G and D pitches, while similar measures 2 and 4 show repetitions of D. The SL three-tone motivic units are structured on the rhyming pitches cipher 2 and 6: 4-3-2, 6-1-2, 1-3-2, 1-7-6, and 4-5-6; notice that the majority of MU are in stepwise melodic motion. A quick view of the transcription of Song One will show that conjunct, small intervals characterize the melody and that larger intervals are usually found between the ending of one phrase and the beginning of another phrase. The fifth interval in measure 3 between pitches G and D is an exception and is intended to emphasize the textual meaning: "and fear (G^4) spring (D^5) departed . . . " (又恐春風歸去). This type of heightened dramatization, which I shall refer to as word painting, also occurs at the last three notes of measure 5. Stanza two is a duplicate of stanza one except for these three pitches which are approximately a minor sixth higher than their counterpart in the first stanza. With the speech tonal levels being quite similar at these two parallel places, it would seem that the high ascending primary pitch contour in measure 5 was intended to describe the text: "dream as cloud" (夢中雲), thus musically capturing the impression of a floating cloud. Song One shows that some correlation exists between the *p'ing* (level) and *chê* (oblique) speech tonal levels and musical direction as based on the following requirements:

(1)   level to level tones correlated with descending motion (see measure 1: 3rd and 4th notes, measure 2: 2nd and 3rd notes, measure 3: 3rd, 4th, and 5th notes, etc.),

(2)   level to oblique tones correlated with descending motion (see measure 1: 3rd and 4th notes, etc.),

(3)   oblique to level tones correlated with ascending motion (see measure 1: 1st and 2nd notes, measure 2: 1st and 2nd notes, measure 3: 2nd and 3rd notes, etc.),

(4)   oblique to oblique tones correlated with ascending motion (see measure 3: 1st and 2nd notes, etc.).

The stress on the level tone imparts a descending tendancy to the general musical contour; however, this is not to say that the melodization is based on the speech-tones. Inconsistencies to the above rules demonstrate that musical factors are more important at times than speech tonal requirements.

A linguistic comparison of Song One is provided by the recitation of Chia-ying Yeh (see bottom lines of Song One transcription). The oral interpretation manifests a general observance of the textual speech tones, but the recited prosodic rhythm is an interesting contrast to the musical rhythm.[10] The speech rhythms consist of four patterns: (1) duple-divided foot ♫, (2) agogic foot ♩♪., (3) half quartal-divided foot with half stop ♫ ⁊, and (4) singular foot ♩, all in duple-meter framework. In comparing the speech rhythms with the musical rhythms, we notice that the greatest dissimilarities occur on the agogic foot and half quarterly-divided foot with half stop. The question on the correlation between the recited prosodic and the musical rhythms is inconclusive, pending additional knowledge on the *tz'u* recitative practice in Sung times and a comparison of oral interpretations by other modern *tz'u* poets.

Analysis of Song Six: "Yangchou Man"

"Yangchou Man" composed in 1176 is an early work, written when Chiang was about twenty-one years old, and is one of the most well-known of his poems. As a poem, *"Yangchou Man"* has two structurally different stanzas. The first stanza has ten lines of the lengths: 4, 4, 6, 5, 5, 7, 4, 4, 7, 4; and the second stanza has nine lines: 4, 4, 5, 4, 4, 6, 7, 7, 4. Moreover, the beginning of the second stanza is structured with an transitional line *huan tou* 換頭 (see transcription of Song Six, measure 11). Unlike the musical similarities found in the two stanzas of Song One (and even in Songs Four, Thirteen, Fourteen, etc.), the music of the two stanzas of Song Six are different, and only in the latter half of stanza two (measures 16-19) is there an approximate similarity to the parallel position in stanza one (measures 7-10).

In spite of the apparent dissimilarities, the analysis on three structural levels (SL, HL, and ML) reveals unifying characteristics. Song Six ends on "fa" (F⁴), a fa or kung mode: 2̲, 3, 4̲, 5, 6̲, 7, 1̇, but since the primary pitch 3 is used only once, the modal scaler impression is really a six-tone scale: 2̲, 4̲, 5, 6̲, 7, 1̇. The HL rhyming pitches as well as the ending and most beginning pitches for the nineteen lines fall on either "fa" (F), "rei" (D) or "la" (A). Besides providing a musical definition to the beginnings and endings of the lines, the triadic HL pitches, D, F, A, or cipher 2, 4, 6 also define the beginnings and endings of the musical phrases. These musical phrases (represented by slurs in Example 5), which are determined by a combination of cadential, prolongational and contour factors, do not parallel the structure of the textual verses.

[10]For the purpose of this study, Prof. Chia-ying Yeh, one of the foremost modern *tz'u* poets, has kindly assisted me by reciting Songs One to Seventeen, and by advising me on some of the critical aspects of the *tz'u* format.

Song Six

Example 5

Example 5 shows 6 phrases (in slurs) and 10 verse lines (in measures) in stanza one, and 7 phrases and 9 verse lines in stanza two. The preponderance of two-lined phrases (4) out of 6) in stanza one, as compared to the majority of one-lined phrases in stanza two (5 out of 7), shows that the stanza one phrases are relatively longer in length. Example 6 below shows the beginning and ending pitches for each phrase as well as calls attention to an overall A B A type structure for each stanza.

The A phrase is defined here as having the same beginning and ending pitch, one of the primary SL pitches; whereas the B phrase has an ending pitch that is different from the beginning pitch, and this latter pitch may not necessarily be one of the primary SL pitches. It seems that the phrasal A B A form is an important compositional criteria for each of the two stanzas in Song Six, although the emphasis of the specific A, B, or A section is different from one stanza to another. Moreover, the compositional attention given to large form and phrase requirements seems to outweigh the consideration for speech tonal rules. Hence in Song Six the

Stanza One   **Stanza Two**

Musical Phrase	Beginning Pitch		Ending (Rhyming) Pitch	Musical Phrase		Beginning Pitch		Ending (Rhyming) Pitch
				Huan-t'ou P7:		2 (D)	–	6 (A)
A { P1:	2 (D)	–	2 (D)	A	P8:	4 (F)	–	4 (F)
P2:	4 (F)	–	4 (F)		P9:	7 (B)	–	2 (D)
P3:	6 (A)	–	6 (A)	B { P10:		1 (C)	–	6 (A)
B { P4:	4 (F)	–	2 (D)		P11:	4 (F)	–	2 (D)
P5:	1 (C)	–	2 (D)		P12:	1 (C)	–	2 (D)
A P6:	4 (F)	–	4 (F)	A	P13:	4 (F)	–	4 (F)

Example 6

correlation between speech tone and melodic contour is not as apparent as in Song One. Another insight into the construction of the melody can be acquired through a diagram (Example 7) of the occurrences of the modally significant HL pitches (in this song referring to the triadic D, F, A pitches, cipher 2, 4, 6). The HL structure of the thirteen phrases show that the intermediate pitch(es) are mostly different from the first and last HL pitches of each phrase for musical variety.

Stanza One   **Stanza Two**

P1: 2 - 6 - 2 - 4 - 2   P7: 2 - 6
P2: 4 - 6 - 4   P8: 4 - 6 - 2 - 4
P3: 6 - 2 - 4 - 6   P9: 2 - 2
P4: 4 - 6 - 2 - 2   P10: 6 - 2 - 4 - 6
P5: 4 - 2 - 6 - 4 - 2   P11: 4 - 6 - 2
P6: 4 - 6 - 4   P12: 2 - 6 - 4 - 2
                                    P13: 4 - 2 - 6 - 4

Example 7

The embellishment practice for Song Six, stanza one, is similar to that of Song One in that the added pitches are applied to form an ornamented cadential motion leading to the end of a phrase (refer to notes in parentheses in Songs One and Six transcriptions). In stanza two, however, the embellishments *also* occur at the initial portion of a phrase, i.e., in measures 11 and 14.

Proceeding to the three tone MU of the SL structure we see that again the rei, fa, la pitches are reinforced in 11 different MU types: 1-4-2, 6-5-2, 1-7-2, 1-6-4, 6-5-4, 2-5-4, 1-7-6, 4-5-6, 1-2-6, 5-7-6, and 4-7-6. (The order of the first and second pitches within a unit is interchangeable, and is called a motivic permutation.) The presence of two HL pitches (cipher 2, 4, or 6) in 8 out of the 11 MU indicates that the D, F, A pitches are essential thematic components to Song Six and occur outside of the absolute rhyming functions as well. As a result of the SL and HL structuralizations, we are able to pursue the question of whether the melodic idea of stanza two was composed independently of stanza one, or whether stanza two is a modification of stanza one. Thus, I have condensed the primary thematic characteristics of the combined SL and HL structuralizations, to form a reduced "fixed" melodization (see Example 8).

Example 8

In the melodization, modificational level pitches are enclosed in parentheses, and embellished (added) pitches have been omitted. The rhythmic density unit is an eighth note for clarity in the analytical process. From the reconstructed melodization of *"Yangchou Man"* (Example 8), it is evident that the phrases (designated by lower case letters) of stanza two are rearrangements of stanza one phrases, and are not in the same sequence. Moreover, a different transitional line *(huan-t'ou)* in stanza two replaces the "a" phrase of stanza one. In terms of compositional procedure, it can be seen that the finished poetic form of *"Yangchou Man"* consists of a prolongational and variational treatment of a limited, pre-set musical idea, to accommodate the stanzaic structure. Thus, the *man-tz'u* differs from the short *ling* not only by its longer stanzaic form, but musically, by the added prolongational-modificational compositional manner.

In comparing the original song with the reconstructed melodization, my impressions are that the latter structure seems more acceptable to our modern musical taste and that the motivic units of the former, with heavy accentuation

upon the absolute and nominal rhyming pitch practices, impart a foreign and some-
times unmusical quality to the original song. Furthermore, we can theorize that the
reconstructed melodization could have been similar to a Kiangsi regional song style
or a late T'ang dynasty popular music style, whereas comparatively the poetic song
would represent the musical style of Chiang K'uei. Only future analysis could prove
or disprove such an idea, but the examination (to follow shortly) of Song Seven,
known to be a pair to Song Six, pursues the question from another angle, that is, by
examining the possibility that Chiang, as a composer, may have had a pre-set musical
idea similar to the reconstructed melodization, which he then used as a com-
positional basis for Songs Six and Seven.

According to Chia-ying Yeh's recitation (see bottom lines of transcription),
there are six prosodic rhythmic patterns in Song Six. Within the duple-meter types
there are the: (1) duple-divided foot ♫, (2) agogic foot ♪♩., (3) half quartal-
divided foot with half stop ♫𝄽, and (4) full quartal-divided foot ♫♫. Within
the triple-meter types there are the (1) triple-divided foot ♫♩, and (2) half sextal-
divided foot with half stop ♫♫𝄽. Although hypothetically the melodic rhythm
could follow the speech meter, it is not likely the case with Chiang's indicated pro-
longational (or diminutive) rhythmic symbols. The speech meter indicates that two
syllables per beat is the speech rhythmic density reference. It should be noted also
that since the triplet rhythmic concept in the speech meter is present, one cannot
rule out the possibility of a triplet rhythmic concept in the melodic interpretation
either.

Comparison with Song Seven: "Ch'ang-t'ing-yüan man" *(Long Pavilion Lament)*

"Ch'ang-t'ing-yüan man", a *man-tz'u* of uncertain date, shares many modal
(same fa mode) and melodic similarities with Song Six and for this reason is referred
to as a pair. The purpose for including Song Seven here is two-fold. First, an
examination of Song Seven illustrates the possibility of two separate songs with
different textual matter being based on the same fixed melody, which in turn
implies that Chiang K'uei did not necessarily compose entirely new music for each
tz'u poem. Second, based on this assumption, we must consider what criteria existed
for the selection of certain "fixed" melodies and by what procedures the musical
adaptations were structurally accomplished, i.e., how was the song completed.

In the limited space of this article it is not feasible to restate details of the
analytical procedures similar to those conducted for Songs One and Six. However,
summarily, the results of the isolation of the three structural levels (SL, HL, and
ML) of Song Seven has led to the "fixed" melodization which is displayed in
Example 9, lines II and III. Since the individual phrases from the Song Seven melodi-
zation proved to be more similar to the phrases of stanza two, Song Six, rather than
to stanza one, the second stanza melodization of Song Six is used as the comparative
model (line I of Example 9). The transitional line *(huan-t'ou)* of Song Six appears
in Song Seven as a modified version and is thus designated as the "a" phrase. The
notes in parentheses are the modificational level pitches. Thus, within the three
reconstructed melodization lines, there are a total of only six different phrases
which are variously modified, repeated, omitted, and even reorganized in a different

Example 9

order within any one of the three lines. (Example 9 shows the phrases in a parallel, vertical relationship which does not represent the sequence of phrases in the actual songs.)

The study of the phrasal isolation and identification in Example 9 implies that each phrase functions are a pre-set musical idea. The selection of certain phrases in Song Six to be correlated with given textual lines in Song Seven seems to be restricted by the conventions and rules manifested in previous analyses, which will be reconsidered in the next section.

Finally, we might inquire into whether the word paintings of Song Six were adopted into Song Seven. The first word painting figure in Song Six is the minor seventh interval (see Example 9; line I, bar 2, phrase "b") which has been altered in lines II and III to a smaller fourth interval, presumably since the latter text no longer required the musical dramatization. In the second word painting figure of Song Six (line I, phrase "e"), the descending minor sixth interval is retained in two stanzas of Song Seven (lines II and III). This minor sixth interval coincides with the ideographs "te-ssu" 得似 (could compare) in line II, and with the ideographs "hung-o" 紅萼 (red flower) in line III. Both these word phrases could be said to occur at the textual climactic points of stanzas one and two respectively, and the coordinating musical figures could therefore have been intended for added tonal articulation. If word painting was indeed practiced by Chiang K'uei, this would seem to reinforce my belief that the application of fixed melodic phrases was a sophisticated practice, not without definable rules and convention.

Chiang K'uei's Compositional Strategy: Rules and Procedures

IN THE ENSUING DISCUSSION I shall delineate a suggestive compositional strategy, including rules and procedures, by which the *tz'u* songs might have been written. Although the present article cannot include the working details of the structual analyses (SL, HL, and ML practices) for the remaining fourteen songs, the results of these findings largely parallel the principles established by the analyses of the previous songs. In Appendix I, I have listed all the motivic units occurring in the seventeen songs and have indicated in modal categories the rhyming and primary non-rhyming pitches for each song. By thus isolating the motivic units and by further reducing their number to include only the most frequently occurring units, I have capsulized the structural-thematic components from which the seventeen songs have germinated. This listing later serves as a source of stylistic reference for the composition of music which would be appropriate to one of Chiang K'uei's *tz'u* poems. The following procedures consist of setting music to stanza one first (parts I-III), and then using the material of stanza one to formulate the music for stanza two (part V).

    I. Pitch determination for the first stanza.

        A. Selection of a key and a final pitch.

            1. The selection of the key is based on the type of melodization one wishes to have, within the limitation of the 11-pitch structural hierarchy (ranging from D^4 to F^5 or $F^{\#5}$, equivocal pitch) in Chiang's style

(refer back to Ex. 1). Therefore the melodic reference and related pitch range of the proposed tune is determined by the root tone (pitch D^4, the lowest pitch of the structural hierarchy) and its definition in a moveable "do" concept, such as naming the root tone as "do", "rei", etc. To elaborate, if a melodic reference requires a 5 or "sol" as the root tone (D^4), then the key in G is suitable, resulting in the cipher moveable "do" scale: 5̣, 6̣, 7̣, 1, 2, 3, 4, 5, 6, 7. Similarly, the root tone on 6 "la" is correlated with the key in F, root tone on 2 "rei" with key in C, root tone on 1 "do" with key in D, root tone on 4 "fa" with key in A, root tone on 7 "ti" with key in E. (Both keys in A and E are rarely used in Chiang's music.) In keeping with Chiang's style, the upper range of the melodic reference is limited to pitch F^5 or $F^{\#5}$.

2. The selection of the final pitch of the song is important since it determines the absolute and nominal rhyming pitches, i.e., the most frequently occurring pitches in rhyming and non-rhyming positions.

B. Selection and placement of the absolute rhyming pitches (usually a fifth above or fourth below the final pitch, or a third above or a third below it). The selection and arrangement of the rhyming pitches at the ends of rhyming lines are determined in the following ways:

1. High and low contrasting placement (refer to scheme of final rhyming pitches in Ex. 6).
2. Textual-emotional criteria of a line.
3. Association of the end rhyming pitches with the selection of three-tone MU (refer to Appendix I) to determine the cadences of the lines. For example, if the rhyming pitch is 2 "rei", the choice of motivic units would be: 4-3-2, 4-5-2, 1.4-2, etc.

C. Placement of the nominal rhyming pitches may also occur on the initial syllables of the lines, although these pitches can be altered after the first stage of pitch placement when another pitch may be more appropriate to the melodic conduct.

D. Determination of the majority speech tonal level for musical contour of each line. Thus a predominance of level speech tones would correlate with a generally descending melodic contour, whereas a predominance of oblique speech tones dictate an ascending melodic contour.

E. Formation of an HL modal pattern by placing the nominal rhyming pitches at key textual words according to the melodic contour.

F. Correlation of level and oblique speech tones to musical pitch direction. For example, between two level-tone syllables, if the pitch for the first syllable is HL pitch G^4, the following pitch should be lower than G^4 to form a descending direction. In this step, the speech-tonal phenomenon would influence the selection of ML (prefix, infix, suffix) pitches which are often used in bridging tone relationship to the nominal rhyming pitches. The selection of ML pitches follows the placement of HL pitches, and should be chosen in consultation with the MU in Appendix I to be stylistically correct.

G. Location of textually significant syllables for word painting, usually in the form of larger intervallic gaps.

H. Musical reshaping of the preceding "mechanically" constructed melodization. Here a re-creative process is called for, that is, the determination of points at which the melodic flow is more important than the "rules". In Chiang's compositions, this reshaping process, noted as inconsistencies, is musically desirable.

II. Placement of prolongation.

Within the normal observance of 1 quarter-note beat per syllabic density reference, a prolongated note (exceeding 1 beat) is usually indicated at the end of a rhyming line, and occasionally at the caesura or end of a non-rhyming line. The prolongation at the end of a non-rhyming line is mostly appropriate in a *man-tz'u*. In the *ling*, I have observed that the prolongation can also occur on the initial pitch of a line.

III. Placement of embellishments.

A. *Chê* embellishments can occur on the syllable preceding an absolute rhyming pitch, or at the beginning or middle syllable of a non-rhyming line. It seldom occurs on the syllable preceding the end of a non-rhyming line and never on the last note of a stanza.

B. *Fan* embellishments (applied only to *man-tz'u*) occur mostly on the syllable directly preceding a prolongated rhyming syllable, and on the syllable that is followed by a third or fourth interval leading to a resolution note. (In the above instances, *fan* frequently appears on pitches D and A, most probably because these two pitches are comparatively easy to embellish on the *hsiao*. Overlapping with the above criteria, *fan* frequently occurs on the note preceding the ending note of either a rhyming or non-rhyming line, particularly if that preceding note is followed by a disjunct interval leading to the last note.

C. *Chih* embellishments (applied only to *man-tz'u*) occur mostly on the syllable directly preceding a short prolongated end-syllable of a rhyming or non-rhyming line. Unlike the *fan*, *chih* can be applied in a consecutive manner on two or three adjacent syllables before the ending syllable of a line. In general, *chih* is applied to a tune in which a faster rhythmic articulation is desired.

IV. Musical similarities and differences manifested by *ling* and *man-tz'u*.

A. In the *ling*, the beginnings and endings of musical phrases and textual lines generally coincide.

B. In the *man-tz'u*, the ends of rhyming lines most often coincide with the ends of musical phrases. Toward this end, the non-rhyming lines may correspond with smaller or partial phrases which combine to form larger phrases, the endings of which coincide with rhyming end-syllables.

C. Although in *man-tz'u* the overlapping of musical phrases and textual lines does occur, it is usually under the condition that one of the nominal rhyming pitches is placed to correspond with the end of the rhyming or non-rhyming line, but not necessarily in a cadential figure. However, by doing so, the modality of the song remains clear.

D. The *man-tz'u* shows a greater distribution of ML pitches within the pitches of the SL motivic units as compared to the *ling*. This characteristic together with the increased incidence of SL pitches seems to constitute a major musical difference between the *ling* and *man-tz'u*.

V. Procedure for completing the second stanza music.

In general, once the music for stanza one has been completed, there are three alternative processes (and combinations) for deriving the music for stanza two: repetition of stanza one, repetition with slight alterations within the confines of phrases, or phrasal reorganization through omissions, repetitions, and altered sequence of phrase segments. A textual precaution that would need to be observed is if the first line of stanza two is a *ch'ung t'ou* 重頭 (repeated head), then its music would be the same as that of line one, stanza one. But if the first textual line of stanza two is a *huan t'ou* (transitional line as in Song Six), then its music is independent of the music in line one, stanza one. Besides these two types, there is the infrequent *shuang-i-t'ou* 雙曳頭 (pair dragged head), a three-stanza form such as found in Song Fifteen.[11] The musical structure of stanzas one and two is similar, whereas that of stanza three is enlarged through repetition of phrasal material, addition of ML pitches, and addition of new material. Briefly, the adoption or adaptation of musical elements from stanza one to stanza two depends upon a clear determination of the modality and musical phraseology of stanza one, and the speech-textual requirements of stanza two, including general speech-tonal contour, emotional content, and length of line. For example, phrasal segments may be rearranged: a-b-c-d in stanza one could become a-c-b-d in stanza two, or phrases may be omitted and repeated: a-b-c-d in stanza one could become a-c-a-d in stanza two. Further, a phrase may be altered by augmentation elaboration (usually accomplished by adding ML pitches to the MU), or by diminution to its simplest SL pitches. The choice of augmentation or diminution technique appears to be related to stanzaic structure. In altering an 8-syllable melodic phrase to fit 5 syllables, obviously diminution would be appropriate, and conversely, in modifying a phrase to include more syllables, augmentation is appropriate. Regardless of either of the two processes, however, the cadential figure of the adapted melodic phrase is generally retained in stanza two, although the initial notes may be altered.

VI. Familiarity through repeated experience.

The last and most essential requirement for understanding Chiang's musical style and direction is to sing the seventeen *tz'u* songs with *hsiao* accompaniment repeatedly (recognizing that Chiang's notation is a tablature rather than vocal notation). Through this musical saturation one can hopefully acquire an almost intuitive sense, a "feeling", for the innate style in Chiang's *tz'u* songs. After all, whenever the music of a *tz'u* song is conceived as a performing expression, as in the case of Chiang's music, the melodic content becomes more important as a song than as a prosodic description. The speech-tonal rules of

[11]In Song Fifteen, stanzas one and two are based on a seven-phrase melodic structure: a, b, c, d, e, f, g; whereas stanza three has a nine-phrase melodic structure: a, e, f, g, a, e, h, d, g.

齊天樂
"Ch'i-t'ien yüeh"

Music by Liang Ming-Yüeh
梁銘越 補曲

黄鍾宮

庾郎先自吟愁賦，　淒淒更聞私語。

露濕銅鋪，苔侵石井、都是曾聽伊處。

哀音似訴。正思婦無眠，起尋機抒。

曲曲屏山．夜涼獨自甚情緒。

西窗又吹暗雨．為誰頻斷續．

相和碪杵．候館迎秋．離宮吊月，

別有傷心無數．幽詩謾與．笑籬落呼燈．

世間兒女．寫入琴絲一聲聲更苦。

the *tz'u* songs, for example, seem to be evident only when the musical-tonal requirements are not being hindered. Moreover, as seen in the analyses of Songs One and Six, the rhythmic structures in the prosodic, recited, and musical versions are related but not homogeneous, and have their separate artistic expressions. Chiang's music thus shows that, in spite of conformity to certain rules and conventions, the aesthetic musical judgement is an important and perhaps the final criterion in the compositional process.

The Applied Experience: "Ch'i-t'ien yüeh" 齊天樂 *(Music Fills the Sky)*

Bringing the foregoing compositional rules and conventions to a practical end, I have followed the procedures and set music to one of Chiang K'uei's own *tz'u* poems, *"Ch'i-t'ien yüeh"* dated 1196 for which there is no surviving *chih-tzu p'u*, notation. (For English translation of the poem see page 246.) My effort is but a gesture to try and revive Chiang K'uei's *tz'u* musical style, in the hope that, together with the knowledge gained from modern *tz'u* scholars, we can begin to appreciate these works in proper perspectives, as music and poetry. Perhaps artists will feel encouraged to create their own music as Chiang K'uei did some 700 years ago.

In historical retrospect, this analytical examination has not only given us some insights into the style of Chiang's *tz'u* music, but it has simultaneously provided some explanation as to why the practice of *tz'u-yüeh* 詞樂 became an archaic expression after the Sung dynasty. The evidence we have before us strongly indicates that 12th-century *tz'u*-song as represented by Chiang K'uei was an extremely intellectualized pursuit with confining rules and conventions which most possibly led to its enjoyment among select literati-scholars. Poets like Chiang who had the musical knowledge to compose *tz'u* songs in accordance with the poetic convention were even fewer. Thus it is not too far-fetched to presume that *tz'u* music's own demanding and esoteric nature led to its obsolescence, precipitated by the anti-intellectual climate of the Yuan dynasty and in conjunction with the rising influence of melodically oriented folk-regional musical styles. This trend is best exemplified by the division of Northern and Southern musical genres during the 14th-15th centuries, the dominance of *K'un-ch'ü* from 16th-18th centuries, and the ongoing tradition of Peking opera since the 19th century. Nevertheless, Chiang's music is sensitive, serene, and personal although appearing somewhat foreign to our taste. And finally, the surviving music of Chiang K'uei enables us to have some understanding of theoretical structures and music practices of 12th-century China.

Acknowledgements

I wish to express my gratitude to Professors Chia-ying Yeh, Jao Tsung-i, and Ts'ao Cheng for the help they have given me. My indebtedness is also due to Professors Yang Yin-liu and Yin Fa-lu, Professor Ch'iu Tsung-sun, Professor Rulan Chao Pian, and Dr. Laurence E.R. Picken for their scholarly research on Chiang K'uei's *tz'u* music, without which the present article would not have been possible. I would also like to acknowledge the generous support of the Social Sciences and Humanities Research Council of Canada, particularly in assisting my research on the ethnographical materials related to the present subject.

Appendix I: Motivic Units

A. Summary of Motivic Units in 17 Tz'u Songs, according to Modes.

1. Mode on 1, rhyming pitches* 1 and 6. (Song 14)

End on 1	*End on 6*	*End on Non-rhyming Pitches*
7 6 1	1 7 6	4 3 2
4 6 1	5 4 6	6 5 4
		5 4 2
		1 2 3

2. Mode on 2, rhyming pitches 2, 4, and 6. (Songs 1, 2, 4, 8, 16)

End on 2	*End on 4*	*End on 6*	*End on Non-rhyming Pitches*
1 4 2 (4 1 2)**	3 2 4	1 5 6	1 2 3 (2 1 3)
3 1 2 (3 1 2)	5 2 4	1 7 6	1 3 5
4 3 2	6 1 4	2 1 6	3 5 1
5 3 2	6 5 4	2 7 6	4 6 5 (6 4 5)
5 4 2	7 5 4	3 2 6	5 6 1
6 1 2		3 4 6	6 5 3
6 4 2		4 2 6 (2 4 6)	6 7 1 (7 6 1)
7 1 2		4 5 6 (5 4 6)	7 6 5
		4 7 6	
		7 5 6	

3. Mode on 4, rhyming pitches 2, 4, and 6. (Songs 6, 7, 10, 11, 12)

End on 2	*End on 4*	*End on 6*	*End on Non-rhyming Pitches*
1 3 2 (3 1 2)	1 6 4	1 5 6	2 3 5
4 3 2	1 2 4	1 7 6	2 7 1
5 4 2	2 3 4	4 1 6	3 2 1
6 1 2	6 5 4	4 5 6	4 2 1
6 5 2	7 1 4	4 7 6	
7 1 2		5 7 6	

4. Mode on 5, rhyming pitches 5, 7, and 2. (Songs 3, 5, 9, 15, 17)

End on 5	*End on 7*	*End on 2*	*End on Non-rhyming Pitches†*
2 3 5	3 2 7	1 7 2 (7 1 2)	1 7 6 (7 1 6)
3 6 5	6 5 7	1 4 2	2 7 6
3 4 5		3 1 2	3 1 6
4 6 5		3 4 2 (4 3 2)	3 2 6
7 1 5		4 5 2 (5 4 2)	3 5 6

7 2 5		5 3 2	4 7 6
7 6 5		5 7 2	5 7 6 (7 5 6)
		6 5 2	5 4 6
		7 3 2	7 2 3
		7 4 2	6 5 3
			5 4 3
			6 2 3
			1 2 3 (2 1 3)
			6 5 4
			3 6 5
			2 7 1
			3 2 7

5. Mode on 6, rhyming pitches 6 and 2. (Song 13)

		End on
End on 6	*End on 2*	*Non-rhyming Pitches*
1 7 6	4 3 2	3 4 5
4 5 6 (5 4 6)	6 1 2 (1 6 2)	

B. Most Frequently Occurring Motivic Units Ending on Rhyming Pitches.

Mode on 1	*Mode on 2*	*Mode on 4*	*Mode on 5*	*Mode on 6*
7 6 1	6 1 2	6 1 2	2 3 5	4 5 6
4 6 1	4 3 2	4 3 2	3 4 5	1 7 6
1 7 6	3 1 2	1 3 2	4 3 2	6 1 2
5 4 6	3 2 4	6 5 4	7 4 2	4 3 2
	4 5 6	1 2 4	5 3 2	
	1 7 6	1 7 6		
		4 5 6		
		5 7 6		

C. Most Frequently Occurring Motivic Units Ending on Rhyming and Non-rhyming
    Pitches.

Mode on 1	*Mode on 2*	*Mode on 4*	*Mode on 5*	*Mode on 6*
7 6 1	6 1 2	6 5 4	2 3 5	1 7 6
4 6 1	4 3 2	1 2 4	3 4 5	4 5 6
	1 3 2	3 2 4		5 7 6

Explanation of Symbols:
  * Rhyming pitches include nominal and absolute types.
 ** Motivic units in parentheses are permutations.
  † Non-rhyming pitches 6 and 3 are closely related to Mode 5 Songs.

Selected Bibliography

Baxter, Glen W. "Metrical Origins of the *Tz'u*." *Harvard Journal of Asiatic Studies*, XVI (1953), pp. 108-145.

Boyce, Conal. "Rhythm and Meter of Tsyr in Performance." Ph.D. Dissertation, Harvard University, 1975.

Chang Wen-hu 張文虎. *"Shu-i-shih yü-pi"* 舒藝室餘筆. In *Chiang-ch'un ts'ung-shu*, vol. XVIII (1862).

Chang Yen 張炎 (1248-ca. 1315). *Tz'u Yüan* 詞源 (Sources of *Tz'u*). In Publications of the Cultural Institute of Ching-ling University, Nanking, 1932.

Chen Yüan-ching 陳元靚 (ca. 1340). *"Shih-lin-kuang-chi"* 事林廣記. In *Chung-kuo ku-tai yin-yüeh shih-liao chi-yao* (Peking: Ching-hua Book Co., 1962), pp. 687-725.

Cheung Sai-bung 張世彬. *Historical Studies of Chinese Music*. Hong Kong: Union Press Limited, 1975.

Chiang K'uei 姜夔. *Pai-shih tao-ren ko ch'ü* 白石道人歌曲 (The Songs of ca. 1202 Whitestone Taoist). In *Ch'iang ch'un ts'ung shu*, vol. XVIII.

Ch'iu Ch'iung-sun 丘瓊蓀. *Pai-shih tao ren ko-ch'ü t'ung-k'ao* 白石道人歌曲通考 (A Comprehensive Examination of the Songs by Whitestone Taoist). Peking: The Music Press, 1959.

Chu Hsi   (1130-1200). "Ch'in-lü shuo" 琴律說 (Discourse on the Ch'in). In *Chu-tzu ta chüan* 朱子大全. Chap. 66, pp. 30a-39b.

Hayashi Kenzo 林謙三. *Tunhuang p'i-p'a p'u ti chieh-tu yen-chiu* 敦煌琵琶譜的解讀研究 (interpretation and Studies on Tunhuang P'i-p'a Notation). Trans. Pang Huei-su 潘懷素. Shanghai: The Music Press, 1957.

Hsia Ch'eng-t'ao 夏承燾. *"Pai-shih tao-ren ko-ch'ü p'ang p'u pian"* 白石道人歌曲傍譜辯 (Varification on the Side Notation in the Songs of Whitestone Taoist). *Yenching Journal of Chinese Studies*, II (1932), pp. 2559-2588.

"Pai-shih tao-ren ko-ch'ü chiao-lü" 白石道人歌曲斠律 (Editing of the Songs of Whitestone Taoist). *Yenching Journal of Chinese Studies*, 16 (1934), pp. 83-117.

"Chiang pai-shih tz'u pian nien chian-chiao" 姜白石詞編年箋校 (A Chronological Study of *Tz'u* by Chiang Pai-shih with Annotations). Shanghai: Chung-hua Book Company, 1958.

Jao Tsung-i 饒宗頤, and Chao Tsun-jo 趙宗嶽. *Tz'u-yüeh ts'ung-k'an* 詞樂叢刊. Hong Kong: Southwind Publication, 1958.

Levis, John H. *Chinese Musical Art*. Peiping: Vetch, 1936. (Reprinted by Paragon Book Reprint Corp., New York, 1963.)

Lin Shuen-fu. *The Transformation of the Chinese Lyrical Tradition*. Princeton: Princeton University Press, 1978.

Pian, Rulan Chao. *Song Dynasty Musical Sources and Their Interpretation*. Cambridge: Harvard University Press, 1967.

Picken, Laurence E.R. "Secular Chinese Songs of the Twelfth Century." *Studia Musicologia Academiae Scientiarum Hungaricae*, 8 (1966), pp. 125-172.

Shen Kua 沈括. *Meng-hsi pi-t'an* 夢溪筆談. ca. 1086 Supplements: *Pu pi-t'an* 補筆談, three chapters; *Hsü pi-t'an* 續筆談, one chapter. Collated and annotated by Hu Tao-ching 胡道靜, *Meng-hsi pi-t'an chiao-cheng* 夢溪筆談校證. Shanghai, 1956.

Tang Lan 唐蘭. *"Pai-shih tao-ren ko-ch'ü p'ang p'u k'ao"* 白石道人歌曲傍譜考 (A Study of the Side Notation in the Songs of Whitestone Taoist). *Tung-feng tza-cheh*, 28 (1931), pp. 65-74.

T'ao Chung-i 陶宗儀 (ca. 1330-1399). *Chuo-keng ch'ü-lu* 輟耕曲錄. *Shin ch'ü-yuan* edition.

Wang Chi-te 王驥德. *Ch'ü lü* 曲律. *Tze-hai* edition. (Preface dated 1610).

Yang Yin-liu 楊蔭瀏, and Yin Fa-lu 陰法魯. *Sung Chiang Pai-shih ch'uang-tso ko-ch'ü yen-chiu* 宋姜白石創作歌曲研究 (Studies of the Composed Songs by Chiang Pai-shih of the Sung Dynasty). Institute of National Music, Peking: The Music Press, 1957.

姜夔詞

Three Tz'u Songs with
Prefaces by Chiang K'uei

Translated by Huang Kuo-pin

鬲溪梅令

丙辰冬自無錫歸作此寓意

好花不與殢香人
浪粼粼
又恐春風歸去綠成陰
玉鈿何處尋

木蘭雙槳夢中雲
小橫陳
漫向孤山山下覓盈盈
翠禽啼一春

To the Tune of *Kê-hsi-mei ling*

Written to express my thoughts on my return from Wuhsi 無錫 in the winter of 1196.

Beautiful flowers are denied to one enamoured of
*   their fragrance.*
The ripples are clear.
When the spring breeze departs I am afraid the
*   shade of the foliage will be complete.*
Where then shall I recover the jade hairpin?

By a pair of magnolia oars, in the clouds of a
*   dream,*
She once gently reclined.
Looking for the fair one in vain, I go to the foot of
*   Lone Hill,*
Where a green bird sings throughout the spring.

鬲溪梅令
丙辰冬自無錫歸作此寓意

好花不與殢香人
浪粼粼
又恐春風歸去綠成陰
玉鈿何處尋

木蘭雙槳夢中雲
小橫陳
漫向孤山山下覓盈盈
翠禽啼一春

247

年年知為誰生
念橋邊紅藥
波心蕩冷月無聲
二十四橋仍在
難賦深情
青樓夢好
縱豆蔻詞工
算而今重到須驚
杜郎俊賞

都在空城
清角吹寒
漸黃昏
猶厭言兵
廢池喬木
自胡馬窺江去後

To the Tune of *Yangchou Man*

揚州慢

On the day of Winter Solstice, in the year 1176, I passed through Yangchou, where the snow that had been falling throughout the night had just stopped. Stretching before my eyes were all shepherd's purse and wheat. On entering the city and looking around, I found it was all deserted, with cold water, unnoticed, shining green. Gradually evening approached, and the garrision's bugles began to wail. Filled with sorrow and moved by the changes that had taken place over the years, I composed the following lyric to a tune of my own, which, in the opinion of "Old Man amidst a Thousand Crags",[1] has the abiding pathos of *Shu li* 黍離 ("Luxuriant is the Broomcorn Millet").[2]

淳熙丙申至日予過維揚夜雪初霽
薺麥彌望入其城則四顧蕭條寒水
自碧暮色漸起戍角悲吟予懷愴然
感慨今昔因自度此曲千巖老人以
爲有黍離之悲也

淮左名都
竹西佳處
解鞍少駐初程
過春風十里
盡薺麥青青

In the famous city south of the Huai River,
On a scenic spot by the West-Bamboo Pavilion,
I unstrap the saddle of my horse to rest awhile on
　　my first trip there.
Travelling for miles in the spring breeze
I see only green shepherd's purse and wheat.

[1]The assumed name of *Hsiao Tê-tsao* 蕭德藻, whose niece was married to *Chiang K'uei*. In his last years, *Hsiao* lived in Huchou 湖州, where, enamoured of the beautiful crags around him, he called himself *Ch'ien-yen Lao-jen* 千巖老人 ("Old Man amidst a Thousand Crags").

[2]A poem in *The Book of Songs*, lamenting the decline of the Chou Dynasty.

揚州慢

淳熙丙申至日予過維
揚夜雪初霽薺麥彌望
入其城則四顧蕭條寒
水自碧暮色漸起戍角
悲吟予懷愴然感慨今
昔因自度此曲千巖老
人以為有黍離之悲也

淮左名都
竹西佳處
解鞍少駐初程
過春風十里
盡薺麥青青

Since the incursions of Chin troops into the Yang-
    tze region,
Even deserted ponds and lofty trees
Loathe the mention of war.
Towards evening,
Wails of plaintive bugles that raise a chill in the air
All come from the empty city.

自胡馬窺江去後
廢池喬木
猶厭言兵
漸黃昏
清角吹寒
都在空城

Tu Mu, who once made his amorous sojourn here,
Would be dismayed if he should revisit Yangchou.
Though his verse on the round cardamom is well
    composed,
His poem on the dream of the blue chamber[3] fine,
He would be hard put to it to express his deep
    feeling.
The Twenty-Four Bridges are still here.
In the centre of the lake, the water ripples,
And the cold moon makes not a sound.
The red Chinese herbaceous peonies by the bridge
    —
For whom do they bloom year after year?

杜郎俊賞
算而今重到須驚
縱豆蔻詞工
青樓夢好
難賦深情
二十四橋仍在
波心蕩冷月無聲
念橋邊紅藥
年年知為誰生

[3]Euphemism for "brothel".

曲曲屏山
夜涼獨自甚情緒

西窗又吹暗雨
為誰頻斷續
相和砧杵
候館迎秋
離宮弔月
別有傷心無數
幽詩漫與
笑籬落呼燈
世間兒女
寫入琴絲
一聲聲更苦

To the Tune of *Ch'i-t'ien yüeh*

齊天樂

丙辰歲與張功父會飲張達可之堂
聞屋壁間蟋蟀有聲功父約予同賦
以授歌者功父先成辭甚美予裒徊
茉莉花間仰見秋月頓起幽思尋亦
得此蟋蟀中都呼為促織善鬪好事
者或以三二十萬錢致一枚鏤象齒
為樓觀以貯之

One evening, in the year 1196, while *Chang Kung-fu* 張功父 and I were drinking in *Chang Ta-k'o* 張達可's reception room, we heard a cricket chirping in the wall. Chang suggested that we each write a lyric about the insect, to be sung by the singer. Chang's piece, written in exceedingly beautiful language, was completed first. Pacing up and down amidst the white jasmine bushes, I looked up and saw the autumn moon, which instantly aroused deep feelings in me. As a result, I also succeeded in completing the following piece. The cricket, called *ch'u-chih* 促織 in Hangchow, is fond of fighting. Sometimes, fans of the game would pay two to three hundred thousand coppers for one cricket, and keep it in a carved ivory mansion.

庾郎先自吟愁賦
淒淒更聞私語
露溼銅鋪
苔侵石井
都是曾聽伊處
哀音似訴
正思婦無眠
起尋機杼

It begins with Yü Hsin chanting his 'Fu on Sorrow" alone.
Plaintive, a low whisper is heard.
Where the dew stains the brass knocker,
Where the moss creeps into the stone well—
These are places where it has been heard.
Its mournful chirps sound as if one were lamenting,
When a woman, sleepless, oppressed with cares,
Rises to look for her loom.

齊天樂

丙辰歲與張功父會飲張
達可之堂聞屋壁間蟋蟀
有聲功父約予同賦以授歌
者功父先成辭甚美予襲
其茉莉花間仰見秋月頓
起幽思尋亦得此蟋蟀中
都呼為促織善鬥好事者
或以三二十萬錢致一枚
鏤象齒為樓觀以貯之

庾郎先自吟愁賦
淒淒更聞私語
露溼銅鋪
苔侵石井
都是曾聽伊處
哀音似訴
正思婦無眠
起尋機杼

Within the winding hills of screens,
Alone on such a cool night, how does she feel?

By the west window, a darkling drizzle is blowing
again.
Chiming with the pounding on the washing-blocks,
Repeatedly, off and on, for whom does the cricket
chirp?
In guesthouses where autumn is seen in,
In imperial lodges where the moon is lamented,
There are other grieved hearts, too numerous to
count.
Writing a poem in the style of the Pin *ballad*[4] *ex-*
tempore,
I envy children of the common folk,
Who, catching crickets, are calling for lanterns by
the hedge.
Once set to music for the ch'in,
The chirps will sound all the more doleful.

曲曲屏山
夜涼獨自甚情緒

西窗又吹暗雨
爲誰頻斷續
相和砧杵
候館迎秋
離宮弔月
別有傷心無數
豳詩漫與
笑籬落呼燈
世間兒女
寫入琴絲
一聲聲更苦

[4]This refers to "The Seventh Month of the Lunar Year" (七月),
a poem in *The Book of Songs*, in which there is a line describing
the cricket.

納蘭性德詞

Eleven Tz'u by Nalan Hsinteh

Translated by John C. H. Wu

菩薩蠻

驚飆掠地冬將半
解鞍正值昏鴉亂
冰合大河流
茫茫一片愁

燒痕空極望
鼓角高城上
明日近長安
客心愁未闌

To the Tune of *P'u-sa man*

A Gale is Blowing*

A soul-shaking gale is sweeping through the earth
    in the depth of Winter.
Alighting from my horse, I see the ravens flying
    pell-mell in the twilight.
The ice has closed up the wide River.
One bleared Immensity of Sorrow!

The scars of the scorched land crash the gates of
    my eyes.
Drums and horns on the Great Wall resound in the
    air.
Tomorrow I shall be nearing Changan,
Bringing with me the sorrow-ridden heart of a
    wanderer.

Professor John C. H. Wu translated many Chinese poems for T'ien Hsia Monthly 天下 which was first published in August 1935. This selection of tz'u poems is reprinted with his permission. The subtitles denoted by asterisks are added by Professor Wu.

采桑子

而今才道當時錯
心緒淒迷
紅淚偷垂
滿眼春風百事非

情知此後來無計
強說歡期
一別如斯
落盡梨花月又西

採桑子

而今才道當時錯
心緒淒迷
紅淚偷垂
滿眼春風百事非

情知此後來無計
強說歡期
一別如斯
落盡梨花月又西

To the Tune of *Ts'ai-sang tzu*

A Regret*

Only now do I realize my former mistake.
My thoughts are running in a hopeless maze.
Red tears are dropping furtively from my eyes.
The Spring mocks my wretchedness with all his
    splendours.

She knew at heart that there was no way for her to
    come back.
But she forced herself to console me with hopes of
    happy reunion.
She is lost to me for ever!
The pear-blossoms have all fallen and the moon is
    waning once more!

夢好難留
詩殘莫續
贏得更深哭一場
遺容在
只靈颺一轉
未許端詳

重尋碧落茫茫
料短髮早來定有霜
便人間天上
塵緣未斷
春花秋月
觸緒還傷
欲結絪繆
翻驚搖落
兩處鴛鴦各自涼
真無奈
把聲聲簷雨
譜出回腸

沁園春

丁巳重陽前三日夢亡婦澹妝素服執手
哽咽語多不復能記但臨別有云銜恨願
爲天上月年年猶得向郎圓婦素未工詩
不知何以得此也覺後感賦長調

瞬息浮生
薄命如斯
低徊怎忘
記繡㡯倚徧
並吹紅雨
雕闌曲處
同送斜陽

To the Tune of *Ch'in-yüan ch'un*

After Seeing Her in a Dream*

In the year 1667, three days before the Double Ninth
Festival (the 9th day of the 9th lunar month), I saw my late
wife in a dream, dressed in a simple style without making
up. Choking with sobs she held my hands. Most of her
words have now slipped my memory. However, I can still
remember the lines she spoke at parting:

Full of regret I wish I were the moon in the sky,
Still shining for you year after year in full splendour.

I simply don't know how she could have composed them,
for she had never been versed in poetry. When I woke up,
I wrote the following slow song:—

Her floating life vanished like a bubble.
Cruel Fate nibbed the frail flower too soon!
I brood over her memory, and cannot forget
How times without number we leaned on the
    embroidered bed
And blew at the showers of roses together,
And how at the bend of the carved balustrade
We watched the setting sun.

沁園春

丁巳重陽前三日夢亡婦淡妝素
服執手哽咽語多不復能記但臨別
有云銜恨願為天上月年年猶得向
郎圓婦素未工詩不知何以得此也
覺後感賦長調

驚怨浮生
薄命如斯
低徊怎忘
記繡牀倚徧
並吹紅雨
雕闌曲處
同送斜陽

夢好難留	The happy dream cannot be prolonged.
詩殘莫續	The unfinished poem will never be continued.
贏得更深哭一場	A bitter weeping at midnight is all my gain.
遺容在	Her image is still vivid in my mind,
只靈飚一轉	But her soul comes and goes like the wind,
未許端詳	Eluding the embrace of man!

重尋碧落茫茫	She must now be threading her way to the azure through the maze of space;
料短髮早來定有霜	Her short hair must have caught some frost in the dawning air.
便人間天上	Though she is in heaven and I on earth,
塵緣未斷	Our *Karma* ties have not altogether snapped!
春花秋月	Before the Spring flowers and the Autumn moon,
觸緒還傷	Our inner chords are touched and sadness fills our hearts.
欲結綢繆	But the more we yearn to renew our union,
翻驚搖落	The more we shudder at our separateness!
兩處鴛鴦各自涼	A pair of love-birds have been torn apart,
真無奈	To bleed in two different worlds from the same wound!
把聲聲簷雨	Ah, what agony!
譜出回腸	The dreary sound of the rain dripping from the eaves Is music to the coils of my sorrowing bowels!

太常引
晚來風起撼花鈴
人在碧山亭
愁裏不堪聽
那更雜泉聲雨聲

無憑踪跡
無聊心緒
誰說與多情
夢也不分明
又何必攛教夢醒

To the Tune of *T'ai-ch'ang yin*

The Tingling of the Flower Bells*

With the eventide a wind has arisen, tingling the
    flower bells.
A man is musing in the bower among the blue hills,
And his heart is tingled with unspeakable sorrow,
As he listens to the bells together with the murmur-
    ing of the streams and the dripping of the
    rain.

Ah me! a rootless waif in the world!
A heart wearied of life!
To whom shall I express the affection of a full
    heart?
Even dreams are vague enough!
What is the need to hasten the awakening?

采桑子　誰翻樂府淒涼曲　風也蕭蕭　雨也蕭蕭　瘦盡燈花又一宵　不知何事縈懷抱　醒也無聊　醉也無聊　夢也何曾到謝橋

采桑子

誰翻樂府淒涼曲
風也蕭蕭
雨也蕭蕭
瘦盡燈花又一宵

不知何事縈懷抱
醒也無聊
醉也無聊
夢也何曾到謝橋

To the Tune of *Ts'ai-sang tzu*

Boredom*

We can sing a different tune from the "Song of Desolation"?
The wind is sighing!
The rain is sighing!
The roseate flower of the candle is wearing itself out for another night!

I know not what is tangling up the skein of my thought.
Sober, I am bored!
Drunk, I am bored!
Even dreams refuse to carry me to the neighbourhood of my love!

興君此夜須沈醉
且由他蛾眉謠諑
古今同忌
身世悠悠何足問
冷笑置之而已
尋思起從頭翻悔
一日心期千劫在
後身緣恐結他生裏
然諾重
君須記

金縷曲
（贈梁汾）

德也狂生耳
偶然間緇塵京國
烏衣門第
有酒惟澆趙州土
誰會成生此意
不信道竟逢知己
青眼高歌俱未老
向尊前拭盡英雄淚
君不見
月如水

To the Tune of *Chin-lü ch'ü*

To Liang Fen

A Vow of Eternal Friendship*

By nature a mad scholar,
By chance born in a rich family,
I have been stained by the dust of the court.

But my heart is with the heroes of Chao,
Wishing to sprinkle their tombs with all my wine!

How could I expect anyone to know this heart of
    mine?
And yet you, O my bosom friend, have seen
    through me!

You and I are both young,
And both take to song and wine.
Before the cups how many tears we have shed,
Sympathetic tears for the poor and down-trodden!
See how the moonlight liquefies in our eyes!

金縷曲
贈梁汾

德也狂生耳
偶然間緇塵京國
烏衣門第
有酒惟澆趙州土
誰會成生此意
不信道竟逢知己
青眼高歌俱未老
向尊前拭盡英雄淚
君不見
月如水

共君此夜須沈醉
且由他蛾眉謠諑
古今同忌
身世悠悠何足問
冷笑置之而已
尋思起從頭翻悔
一日心期千劫在
後身緣恐結他生裏
然諾重
君須記

Let us drink our fill tonight!
Let the garrulous women backbite!
Now as before, gossip is their sole delight!

Worry not over the vicissitudes of our floating life.
We shall leave them to Fate with a cold smile.
As to the past, I wish it could be blotted out
From the very beginning of my life!

The heart-throb of a single day ripples through all
the Cycles of Existence!
I am only afraid that the *Karma* ties of our next
life
Are already tangled up in our former incarnations.
But don't forget our vows
We've made today!

菩薩蠻

新寒中酒敲窗雨
殘香細學秋情緒
才道莫傷神
青衫有淚痕

相思不似醉
悶擁孤衾睡
記得別伊時
桃花柳萬絲

To the Tune of *P'u-sa man*

Yearnings of Love*

The weather is getting cold.
The wine lies like poison on my heart.
On the window beats the rain.

The fading fragrance, like a little pupil,
Is simulating the feelings of Autumn.

"Cheer up, cheer up!" I said to my heart,
But tears have stolen into my blue gown.

Yearnings for my love keep me sober
In defiance of the wine.
I lie listlessly in my lonely bed.
I remember when I parted from her,
The peach-trees were flowering,
And the willows waving their tender locks.

采桑子

明月多情應笑我

笑我如今

孤負春心

獨自閑行獨自吟

近來怕說當年事

結徧蘭襟

月淺燈深

夢裏雲歸何處尋

To the Tune of *Ts'ai-sang tzu*

The Moon is Mocking Me*

The bright moon, full of love, ought to laugh at me,
Laughing at my present plight.
I failed miserably to respond to the heart of Spring,
And now I am wandering all alone and whimpering to myself.

Of late, to shun the memories of the past,
I have sought solace in friendships everywhere.
But when the moon is pale and the lamp is burnt to its socket,
In my dream I still try to trace the vanished cloud.

浣溪沙

誰道飄零不可憐
舊遊時節好花天
斷腸人去自經年

一片暈紅疑着雨
幾絲柔柳乍和煙
倩魂銷盡夕陽前

To the Tune of *Huan hsi sha*

*A Waif**

Who can gainsay the wretchedness of a waif?
The season of flowers has come again to remind
    me of the happy hours.
The sweet tormentor of my heart has been gone
    for a whole year!

A petal of haloed red seems diluted in the rain.
A few threads of tender willow leaves
Are just harmonizing with the smoke.
The soul of a lover is dissolved into the eventide.

蝶戀花
散花樓送客

又到綠楊曾折處
不語垂鞭
踏徧清秋路
衰草連天無意緒
雁聲遠向蕭關去

不恨天涯行役苦
只恨西風吹夢成今古
明日客程還幾許
霑衣況是新寒雨

蝶戀花

（散花樓送客）

又到綠楊曾折處
不語垂鞭
踏徧清秋路
衰草連天無意緒
雁聲遠向蕭關去

不恨天涯行役苦
只恨西風吹夢成今古
明日客程還幾許
霑衣況是新寒雨

To the Tune of *Tieh lien hua*

Seeing Guests off at San-hua lou

*The Pathos of Autumn**

I have again come to the place where I used to
    break the willow sprigs.
Speechless, I let my whip droop,
And walk all over the Autumn-swept roads.
My heart is as desolate as the wilderness of wither-
    ing grass.
The cries of the wild swans faint away toward the
    Pass of Hsiao.

I do not complain of the hardships of a wanderer,
I only complain of the West Wind,
Whose breath transforms the dreams into past and
    present!
Tomorrow, how many more miles shall I have to
    cover?
My clothes are soaked in the cold rains of a new
    season.

憶江南
宿雙林禪院有感

心灰盡
有髮未全僧
風雨消磨生死別
似曾相識只孤檠
情在不能醒

To the Tune of *I chiang-nan*

*Thoughts After Spending the Night
at Shuang Lin Temple*

*Nocturnal Thoughts in a Temple**

The fire in my heart is turned to ashes.
I feel like a monk;
Only my head is still unshaven.

O poor heart!
How the wind and rain have worn you out!
How the partings from friends, dead and alive,
Have torn you to pieces!

This orphan-like candlestick
Appears like an old friend to me.

There remains one thing alone
That keeps me from a complete Awakening:—
Love still smoulders in the ashes of my heart!

"The River at Dusk Is Saddening Me":
Cheng Ch'ou Yü and *Tz'u* Poetry

By **Wai-leung Wong**

A POPULAR BUT NOT prolific poet, Cheng Ch'ou-yü 鄭愁予 (1933-)[1] is noted for his cute and charming lyricism, which is well exemplified by *Ts'o-wu* 錯誤 (A Mistake):

> *I pass the country south of the River,*
> *Where the face waiting in the seasons, lotus-like,*
> > *blossoms and withers.*
>
> *No east wind, the willow catkins of March do not drift;*
> *Your heart is a tiny lonely town,*
> *Like a green stone street, toward evening.*
> *No footfalls, the spring curtains of March do not part;*
> *Your heart is a tiny casement tightly closed.*
>
> *Clip-clop, the clatter of my horse's hoofs is a beautiful mistake:*
> *I am not coming home, I'm a passer-by . . .*
> > —"A Mistake"

Author's Note: I would like to thank Mr. Stephen C. Soong for his enlightening comments, which have improved the quality of this essay, but I assume full responsibility for all the views expressed.

[1] Cheng Ch'ou-yü, whose real name is Cheng Wen-t'ao 鄭文韜, was born in 1933 in Hopei. After graduating from Chung Hsing 中興 University, he worked at the Harbor Bureau of Keelung, where he wrote his famous marine poems. In 1968 he attended the International Writing Program at The University of Iowa. Currently he is teaching Chinese at Yale University. His poems are gathered in *Cheng Ch'ou-yü shih hsüan-chi* 鄭愁予詩選集 *(Selected Poems of Cheng Ch'ou-yü)* (Taipei, Chih-wen 志文, 1974), with an introduction by Yang Mu 楊牧 (the pen-name of C.H. Wang 王靖獻). The introduction, running more than thirty pages, is loaded with insights into Cheng's poetry. Since the appearance of his *Selected Poems*, Cheng has published only a few poems. When this present essay was near completion, a new edition of Cheng's poems came out. The volume, *Cheng Ch'ou-yü shih chi* 鄭愁予詩集 (Taipei, Hung-fan 洪範, 1979), advertised as the "definitive edition . . . compiled by the poet himself", collects a total of 153 poems written from 1951-1968.

我打江南走過
那等在季節裏的容顏如蓮花的開落

東風不來，三月的柳絮不飛
你底心如小小的寂寞的城
恰若青石的街道向晚
跫音不響，三月的春帷不揭
你底心是小小的窗扉緊掩

我達達的馬蹄是美麗的錯誤
我不是歸人，是個過客⋯⋯
　　　　　　——「錯誤」

Put in a collection of Sung *tz'u* poetry (or lyrics) in English translation, the poem is likely to be mistaken by readers with little or no knowledge of modern Chinese poetry for a *tz'u* composition, undistinguishable from the rest of the collection. Indeed, in terms of imagery and sentiment, "A Mistake" comes extremely close to a *tz'u* poem of the *wan-yüeh* 婉約 (beautiful and refined), as opposed to the *hao-fang* 豪放, (powerful and free) category.

But what does a *tz'u* poem of the *wan-yüeh* category look like? According to Miao Yüeh 繆鉞, one of the characteristics of *tz'u* is its "smallness" in diction. What the reader often encounters in *tz'u* poetry, says Miao, are "breeze," "broken clouds," "sparse stars," "distant mountains," "misty isles," "orioles," "withered flowers," "flying catkins," etc., all related to "smallness."[2] To illustrate his point, he cites the following lyric to the tune *Huan hsi sha* 浣溪沙 by Ch'in Kuan 秦觀 (1049-1100):

A misty light chill ascends the small tower.	漠漠輕寒上小樓
The morning sky, cloudy, with a touch of ennui, reminds one of late autumn.	曉陰無賴似窮秋
Pale smoke, flowing water—the painted screen looks gloomy;	淡烟流水畫屏幽
Free and easy, the flying petals are light as a dream.	自在飛花輕似夢
From the vast sky falls a drizzle, fine as sorrow.	無邊絲雨細如愁
From the precious curtain, restfully hangs a tiny silver hook.	寶簾閒掛小銀鉤

The poem, written in the *wan-yüeh* style, reminds one of Cheng's "A Mistake", which is characterized by such words of "smallness" as "lotus," "east wind," "willow catkins," "tiny lonely town," "green stone street," "spring curtains" and "tiny casement."

In Miao Yüeh's opinion, *tz'u* is "light" in substance, "limited" in scope and "elusive" in meaning.[3] The word "light" is used in both its physical and psychological senses. Physically, since it is "small," it is "light." A *tz'u* poem is not designed to arouse emotionally awe-

---

[2] Miao Yüeh, *Shih tz'u san lun* 詩詞散論 *(Essays on Shih and tz'u Poetry)* (Taipei, K'ai-ming 開明, 1953, rpt.), P. 5. Miao comments on *tz'u* poetry as a whole. However, I think his remarks best illuminate the *wan-yüeh* 婉約 category of *tz'u*, but not all *tz'u* poetry.

[3] *Ibid.*, pp. 6-10.

some and powerful reactions on the part of the reader and is therefore "light" in its psychological aspect. Since many examples can be drawn from classical lyrics as well as from Cheng's poems to support the "lightness" statement, further elaboration on this point seems unnecessary.

As for Miao's comment that *tz'u* is "elusive" in meaning, I have decided to put it aside for two reasons. First and foremost, a thorough discussion would require elaborate and lengthy explanations. Second, I have some reservation about Miao's comment. At this point, I can only say that there are a large number of elusive *tz'u* and *shih* 詩 poems in Chinese literature; yet I am not quite sure whether *tz'u* or *shih* is more elusive.

In connection with the "limited" scope of *tz'u* poetry, Miao Yüeh has remarked that "*tz'u* is capable only of depicting feelings and scenery; it is absolutely not suitable for argument and narration."[4] Here Miao is actually prescribing the nature of *tz'u*. It is true that a large number of famous *tz'u* poems depict feelings and scenery instead of arguing an idea or narrating a story; but it is unjust to say that *tz'u* is incapable of arguing and narrating. In respect of scope, Miao Yüeh says that "of all Chinese literary genres, *tz'u* is the most refined; one cannot deal with elusive and sad feelings if one does not write in the form of *tz'u*.[5] Again I take this comment, especially the second half of it, with some reservation, for, even in expressing elusive and sad feelings, one does not always have to turn to *tz'u*. However, although the whole statement needs qualification, Miao has pointed out an important characteristic of *tz'u*: the feeling of sadness. In fact, it would not be an exaggeration to say that sadness is the predominant sentiment of this genre. In the following paragraphs we shall discuss how the theme of sadness dominates *tz'u* and Cheng Ch'ou-yü's poetry, and examine the recurrent images related to this theme.

We find sadness in *shih* poetry and other genres of Chinese literature, too, to be sure, but it is in *tz'u* poetry that sadness prevails, and this sadness is often gentle and abiding. The failure to serve and hopefully save one's country, the decline and fall of a dynasty with which one has cast one's lot—these and other similar situations usually result in sadness of a more intense type, in the tragic sense that marks the poetry of Ch'ü Yüan 屈原 (343?-278 B.C.) and Tu Fu 杜甫's (712-770), as well as the works of Hsin Ch'i-chi 辛棄疾 (1140-1207) and other patriotic *tz'u* poets. In *tz'u* poems written in the *wan-yüeh* style, however, we do not encounter this kind of sadness. Instead, we find a sadness caused directly or indirectly by love—either the longing for love, love-sickness, or the parting of lovers. An example is Wen T'ing-yün 溫庭筠 (813?-870)'s *Pu-sa man* 菩薩蠻, in which the poet depicts a woman longing for love:

Like hills upon hills the golden screens reflect a glittering sun.	小山重疊金明滅
	鬢雲欲度香腮雪
On her fragrant cheeks, white as snow, her hair drifts.	嬾起畫蛾眉
Languidly she gets up to draw her eyebrows	弄妝梳洗遲
And dallies with her make-up.	
A mirror in front and a mirror at the back reflect the flowers;	照花前後鏡
	花面交相映
They and the face dazzle each other.	新貼繡羅襦
On her new topcoat of silk	雙雙金鷓鴣
A pair of golden partridges are embroidered.	

[4]*Ibid.*, p. 8.

[5]*Ibid.*

Getting up late in the morning, she is langorous and alone. By focusing on a pair of golden partridges, the poet suggests that she is lonely, longing for her companion.

In Li Ch'ing-chao 李清照 (1084?-1151)'s lyric to the tune *I chien mei* 一剪梅, we can find the same kind of sentiment:

The pink lotus withers, the jade mat is autumn-cold.	紅藕香殘玉簟秋
Gently I unfasten my silk skirt	輕解羅裳
And alone board a magnolia boat.	獨上蘭舟
Who is to send me a letter of love via the clouds?	雲中誰寄錦書來
When the wild geese return,	雁字回時
The moon is full over the West tower.	月滿西樓
The petals drift and the water flows as usual—	花自飄零水自流
The same love-sickness:	一種相思
Sorrow at two places.	兩處閒愁
This feeling cannot be rid of;	此情無計可消除
It falls to my heart	才下眉頭
No sooner than it is relieved from my eyebrows.	卻上心頭

The poetess wrote this lyric when her husband was far away from home; and hence the love-sickness of separation. Another one dealing with a similar situation is Wen T'ing-yün's lyric to the tune *I Chiang-nan* 憶江南, in which the poet speaks on behalf of the woman waiting, in vain, for her lover:

Washed up and the hairdo completed,	梳洗罷
She alone leans out from the tower overlooking the river.	獨倚望江樓
A thousand sails have passed, no one brings back her lover.	過盡千帆皆不是
The setting sun lingers, the water gently flows.	斜暉脈脈水悠悠
Heart-broken she is, at the sandbank covered with white duckweeds.	腸斷白蘋洲

The woman in this poem has waited for the whole day—from the morning, after she has washed up herself, until the evening. The rails on which she leans must have been made warm, just like the bar in Dante G. Rossetti's poem "The Blessed Damozel":

> *The Blessed Damozel leaned out*
> > *From the gold bar of Heaven;*
>
> ......
>
> *And still she bowed herself and stooped*
> > *Out of the circling charm;*
> *Until her bosom must have made*
> > *The bar she leaned on warm,*

but her heart certainly gets colder and colder toward the end of the long wait in vain. Besides sharing the common waiting-in-vain theme, Cheng Ch'ou-yü's "A Mistake" resembles Wen T'ing-yün's *I Chiang-nan* also in terms of plot, only the woman in Wen's lyric is saved from the additional grief her counterpart in "A Mistake" has to experience. In the latter poem, the heroine's high hope of welcoming the man home is dramatically shattered when the man on horseback declares, "I'm not coming home, I'm a passer-by."

However, different as they are in other respects, the above *tz'u* poems, two by Wen T'ing-yün, one by Li Ch'ing-chao, and Cheng Ch'ou-yü's "A Mistake", all belong to the category of *kuei-yüan* 閨怨 (boudoir sadness) poems, which constitute a large corpus in Chinese literature.

The third kind of sadness springs from the parting of lovers, as is exemplified by Liu Yung 柳永 (fl. 1034)'s renowned lyric to the tune *Yü lin ling* 雨霖鈴:

Cold cicadas sound sad and desperate;	寒蟬淒切
It is twilight, at the long pavilion,	對長亭晚
When the showers have just stopped.	驟雨初歇
Outside the city, we drink in the tent without cheer.	都門帳飲無緒
I want to linger awhile,	方留戀處
But the magnolia boat urges me to leave.	蘭舟催發
We hold each other's hands, and look at each other's tearful eyes,	執手相看淚眼
Choking, unable to utter a word.	竟無語凝噎
This journey covers a thousand miles of mists and waves,	念去去千里烟波
Where the evening clouds are gloomy and the southern sky vast.	暮靄沉沉楚天闊
Since ancient times, passionate lovers have suffered the sorrows of parting.	多情自古傷離別
How could I stand my loneliness in this cold autumn?	更那堪 冷落清秋節
When I sober up from wine tonight, where shall I be?	今宵酒醒何處
—Willow banks, morning breeze and the waning moon.	楊柳岸 曉風殘月
I shall be away for years,	此去經年
The sweet moments and scenes will signify nothing.	應是良辰好景虛設
Even if there are tender feelings of a thousand varieties,	便縱有千種風情
Who is going to share them with me?	更與何人說

Apart from the above three kinds of sadness, which are all love-oriented, there is yet another kind which is not easily identifiable. Ch'in Kuan's *Huan hsi sha*, as previously cited, belongs to this last category. In such *tz'u* poems, the unhappy sentiments are caused by ennui, nostalgia, self-pity or self-lament, examples of which are too numerous to cite.[6]

THUS SADNESS IS THE archetypal sentiment in *tz'u* poetry written in the *wan-yüeh* style. Cheng Ch'ou-yü shares this sad sentiment with many traditional *tz'u* writers. The woman in his "A Mistake" is waiting for her love in vain; her lonely heart is "a tiny casement tightly closed." In sentiment this poem does not differ much from the "boudoir sadness" verse by Wen T'ing-yün and other *tz'u* writers. But in terms of artistic achievement, the fine lines in this poem

> Clip-clop, the clatter of my horse's hoofs is a beautiful mistake:
> I'm not coming home, I'm a passer-by . . .

[6]Cf. James J.Y. Liu, "Some Literary Qualities of the Lyric *(Tz'u)*," in Cyril Birch ed., *Studies in Chinese Literary Genres* (Berkeley, University of California Press, 1974), pp. 137-143.

are so dramatic and epigrammatic that it outshines many other lyrics belonging to the same category.

The heroine in a number of Cheng's poems is the typical solitary woman in endless waiting. Sometimes, the solitude is imposed by a proud, manipulating man, as is shown in his *Ch'ing-fu* 情婦 (Mistress):

> *In a small town with green stone streets lives my mistress*
> *Whom I left without a thing*
> *Except a bed of gold-thread chrysanthemums and a high*
>   *window*
> *Which perhaps admits lonesomeness from the blue.*
> *Perhaps . . . but chrysanthemums are patient in waiting.*
> *I suppose lonesomeness and waiting are good for women.*
>
> *So I never went there but in a gown of blue*
> *That she might feel it was the season*
> *Or the bird's migration,*
> *For I'm not the kind of person who keeps going home.*

tr. by Yü Kwang-chung 余光中[7]

在一青石的小城，住着我的情婦
而我什麼也不留給她
祇有一畦金綫菊，和一個高高細窗口
或許，透一點長空的寂寥進來
或許……而金綫菊是善等待的
我想，寂寥與等待，對婦人是好的

所以，我去，總穿一襲藍衫子
我要她感覺，那是季節，或
候鳥的來臨
因我不是常常回家的那種人

Here again is the man, proud and lordly:

> *In the tiny Sister Harbor, when the men mooring there are*
>   *raptured*
> *You will heave a gentle tide,*
> *Which is the swell of a girl's passionate tears.*

---

[7]This translation and the following other translations of Cheng's poems by Yü are quoted from Ch'i Pan-yüan 齊邦媛 *et al*, ed., *An Anthology of Contemporary Chinese Literature; Taiwan: 1949-1974* (Taipei, National Institute for Compilation and Translation, 1975), Vol. I. The translator, Yü Kwang-chung, is a very important poet himself. For an analysis and evaluation of Yü's works, see *Huo-yü te feng-huang: Yü Kwang-chung tso-p'in p'ing-lun chi* 火浴的鳳凰: 余光中作品評論集 *(The Phoenix Bathing in Fire: A Collection of Critical Essays on the Works of Yü Kwang-chung)* (Taipei, Ch'un Wen-hsüeh 純文學, 1979), edited by myself. The rest of Cheng's poems and other poems quoted in this present essay are my own translations.

Nestling against all the helms and clinging to the edge of
　　mooring men's dream,
Perhaps you will move me and cause me to slowly cast the
　　long anchor in spite of myself.
　　　　　　　　　　—"Chieh-mei kang" (Sisters Harbor)

小小的姊妹港，寄泊的人都沉醉
那時，你興一個小小的潮
是少女熱淚的盈滿
偎着所有的舵，攀着所有泊者的夢緣
那時，或將我感動，便禁不住把長錨徐徐下碇
　　　　　　　　　　——「姊妹港」

The element of male chauvinism is most clearly revealed by *Ch'uang wai te nü-nu* 窗外的
女奴 (Slave-girls Outside the Window) where, in the form of metaphor, the man regards
his girls as slaves:

　　I am God facing south. My naked arms are wrapped with
the gauze-like night, so that the stars hanging down the wrists are
my slave-girls.

　　　我是南面的神，裸着的臂用紗樣的黑夜纏繞。於是，垂在腕上
　的星星是我的女奴。

Such poems with lordly attitudes might appear offensive to some modern readers. But this
is what Cheng Ch'ou-yü is.

Cheng has written about the parting of lovers in the traditional vein of "beautiful and
refined" *tz'u* poetry as well. The following is quoted from his *Fu-pieh* 賦別 (Parting):

This time I take leave of you; it is wind, rain, and evening.
You smile and I wave my hand,
And a lonely road extends in two directions.
By now you must have returned to your home by the river
　bank,
Combing your long hair or putting your wet overcoat in
　order.
Yet my return journey in the wind and rain is still long.
The mountain recedes into the distance, the plain expands
　wider and wider.
Alas, in this world, I am afraid, darkness has indeed taken
　shape . . .

這次我離開你，是風，是雨，是夜晚；
你笑了一笑，我擺一擺手，
一條寂寞的路便展向兩頭了。
念此際你已回到濱河的家居，
想你在梳理長髮或是整理濕了的外衣，
而我風雨的歸程還正長；

山退得很遠，平蕪拓得更大，
哎，這世界，怕黑暗已真的成形了……

The setting of this poem—"it is wind, rain, and evening"—is identical with that of Liu Yung's *Yü lin ling*.

Cheng Ch'ou-yü is the pen-name of Cheng Wen-t'ao 鄭文韜. The characters *Ch'ou-yü* 愁予 appeared at least in two famous pieces of traditional Chinese poetry. One is *Hsiang Fu-jen* 湘夫人 in *Ch'u-tz'u* 楚辭; the other is *P'u-sa man* 菩薩蠻, "Written on a Wall at Tsao-k'ou in Chiang-hsi 書江西造口壁" by Hsin Ch'i-chi. They read respectively:

The Child of God descends on the northern isle.	帝子降兮北渚
Looking afar, I am saddened.	目眇眇兮愁予
Gently the autumn wind blows;	嫋嫋兮秋風
On the Tung-t'ing Lake leaves are falling.	洞庭波兮木葉下

The river at dusk is saddening me;	江晚正愁予
Deep in the mountains I hear the sound of partridges.	山深聞鷓鴣

The line "The river at dusk is saddening me" is especially significant in our present discussion for two reasons. First, the poet's surname 鄭 and the character 正 in *cheng ch'ou yü* 正愁予 (is saddening me) are homonyms; it is very likely that the pen-name Cheng Ch'ou-yü was adopted from this line. Second, the word *wan* 晚 (at dusk; evening) and a cluster of words with meanings similar to it appear again and again in *tz'u* poetry in general and in Cheng Ch'ou-yü's poetry in particular. *Wan* as a recurrent image is a key to understanding the unique mood and sentiment of *tz'u* poetry; it is also a key to understanding the similarity between Cheng Ch'ou-yü's work and *tz'u* lyricism.

IN THE ARTICLE, WE have so far quoted in entirety or in part six *tz'u* poems, all taken from anthologies at random:
  (1) *Huan hsi sha* by Ch'in Kuan;
  (2) *P'u-sa man* by Wen T'ing-yün;
  (3) *I chien mei* by Li Ch'ing-chao;
  (4) *I Chiang-nan* by Wen T'ing-yün;
  (5) *Yü lin ling* by Liu Yung;
  (6) *P'u-sa man* by Hsin Ch'i-chi.

Of these, four (poems three to six)—in other words, a two-third majority—deal with events happening in the evening and/or night. In fact, wherever the time element can be identified with certainty, the vast majority of *tz'u* poems are found to depict things that happen in the evening and/or night. Evening (and/or night) is the archetypal time in *tz'u* poetry.

Northrop Frye, dean of the school of archetypal criticism, rightly states that the thematic mode of tragedy is one of fall and death; tragedy is comparable to the evening of a day, and to the autumn season of a year, both of which symbolize fall and death in the cyclical movement of nature. (In contrast, according to Frye, comedy is comparable to morning or spring, while romance is noon or summer.) Frye's archetypal criticism is a huge framework within which the critic has built a hierarchic world of literature.[8] Though Frye

---

[8]See the third essay in Northrop Frye, *Anatomy of Criticism* (Princeton, New Jersey, Princeton University Press, 1957).

draws little from Chinese literature in building his theoretical framework, it does not mean that Chinese literature cannot fit into his framework. In Chinese literature, evening sadness has a long tradition; so does autumn sadness. It is late in the day when the sun sets and then "dies" in the west. It is late in the year when autumn comes, with the plants withering, the animals and birds hiding themselves and most living things decaying. In traditional China, criminals were often executed in autumn rather than in other seasons. Naturally, evening and autumn are the "objective correlatives" of sadness. The blending of sadness, autumn and evening together is the fusion of emotion with external objects (*ch'ing ching chiao jung* 情景交融), which is one of the most important canons in Chinese poetics.[9] Substitute sadness for tragicness, and we will find Frye's archetypal theory very helpful in illuminating the correlation between the sentiment of *tz'u* and its imagery. Very often, evening, autumn, and all the elements of sadness may appear in a single lyric. For example, the season of two of the four "evening" lyrics (that is, poems three and five) can be unmistakably identified as autumn.

Though there are archetypes in literature, creative writing is by no means a mere complying with cut and dried formulas. Spring, instead of autumn, can also make people feel sad; but the effect is always achieved by ironic contrast, or by focusing on the lateness of the season. Here is the first part of Ch'in Kuan's *T'a so hsing* 踏莎行:

In the fog, the towers and terraces are lost.	霧失樓台
In the moonlight, the pier can hardly be seen.	月迷津渡
Though I have strained my eyes, the Peach Blossom Utopia	桃源望斷無尋處
is nowhere to be found.	可堪孤館閉春寒
How could I bear to live in a lone inn locked in spring chill?	杜鵑聲裏斜陽暮
Amid the cries of cuckoos, the sun is setting.	

The season is spring, but it is a chilly spring, with the weather completely contrary to that of the archetypal spring day, when the breeze is gentle and the sun warm. Then there is the lateness of spring that causes sadness, as is found in Yen Shu 晏殊 (991-1055)'s famous *Huan hsi sha*:

A newly composed lyric, a cup of wine.	一曲新詞酒一杯
Last year's weather, at the same pavilion.	去年天氣舊亭台
The sun is setting—when will it return?	夕陽西下幾時回
It can't be helped: the flowers are falling.	無可奈何花落去
They look familiar: the swallows are coming back.	似曾相識燕歸來
In the fragrant garden path, alone I linger.	小園香徑獨徘徊

Morning, instead of evening, can also bring about sadness; but, again, the result is always achieved by ironic contrast or by focusing on its lateness. In Ch'in Kuan's *Huan hsi sha*, quoted above, the morning is not the archetypal morning, when the sunshine is bright and warm; rather, it is a cloudy and chilly morning, "like late autumn." In Wen T'ing-yün's *P'u-sa man*, also quoted above, it is late rather than early in the morning that the action takes

---

[9] For a discussion on the correlation of imagery and emotion, see *"Chung-kuo shih-hsüeh-shih shang te yen-wai-chih-i shuo"* 中國詩學史上的言外之意說 ("Concepts of the Ulterior Significance in the History of Chinese Poetics") in my book *Chung-kuo shih-hsüeh tsung-heng lun* 中國詩學縱橫論 *(Essays on Chinese Poetics)* (Taipei, Hung-fan, 1977).

place ("And dallies with her make-up late"). Borrowing Frye's theory of displacement,[10] we may say that in these poems, since spring is chilly and morning cloudy, since spring and morning are both in their late periods, they assume the moods of autumn and evening.

GOING BACK TO CHENG CH'OU-YÜ'S poems, we see that the time of "A Mistake" is "toward evening." Although the season of the poem is spring, it is not in the spring mood, because there is "no east wind": "the willow catkins of March do not drift . . . the spring curtains of March do not part." As the first line indicates, the time of "Parting" is clearly evening, which is the favorite time of the day in Cheng Ch'ou-yü's poetry.

The speaker in Cheng's poems is usually a vagrant-minstrel, who takes leave of his girls and travels alone, writing his poems and drinking his wine. At one time, he sees a deserted fortress, around which are

> *The nervous and hollow loophole eyes,*
> *The nails on which bugles were hung,*
> *The lookout tower battlements*
> *Worn flat by evenings and homesick boots.*

> 怔忡而空曠的箭眼
> 掛過號角的鐵釘
> 被黃昏和望歸的靴子磨平的
> 戍樓的石垛啊

He laments the decaying place, is nostalgic about its heroes and warriors, and then,

> *In the moonlight let me deliver "The General's Order"*
> *Plaintive on my lute . . .*
>
> —"Ts'an pao"
> "Deserted Fortress"
> tr. by Yü Kwang-chung

> 趁月色，我傳下悲戚的「將軍令」
> 自琴絃……
> ——「殘堡」

Here the time is his favorite evening. At another time, again in the evening, he joins the lonely travellers in a country inn, a "home" lit by campfire, where wine and meat are served, where men talk with each other about their vagrancy. This is his *Yeh tien* 野店 (Country Inn), which begins with the following couplet:

> *Who passed to us the poet's profession?*
> *Hoisting a lamp in the evening.*

> 是誰傳下這詩人的行業
> 黃昏裏掛起一盞燈

At sunset, when the color of the sky quickly changes, the passage of time is most

---

[10]By "displacement" Frye means "the adaptation of myth and metaphor to canons of morality or plausibility"; see Frye, p. 365.

conspicuous. Time passes; and with time the hero, the beauty, and indeed history and life.
These are causes of sadness in much of Cheng's poetry. But Cheng the contemplative poet is
sometimes fascinated merely by the passage of a colorful scene in the evening. In his *Wan
hung chih shih* 晚虹之逝 (Passage of an Evening Rainbow) the short-lived color belt is in
the western sky,

> *But evening says it is now cold*
> *And covers the pretty red tie with his big gray lapel.*

但黃昏說是冷了
用灰色的大翻襟蓋上那條美麗的紅領帶

Another "evening" poem is *Wan Yun* 晚雲 (Evening Clouds):

> *Here comes July, craggy are the evening clouds of July.*
> *Look up at the blue river tender and slow through the*
>   *canyons.*
>
> *Suddenly, autumn droops her girdle and unties her brocade*
>   *purse:*
> *Small hands all across the plain waving, are filled with gold.*
>
> *Or as if in winter,*
> *Busy partridges trudging for miles in the snow at night*
> *To catch the last fair of the year...*
>   (tr. by Yü Kwang-chung)

七月來了，七月的晚雲如山，
仰視那藍河多峽而柔緩。

突然，秋垂落其飄帶，解其錦囊，
搖擺在整個大平原上的小手都握了黃金。

又像是冬天，
匆忙的鵪鶉們走卅里積雪的夜路，
趕年關最後的集……

Like the previous one, this poem is purely a description of the evening scene.

Thus we see that Cheng Ch'ou-yü shares with traditional *tz'u* poets the obsession with
evening; both the modern poet and his classical counterparts use diction that is "small" and
the substance of their poems is usually "light." Is Cheng's preoccupation with evening and
"smallness" descended from the *tz'u* tradition? Or is their similarity a mere coincidence? It
is difficult to tell. But as far as tradition is concerned, one thing is clear: Cheng has drawn
phrases and ideas from some of the most famous *tz'u* poems. Apart from his pen-name,
which we have discussed above, the line "Autumn droops her girdle and unties her brocade
purse" from *"Wan yün"*, for instance, is obviously borrowed from "the fragrant bag is
secretly untied, the silk girdle lightly detached," (香囊暗解，羅帶輕分) which are lines in
Ch'in Kuan's *Man T'ing fang* 滿庭芳 .

Autumn appears in Cheng's poems—*Tang hsi-feng tsou kuo* 當西風走過 (When the
West Wind Passes) and *Tz'ao-li-ch'ung* 草履蟲 (Paramecium), for example—too, but not as

often as evening. Evening is sad; so is autumn. When it is autumn evening, sadness in the poem becomes more poignant. However, as we have seen, sadness is the sentiment that dominates only some of Cheng's poems. Cheng is not a poet writing in Su Shih 蘇軾 (1037-1101)'s or Hsin Ch'i-chi's "powerful and free" style; neither is he a Ch'in Kuan chanting his sadly "beautiful and refined" lyrics. His poems are "beautiful and refined", but only with an occasional touch of sadness. Few modern Chinese poets resemble the traditional *tz'u* poets as closely as Cheng, whose work is a worthy continuation of the *tz'u* tradition. A poet writing entirely in the shadow of his predecessors would have no significance of his own. Cheng is not such a poet. His modern vocabulary and syntax, together with his sensibility and skill, have created a distinguished style. He borrows phrases and ideas from the tradition, but is original in his art, especially in creating his own metaphors.

Since the literary revolution, the language of modern Chinese poetry has been in the main what is called vernacular as opposed to the classical. Vernacular Chinese, characterized by its use of modern syntax and vocabulary, has indeed injected vitality into classical Chinese. But, in the hands of inferior writers, the vernacular language often appears crude and clumsy, sometimes even outrageous, to discerning eyes.

However, with Cheng Ch'ou-yü's language, we find a remarkable maturity to which not many Chinese poets up to the fifties could have aspired. For example, in Cheng's *Hsiao-hsiao te tao* 小小的島 (A Small Small Island), a lovely piece which reminds one of W.B. Yeats's "The Lake Isle of Innisfree," the vocabulary and syntax are unmistakably modern, yet the use of words is beautifully economical, as can be seen in the first stanza of the poem:

> *The small, small island where you live I'm now thinking of.*
> *It belongs to the tropics, to the kingdom of green.*
> *On the shallow sand, fishes of five colors*
> > *always dwell,*
> *Little birds leap and sing on the branches, like piano keys*
> > *going up and down.*

> 你住的小小的島我正思念
> 那兒屬於熱帶，屬於青青的國度
> 淺沙上，老是棲息着五色的魚羣
> 小鳥跳響在枝上，如琴鍵的起落

Another example, Cheng's famous line and a half, which have already been cited, reflects the same virtue:

> *In the moonlight I deliver the "General's Order"*
> *Plaintive on my lute . . .*

The following epigrammatic couplet from *Pieh-chieh chiu-tien* 邊界酒店 (Tavern on the Border), again a combination of modern vernacular features with poetic refinement,

> *How he desired to step across! One single step, and it's*
> > *homesickness.*
> *That beautiful homesickness, tangible at an arm's stretch.*

> 多想跨出去，一步即成鄉愁
> 那美麗的鄉愁，伸手可觸及

would in inferior hands become

他多麼地想要跨出他的腿啊，他的一個步伐
就可以使他感染到鄉愁了
那個美麗的鄉愁呀，他的一隻手伸出去
就可以觸摸到它了

Cheng is skillful at creating metaphors, the capacity for which is generally regarded as a sign of poetic genius. Cheng compares an evening rainbow to a "beautiful red neck-tie" and the vanishing of this rainbow to the tie's being covered by "A big gray lapel" ("Passage of an Evening Rainbow"). The first stanza of *Yeh ke* 夜歌 (Night Song) is based on a metaphor:

> *Now our harbor is quiet*
> *The tall cranes point their long noses at the sky*
> *Like giant elephants reaching for food*
> *And the stars everywhere in the sky are drooping like fruits*

這時，我們的港是靜了
高架起重機的長鼻指着天
恰似匹匹探食的巨象
而滿天欲墜的星斗如果實

The image of elephants reaching for fruits is quite a lovely one; modern poets with anti-industrialization sentiments (Robert Lowell, for instance) would hardly look at the operation of the "ugly" cranes from such an angle. However, having gathered a bundle of beautiful images during the years he was working at the Harbor Bureau of Keelung, and following in the steps of traditional Chinese *tz'u* poets, who often tended to romanticize the things they saw, Cheng Chou-yü has chosen to view industrialization with a friendly eye.

Of all the poems Cheng wrote at the harbor, "As Though in a Mist" is perhaps the prettiest:

> *I came back from the sea, bringing the mariner's stars two*
> *and twenty.*
> *You ask me about the voyage; I look up at the sky and*
> *smile . . .*
> *As though in a mist,*
> *The earrings ringing, we groped through the dark tresses,*
> *Parting the eyelashes with the lightest of breaths, for the*
> *lighthouse light.*
>
> *The equator was a streak of moist red, fading as you smiled.*
> *The meridian was a string of dark blue pearls*
> *That shed for dividing time when you fell fast in thought.*
>
> *I come back from the sea whose treasures you own*
> *aplenty . . .*
> *The approaching shells, the reproaching sunset clouds,*
> *And the coral reef I wouldn't risk steering near.*
> — "As Though in a Mist"
> tr. by Yü Kwang-chung

我從海上來，帶回航海的二十二顆星。
你問我航海的事兒，我仰天笑了⋯⋯
如霧起時
敲叮叮的耳環在濃密的髮叢找航路；
用最細最細的噓息，吹開睫毛引燈塔的光。

赤道是一痕潤紅的線，你笑時不見。
子午線是一串暗藍的珍珠，
當你思念時即為時間的分隔而滴落。

我從海上來，你有海上的珍奇太多了⋯⋯
迎人的編貝，嗔人的晚雲，
和使我不敢輕易近航的珊瑚的礁區。
　　　　　　——「如霧起時」

In this poem, readers can still find such words as "stars", "earrings", "lightest", "streak", "pearls" and "shells", which are similar to those in classical *tz'u* in their "smallness". But it hardly resembles *tz'u* poems written in the *wan-yüeh* style. Such terms as "lighthouse", "equator", "meridian" and "coral reef", unknown to people about 1,000 years ago, are only used by modern men. The life of a mariner too, as far as I know, never appeared as a theme in *tz'u* poetry of the Sung dynasty. As it is, the above poem is the work of a modern Chinese poet who has succeeded in assimilating the "short song" (小令) technique of classical *tz'u* poetry. It begins with a mariner coming back from the sea, who when asked about the voyage in a rendezvous with his girl, only smiles and answers the question indirectly. With the girl apparently in his embrace, the mariner tells her how he groped through the thick mist, ringing the bells to look for the light of the lighthouse; how the equator and the meridian are alike; what the shells, the evening clouds and the coral reef signify to him. All the things the mariner recounts are metaphors: the mist is the girl's tresses, the bells her earrings, the lighthouse her bright eyes, the equator the thin line between her lips in their closure, the meridian her tear drops, the shells her teeth, the evening clouds her cheeks, and the coral reef (which the mariner wouldn't risk approaching) her body. What the mariner perceived and conceived on his voyage are all related to his girl. In such a short poem, colors (red, blue, black and white), lines (vertical as well as horizontal), sounds and emotions (sorrow and gaiety) are richly interwoven. With its language so refined, its images so evocative, it can certainly rank with the most beautiful love poems written in Chinese. Indeed, it can be regarded as a triumph of metaphors.

In "A Mistake", quoted at the beginning of this essay, metaphors again play an important role: "... the face waiting in the seasons, lotus-like, blossoms and withers," "Your heart is a tiny lonely town/Like a green stone street, toward evening," and "Your heart is a tiny casement tightly closed" are all metaphors. But what Cheng Ch'ou-yü has achieved in "A Mistake" is not merely its metaphorical language. Its structure and the paradox at the end, too, are excellent. The poem begins with the vast country south of the River, then zooms to the town, the street, the curtain, the casement, the invisible, yet central, figure— the woman who has been waiting for seasons in loneliness—and then to her dramatic encounter with the man. The climax of the story comes briefly but forcefully when the "beautiful" hope is shattered: the hope is "beautiful" but it is a "mistake", for the man is not coming home. The poem does not tell us how the merciless man leaves the woman and continues his journey, but with the word "passer-by" we can imagine that, as he leaves, the scene shifts from the casement to the street, to the town and to the vast country, and the story ends where it began. Whereas the words "pass" in the first line and "passer-by" in the last complete the circular structure of the poem, the "tiny lonely town," the "green stone street" and the "tiny casement tightly closed", with sizes varying from big to small, occupy strategic points in this structure. The objects, either "tiny," "closed" or "green" (obviously a cold color), apart from providing the poem with the setting, also describe the woman's feelings of loneliness and alienation. That these words can perform a double function testifies fully to Cheng's fine and subtle craftsmanship. The theme and sentiment of "A Mistake" are very traditional; it is one of the numerous *guei yüan* (boudoir sadness) poems depicting the loneliness of women in their endless waiting for men. There is little difference between the woman in this poem and those in *tz'u* pieces. One cannot, for instance, tell the woman in "A Mistake" from her counterpart in Wen T'ing-yün's *I Chiang-nan*, cited above. Yet, despite all these similarities, "A Mistake", with its modern syntax and verbal paradox ("a beautiful mistake"), has an unmistakable modern ring. For the verbal paradox, though a favorite rhetorical device in modern Western and Chinese poetry, is rare in classical Chinese poetry. It is precisely in this sense that "A Mistake" can lay full claim to modernity.

Cheng is not yet a major poet, for, up to the present, his scope (both thematically and technically speaking) is still limited, and the quantity of his work is less than impressive.[11] Yet surely impressive is his charming lyricism, which is a worthy continuation and development of the classical *tz'u* tradition.

[11]He has written about 160 poems in some thirty years.

NOTES ON CONTRIBUTORS

RUTH W. ADLER (安露絲) received an M.S. in nutrition from Columbia University, did graduate research in biochemistry at Cornell University Medical College and published some 100 review papers on nutrition and biochemistry before becoming interested in Chinese language and literature and returning to Columbia University where she received an M.A. in Chinese and Japanese literature. She is at present preparing an anthology of modern Japanese fiction in translation and pursuing independent studies in Tibetan. Her translations of Japanese fiction have appeared in *Short Story International* and in *Translation.*

YING-HSIUNG CHOU (周英雄) formerly Research Associate at the Institute of Chinese Studies, The Chinese University of Hong Kong, is now Lecturer in the Department of English, teaching English and Comparative Literature. He is author of *A Study of the Return Motif in Fiction*, in addition to a number of articles in English and Chinese on *Yüeh-fu* ballads and Structuralism. He also co-edited *New Asia Academic Bulletin*, I (1978), which is a special issue on East-West Comparative Literature.

JAMES R. HIGHTOWER (海陶瑋) was born in 1915. He attended the University of Colorado and Harvard University, where he took his Ph.D. in 1946. He is at present Professor of Chinese Literature at Harvard, having taught there since 1948. He studied in Peking from 1940 to 1943 and again 1946-1948. He was at the Academic Sinica in Taipei in 1965-66. He is currently collaborating with Chia-ying Yeh Chao on a historical and critical study of *tz'u* of which several installments have appeared in the *Harvard Journal of Asiatic Studies.*

C.Y. HSU (徐兆鏞), B.A., Yenching University and M.A., University of Michigan, journalist, editor and translator, is well-versed in English and Chinese literature and journalism. He has been editor of an English news service, correspondent in France and Australia, editor of a translation service, correspondent of an English daily and a Chinese journal, radio news writer, editor and correspondent, and editor of *The Asian Student* in San Francisco. He has published many articles in English and Chinese newspapers and periodicals, including *Renditions* and is doing a new English translation of *Liao Chai Chih I* (聊齋誌異).

HUANG KUO-PIN (黃國彬) graduated from the University of Hong Kong in 1971, obtained his M. Phil. in English in 1976, and, as Tutor, taught English at New Asia College, The Chinese University of Hong Kong, from 1974 to 1978. At present he is Production Manager of *Renditions.*

JULIE LANDAU writes stories, poems, essays and criticism for various journals and anthologies, and the BBC. The Chou Pang-yen translations are part of a book of Sung *Tz'u* she has just completed. Born in Zurich, Switzerland, she has a B.A. *cum laude* from Harvard in Philosophy and Mathematics. She studied Chinese at the China Institute in New York and privately in Hong Kong. Since 1975, she has done graduate work in Chinese Literature at Columbia University. Her translations have been assisted by a grant from the Asian Literature Program of the Asia Society and the New York State Endowment for the Arts.

D.C. LAU (劉殿爵) was born in Hong Kong in 1921. He read Chinese at the University of Hong Kong, and in 1946 went to Glasgow, where he read philosophy. He taught Chinese philosophy at the School of Oriental and African Studies in London from 1950. In 1965 he was appointed to the Readership in Chinese Philosophy, and in 1970 to the Chair of Chinese, in the University of London. In 1978 he returned to Hong Kong to take up the Chair in Chinese Language & Literature at The Chinese University of Hong Kong. He has made new translations of the *Lao Tzu* (1963) and of the *Mencius* (1970), both published in the Penguin Classics. His translation of the *Analects of Confucius* was published in 1979 in the same series.

WINNIE LAI-FONG LEUNG (梁麗芳) was born in China and grew up in Hong Kong. She received a B.A. from the University of Calgary in 1972 and an M.A. from the University of British Columbia in 1976. Currently Library Assistant of the University of British Columbia, she has published poems in several Chinese periodicals and articles in *Chung-wai Wen-hsüeh* (中外文學), *Tamkang Review*, and *The Seventies*. Her book on Liu Yung's *Tz'u* will be published by The Cosmos Book Ltd. At present she is working on the literary theories of Ku Sui.

LIANG MING-YUEH (梁銘越), born 1941 in China, received his Ph.D. degree with distinction from the University of California, Los Angeles, and presently teaches at the University of British Columbia. Being one of few scholars equally well-schooled in both the Chinese music and Western academic traditions, Liang's contribution to the study and interpretation of Chinese music is unique. As an ethnomusicologist, composer, and performer of Chinese musical instruments, his lectures and recitals have been widely acclaimed throughout North America, Asia, and Europe. His works include articles, recordings, symphonic, and chamber compositions, notably his book *The Chinese Ch'in: Its History and Music*, the recording *Ch'in Music of Ten Centuries*, and contributions to the *Grove's Dictionary of Music and Musicians*, (6th edition). He is currently completing a book on the music before 10th century China, based on interpretations and structural analyses of the *Shen-ch'i mi-p'u*.

JOHN MINFORD (閔福德), born in 1946, studied Chinese at Oxford and is currently completing a Ph.D. dissertation on Kao E and *The Story of the Stone*, at the Australian National University. His translation of Volumes Four and Five of the novel will be published by Penguin Classics in 1981-2.

JAMES P. RICE (米傑), born in 1950, read English Literature and Foreign Language Education and obtained a B.A. and an M.A. from the University of Texas. His interest in Asian languages and literatures began while in the Peace Corps in Korea. He is presently living in Japan.

FREDERICK C. TSAI (蔡濯堂), essayist and translator, better known by his pen-name Ssu-kuo (思果), was born in Chenkiang, Kiangsu, in 1918. He was editor, Hong Kong Management Association, Federation of Hong Kong Industries, and the *Reader's Digest*, Chinese